Robert L

Working and Living
USA

CADOGANguides

Contents

About the authors

Christian Williams has been in and out of the USA for the past decade, including spells based in Colorado and New Jersey. He has worked as a travel writer for various publications, including the *Daily Telegraph*, and has written and co-authored several guidebooks. These have included *The Rough Guide to the Rocky Mountains* and *The Rough Guide to Skiing and Snowboarding*. He has also written extensively about Canada, Tenerife and his home town, Berlin.

New York native **Robert Rhatigan** has lived and worked in many different states. His working life started with a job in New York, before he headed west to seek out a fortune in the foothills of the Rocky Mountains. He is currently pursuing a career in academic geography.

Hunter Slaton is a writer and editor who has, among other pursuits, spent six months washing dishes at McMurdo Station on Antarctica. He lives in New York City and is currently working on a cookbook called *How to Be a Rock Star in Your Own Kitchen*.

Conceived and produced for Cadogan Guides by **Navigator Guides Ltd**, The Old Post Office, Swanton Novers, Melton Constable, Norfolk, NR24 2AJ
info@navigatorguides.com
www.navigatorguides.com

Cadogan Guides
2nd Floor, 233 High Holborn
London WC1V 7DN
info@cadoganguides.co.uk
www.cadoganguides.com

The Globe Pequot Press
246 Goose Lane, PO Box 480, Guilford,
Connecticut 06437–0480

Cover design: Sarah Rianhard-Gardner
Cover photographs: © Dynamic Graphics Group / Creatas / Alamy, Authors Image / Alamy, Robert Harding Picture Library Ltd / Alamy, Janine Wiedel Photolibrary / Alamy, Brand X Pictures / Alamy, Barry Mason / Alamy
Webstream / Alamy, AGStockUSA, Inc. / Alamy
Colour essay photographs © Christian Williams
Editor: Susannah Wight
Proofreader: Mary Sheridan
Indexing: Isobel McLean

Printed in Finland by WS Bookwell

A catalogue record for this book is available from the British Library
ISBN 1-86011-197-1
ISBN 13: 978-1-86011-197-6

The author and publishers have made every effort to ensure the accuracy of the information in this book at the time of going to press. However, they cannot accept any responsibility for any loss, injury or inconvenience resulting from the use of information contained in this guide.

Please help us to keep this guide up to date. We have done our best to ensure that the information in it is correct at the time of going to press. But places are constantly changing, and rules and regulations fluctuate. We would be delighted to receive any comments concerning existing entries or omissions. Authors of the best letters will receive a copy of the Cadogan Guide of their choice.

Introduction

As the world's fourth-largest country, America contains both abundance and immense variety, making it famous as a land of opportunity that has lured immigrants from every major culture and nation on earth for the past five centuries. And its numbers continue to swell with those seeking prosperity and freedom; estimates suggest America may have a population of over 440 million by 2050, larger than the entire European Union.

The last thing this book needs to do, therefore, is sell the USA. Its purpose is to accompany you at the start of your new life. As you settle in, you'll find a world of difference between reality and the excitement and glamour of the movies or your holiday experiences, which may have shaped your ideas about the country. Though at first glance the USA seems a lot like the UK, differences outweigh similarities; some social dislocation is inevitable. This book aims to give you a head-start in unravelling these differences and provides friendly guidance through the maze of oddities and obstacles that hinder settling in.

Chapter 01, **Getting to Know the USA**, orientates you in the basics: the country's history, its geography, its regional climates and the foods they produce. Peeling off the next layer of complexity, Chapter 02, **Profiles of the Regions**, looks closely at America's states and regions and should be particularly helpful if you're free to choose where to move – or for planning holidays later on. Chapter 03, **The USA Today**, provides background information on areas such as politics, economics, religion and the arts. It should help you begin to understand America's key issues and enable you to interpret its cultural landscape.

With the vital background information in place, the remaining chapters focus on practical matters: Chapter 04, **First Steps**, looks at the basics of getting there and reasons for moving; Chapter 05, **Red Tape**, unravels the complex system of visas; Chapters 06 and 07, **Living in the USA** and **Working in the USA**, then deal with everyday life, at home and in the workplace, giving plentiful insider tips. Chapter 08, **References**, concludes with useful reference material, including recommended books and films.

As your first point of reference for all things American, this book should become thoroughly dog-eared. Your experience of exploring and settling in the USA as a foreigner – a so-called *alien* – will be different from that of the authors, but we hope enough common threads will run through this experience that this book can help make life easier.

Getting to Know the USA

01

Arriving in America can feel like walking on to a movie set. Thanks to the global export of American movies and television, many of your first impressions may well also seem eerily familiar. Treading between hydrants, yellow cabs, diners and huge cars, and seeing international landmarks like the Golden Gate Bridge, the White House or the Statue of Liberty, can be a dizzying yet unnervingly familiar experience. And once you leave the cities you'll find the equally foreign yet recognisable wide-open road, country music and low-slung wooden houses.

Yet truly getting to know the USA means facing all your preconceptions and unravelling the flimsy cultural stereotypes. Beneath the solid, unified and stereotyped image that the USA tends to project onto the world is a huge and geographically varied country and one in which diversity and difference routinely loom larger than similarities. The country is built on an ethnic diversity that mirrors the world and its spectrum of attitudes and lifestyles.

Appreciating some of its history is a key way of getting to grips with contemporary America. The process of European discovery and colonialism followed by independence and expansion was an uneven one and affected different parts of the country in varying ways. But one common element across the continent is the pioneering spirit that was demanded of settling immigrants and which has since become ingrained, creating an overwhelmingly dynamic and driven society. The vitality of stubborn independence and a strong sense of fighting for personal justice continues, coupled with a patriotic pride, as part of the American psyche.

After its independence and expansion into its present form, all parts of the country began to share a history by strongly weaving together an economy, culture and common identity. The media has been a crucial homogenising influence in this process. Nevertheless, many regional differences have been maintained, and those that don't have historical roots are the result of geographical differences within the country. The terrain, climate and even the local soils still determine patterns of settlement and activity. And the menus of the best restaurants have increasingly come to concentrate on making the most out of fresh, locally grown ingredients.

Climate and Geography

Climate varies enormously in the USA. The country contains elements of almost all of the world's environments and ecosystems and is so big that it can harbour several major weather systems at once. Generally areas in the south are warmer than those in the north and coastal areas have milder weather than inland areas, but no single weather pattern governs the whole country. The deep snow and frozen lakes of the Midwest winter seems worlds away from

Florida's sunbathers. Variation occurs not only between regions and seasons, but also from day to day and even hour to hour. Yet, broadly, the bulk of USA can be said to have a temperate climate, while Hawaii and Florida are tropical, much of the Great Plains semi-arid, and the bulk of the southwest is desert.

Though not without its extremes, the American climate is however mostly a bearable one, and the great wealth of the country means that powerful heating and air-conditioning systems are in place to make life comfortable almost everywhere.

Topography

North American topography was largely shaped 50–60 million years ago, when ice sheets smothered the continent and the Rocky Mountains first began to rise. Since then the landscape has been sculpted by rain, ice, rivers and wind, to produce today's surface characteristics. The three main mountain systems that cut through the USA run north–south and are the product of land masses colliding and crumpling the earth into mountain ranges. This plate movement is also the source of California's ever-present earthquake danger. The most significant ranges are the Appalachians in the east, the Rocky Mountains just west of the centre and the Sierra Nevada range in the west. Between these ranges the land is relatively flat, with much of the north the work of glaciers that have left behind vast numbers of lakes. On a continental level, these major mountain ranges and the Great Lakes, along with the presence of the neighbouring oceans, are America's most significant climatic factors.

Regional Climate

The continent's layout and topography create a number of climatic regions, many of which hinge on the prevailing westerly winds that sweep across the continent from the Pacific. These give the west coast a largely damp maritime climate, shielding those regions immediately east of the Sierra Nevada mountains from much of the rainfall and so producing deserts like those of Nevada. The Rocky Mountains also produce a 'rain shadow', which leaves the plains to the east relatively dry and fairly predictable. Further east, elements of an unpredictable and damp maritime climate reappear on the east coast. This is at its most extreme in the climate of Florida.

The East

Among the temperate areas of the USA, the northeast has the lowest rainfall, but at the same time temperatures in areas like New England and Washington can vary from piercingly cold in winter to uncomfortably hot and humid in summer. Generally, though, snowfall is light and restricted to several large storms. Summers in the region are relatively short, but get longer the further south you travel. Chesapeake Bay has hot, sunny summers and crisp winters with little snowfall. Florida is so far south that it's not bothered by any real winter, while in summer some of its tropical heat is tempered by the surrounding seas. Summer in Florida, as in most of the rest of the south, is also by far the wettest period, and one or two annual hurricanes are a regular part of life in the state.

The Midwest and the Rocky Mountains

Covering the Great Plains between the Appalachians and the Rocky Mountains, the Midwest is at the middle of several converging weather patterns. Generally, the further west and south you go within the region, the drier and warmer it gets. But with very little notice, Arctic air flows from Canada, or tropical winds streaming in from the Caribbean and Gulf of Mexico change local weather considerably – by as much as 50°F in a few hours. The Midwest is also home to the bulk of America's violent lightning storms and many of the continent's tornadoes (or 'twisters'). Snowfall is typically heavy, especially in the north, where blizzards sweep down from the Arctic without mountains to divert them. The Rocky Mountains have a similar climate but more highly localised weather patterns, within which altitude is as important as latitude: the higher you are, the colder, wetter and snowier it is.

The Southwest

In the southern USA, between the Rocky and Sierra Nevada mountains lie hot deserts, which no amount of irrigation, dam-building and water reclamation have been able to make fit for agriculture, although these projects have been exceptionally useful in providing supplies for cities like Los Angeles, Las Vegas and Phoenix. The extraordinary temperatures, that regularly bridge the 100°F mark, are made bearable only by the region's low humidity.

California and the Pacific Northwest

As it covers the lion's share of the USA's west coast and is flanked to the east by the Sierra Nevada mountains, California contains a wide variety of climates. In southern California you can expect consistent sunshine, while further north coastal fog often lowers temperatures. Generally, though, it lives up to its idyllic reputation and the mountains get enough snow to harbour some inter-nationally important skiing destinations.

The climate of the Pacific Northwest is determined largely by storms coming inland from the Pacific and the presence of the Cascade Range. To the east of the mountains you can expect blue skies, but along the western seaboard and in the mountains you can expect plentiful rain – snow in winter – at more or less

Movers and Shakers: Tornadoes, Hurricanes and Earthquakes

Tornadoes, though rare, can occur anywhere in the USA, but are most common in Kansas, Oklahoma and Nebraska. Also called cyclones or twisters, these highly unpredictable rotating air masses are usually recognisable by their cone-shaped cloud, whose point dances along the ground. Tornadoes frequently accompany thunderstorms and can generate wind speeds of around 300mph in the inner vortex, which tear up everything in their way. Thankfully they rarely move along the ground any faster than 40mph, so usually there is plenty of time to get out of the way. Listen out for tornado warnings in weather reports and steer well clear of them. If you do end up in the possible path of a tornado, take cover in a cellar or sturdy, preferably brick or concrete building and stay away from windows. If travelling in the wake of a tornado, be sure to check for potentially lethal live power-lines that might have been downed.

In the southwestern USA, and particularly Florida and most recently Texas and Louisiana, strong winds are more likely to occur in the form of **hurricanes** surging in from the Caribbean. These are usually fairly easy to predict days in advance and are well publicised on TV and radio, but should you see large numbers of people boarding up their houses it's certainly worth asking if one is expected. The course of action is as for tornadoes, but be sure to also seek local advice. If an evacuation order is issued, do not hesitate to follow it.

Earthquakes are another climatic fact of life in the USA, though their tangible effects are limited to the states along the Pacific Rim, and particularly California, which sits above the San Andreas Fault, where two gigantic parts of the earth's crust rub against one another. This rubbing is a jerky and not a smooth process, and each jerk is an earthquake. These can come suddenly and at any time, although through careful ongoing monitoring scientists have become good at predicting them. Minor tremors from mild earthquakes shouldn't cause alarm, but once things begin to sway or topple then you should find somewhere protected. A good place to take cover is under a sturdy table or doorframe for protection against falling objects. Stay away from windows and don't rush outside, as masonry, glass or even power lines may be falling. If driving, pull off the road and stop; controlling a vehicle when the ground is moving can be very difficult. After the initial quake, prepare for the inevitable, but always smaller, aftershocks.

any time. Fog is also common, but from May to September the vast majority of days will see some sunshine.

Historical Overview

The main landmarks in the relatively short but extraordinarily well-documented history of the United States of America have evidently shaped life in the USA today. Some aspects of contemporary culture can be traced back to the era of colonialism, when all the great European powers carved their niches in the newly discovered lands, but it was only in the late 18th century that the USA became a country in its own right. The infant nation almost immediately made up for its late start by growing energetically across the entire lower half of the North American continent. Through a combination of luck, wars and purchase, it came to dominate a continent that contained riches beyond anyone's wildest dreams. Within a hundred years, the USA had grown to its present boundaries, stabilised the fissures in its fledgling government that had caused a civil war, and industrialised at a furious and extraordinary rate. By the turn of the 20th century its economy, fuelled by waves of immigrants, had become a global powerhouse. During the 20th century, the USA was increasingly though at first unwillingly dragged into global politics, until by the end of the century it had become the world's major player in political, economic and military terms. During the same century the USA also created the world's greatest consumer society, one which inadvertently underwrote a generation of counter-cultural questioning. By the start of the 21st century, however, the capitalist consumer credo was stronger than ever, and had stimulated a hi-tech revolution that transformed global communications.

Early Settlement

Archaeological findings suggest that the first human settlers to arrive on the American continent did so by foot or boat from Siberia, over the Baring Straits, at least fifteen thousand years ago. They would have been greeted by a vast landscape of treeless tundra. Yet the lands came with an abundance of large mammals, which promised successful hunting and good prospects for survival, making human settlement attractive. So easy was the hunting that it took only two thousand years for these nomadic hunter-gatherers to spread throughout both the North and South American continents. Their success was at the expense of much of the easiest prey, however, with the likes of mammoths and huge ground sloths hunted into extinction.

As a result, the ever-adaptable humans developed agriculture and, in so doing, created a more settled existence. Tribes began to form around specific cultural traditions and ways of life reflecting their environments. The tribes' co-existence seems to have been generally harmonious, helped, no doubt, by the continent's exceptionally low population density.

European Exploration

Columbus sailed the ocean blue, In fourteen hundred and ninety-two – and discovered America, as every schoolchild knows. What many know too is that the Vikings actually got there first. The first Europeans to set foot in the

Americas, the Vikings established a colony in Greenland, sailed around the Labrador coast and possibly visited New England in AD 982. Norse sagas tell how Norwegian missionary **Leif Ericsson** was blown off course returning from Greenland, landing in 'Vinland' – somewhere on the east coast of North America – where he found wheat and grapes. Icelandic leader **Thorfinn Karlsefni**, according to the same sagas, tried to establish a colony there (scholars have been unable to identify exactly where). But in unfamiliar terrain, faced with native hostilities and internal dissension, the Viking colonies quickly foundered.

It was another five hundred years before the Europeans, now more advanced in long-distance seafaring and trade (ship technology was much improved, for one thing), again felt the impetus to explore westwards. Sailing west in search of a route to India, with the backing of the Spanish Crown of Ferdinand and Isabella, Genoese chart-maker and seafarer **Christopher Columbus** famously stumbled on the Caribbean islands instead, so 'discovering' the Americas. In that first and three subsequent voyages, Columbus found Cuba, Hispaniola, Jamaica and Trinidad (among others), but failed to land on the continent, which he glimpsed at the mouth of the Orinoco River in what is now Venezuela. In the end shipwrecked on Jamaica and forced to abandon his 'Enterprise of the Indies', Columbus was nonetheless soon followed by others. Among them was the Florentine **Amerigo Vespucci**, who explored 6,000 miles of South American coastline in the service of the Spanish and Portuguese between 1499 and 1502; the continent was first named America, in his honour, in 1507.

In this golden age of exploration, all the great European powers were soon funding explorers to head west in a scramble for riches. Spain concentrated its efforts around the Caribbean, Mexico and South America, where it located and plundered all the gold and silver it could find. Part of this process included sending expeditions into the American interior in search of fabled, yet ultimately non-existent, cities of gold. **Francisco Vázquez de Coronado** explored the southwest in 1539, then in 1542 **Juan Cabrillo** sailed up the Pacific coast. The Spanish also started permanent North American settlements, the first of which was **St Augustine** on the coast of Florida in 1565. As elsewhere in the New World, the early history of the settlement was extremely difficult; here, the difficulties of subsistence were exacerbated when St Augustine was burnt to the ground in 1586 by **Sir Francis Drake**, acting for Queen Elizabeth I of England, one of Spain's greatest imperial competitors. (The oldest European-style building in the USA, dating back to the late 1500s, still stands in St Augustine.)

While the Spanish developed a foothold in the south of the present-day USA, the English, along with the Dutch and French, operated in the north. In 1496 **John Cabot** explored the coast of Newfoundland, paving the way for British fishermen to set up camp in New England, where they spent winters curing their fish. Meanwhile, the French were busily exploring the continent via a series of expeditions in search of the fabled Northwest Passage – a sea route to China believed to pass north of the American continent. These searches led to voyages down the St Lawrence River, through the heart of present-day Québec and into the Great Lakes region. Early attempts at settlement were unsuccessful, but a few hardy and intrepid traders and trappers made a go of it.

European Settlement

As the 17th century dawned, so did the era of European colonisation. Despite problems with the harsh terrain, early Spanish missionary activity along the Rio Grande, in the colony of New Mexico, proved successful, and in 1609 work was started on a capital at Santa Fe. With the exception of rebellions that drove them out in the 1680s, the Spanish were remarkably effective in consolidating their power here and a unique hybrid culture emerged, combining elements of both Spanish and native traditions. The Spanish also became entrenched in modern-day Florida, Texas and as far west as California. In the long term, however, for the purposes of finding precious metals and converting heathens to Catholicism, the Spanish found their colonies in the USA relatively unfruitful.

By contrast with the Spanish settlers, the early attempts of the northern European powers and peoples to settle in the northeast were naïve, ill-prepared and frequently disastrous. Many early settlers came to escape religious persecution in Europe, others were simply adventurous fortune-hunters, but neither group had the vital know-how to survive or farm the New World; in the earliest days of settlement six out of seven colonists died within a year of arrival. It was only with the help and local agricultural expertise of native tribes, who were typically friendly and rarely hostile, that most early settlements succeeded at all.

The first enduring British colony was **Jamestown** in Virginia, founded in 1607. Once survival became more secure, it was export rather than subsistence agriculture that the colonists sought. After early experiments with rice and sugar, the Virginian colonies finally struck it rich with tobacco in 1615. The crop took off so well that the demand for more land and more labour soared. As a consequence, neighbouring native peoples were removed from their lands and slaves began to be imported from Africa, following patterns already well established in South America.

Encouraged by the success of tobacco farming, and by the possibility of religious freedom, other colonies attempted to follow Jamestown's lead. These included the colony at **Plymouth**, started by those now known as the Pilgrim Fathers. Puritans fleeing persecution, they disembarked from the leaky *Mayflower* in New England in 1620, so weak and unprepared that half of the 102 colonists died within the first year. The survival of the remaining few was possible only through the help of native peoples and particularly that of the remarkable **Squanto** (*see* box, right). In acknowledgement and as thanks the settlers threw an almighty feast and harvest festival for all, in an annual event celebrated as the modern Thanksgiving holiday. Although the most famous,

Mothering the Pilgrim Fathers

Of all the natives who helped colonists survive in their strange new surroundings, one of the best documented is the extraordinary Squanto (or Tisquantum). Having been kidnapped and taken to Europe to be sold as a slave, he ended up living in Spain before a successful spell working as a merchant in London, where he learnt to speak English well. Eventually he made his way home, only to find that his tribe had been wiped out by smallpox, leading to his moving in with a neighbouring tribe.

Within two years of his return the pilgrims arrived at Plymouth Rock and set up home on what had previously been his tribal homelands. Squanto became vital in coaxing the colonists through their early years. Acting as their interpreter and guide, he helped negotiate a peace with local tribes and taught the colonists how to manure their corn and where to catch fish and eels. Without Squanto's help, the pilgrims would probably have suffered severe famine over the next year, and would have lived in constant fear of their Indian neighbours (though the Native Americans were generally peaceful, the kidnapping of their people had made them justifiably suspicious).

Squanto spent the rest of his short life in the Plymouth colony, before dying of influenza in 1622. He might have gone down in history as a wholly forgiving, selfless and helpful individual had his unique position not corrupted him. In his last years he attempted to enforce his authority over neighbouring tribes, threatening that he would 'release the plague' against them if they did not do as he told them. But the pilgrims remained his firm friends to the end, and wrote of their powerful sense of loss when he died.

Plymouth was just one of many small colonial enterprises in New England, the most successful of which became **Boston**, founded in the 1630s. Further south, the Dutch were also busy exploring the new lands and setting up colonies, the most famous of these being the settlement at the mouth of the Hudson River, founded in 1624, which later became **New York**. While some of the early English colonies were royal (Virginia), many were corporate in character, controlled by their own resident corporation (Massachusetts), or proprietary, founded under quasi-feudal grants from the king (Pennsylvania, founded by William Penn) – although most were later brought back under royal control.

While the British and Dutch settled the coast, the interior of the continent remained largely wild and unmapped. But it was slowly being discovered by the French, who had begun to develop a foothold in the Great Lakes region, from where they continued to engage in exploratory expeditions. The most famous and successful of these was that of **Joliet and Marquette** in 1673. By mapping the course of the Mississippi and successfully determining that it flowed into the Gulf of Mexico, they nominally gave France a poorly defined yet gigantic area, which extended from Louisiana and its capital New Orleans, spreading as far west as the Rocky Mountains. In the centuries to come, this region and the river flowing through it became economically crucial to the country, with agricultural produce shipped out down the Mississippi for export and raw materials fo industry shipped in along the same route. New Orleans, sited on swampland at the river mouth, flourished. The French colonies, failed, however, to attract as many colonists, largely due to the feudal structures and rigid Catholicism imposed by the French government.

In the vast, mainly unexplored lands of the interior, native populations still thrived, though early and often indirect contact with European culture had begun to leave its mark and change tribal societies forever. One of the greatest impacts was made by smallpox, an Old World disease to which indigenous populations had no resistance, which slaughtered untold numbers and appears to have caused great population migrations. The arrival of the horse, thought to have been captured by the natives from the Spanish, caused a culture change for many of the tribes. Many turned their back on their settled agricultural lifestyles to return to the nomadic hunter-gatherer way of life of their earliest ancestors, at the same time developing close trading ties with the colonists.

Growth and Unrest

By 1700 there were more than 250,000 colonists living in the USA, and news of the opportunities attracted immigrants in ever greater numbers. Northern Europeans were particularly attracted by a new life, with many Irish, Scots and Germans making the move across the Atlantic. Hopes of economic betterment brought thousands from the English rural middle class, the poorest of whom were indentured for years to colonial masters to pay for their passage. By the 1760s the population had swollen to 1.6 million.

In the early 1700s all colonies but Rhode Island and Connecticut were brought back under royal control (although some, such as Maryland, remained nominally proprietary), in part to stem dissension caused by religious differences between Puritans, Anglicans and other sects within the colonies, but more largely because of England's desire to control the colonies' thriving economic life and to co-ordinate empire defences against France. Colonial assemblies frequently clashed with the English governors, especially over tax. As the 18th century progressed, colonial grievances were exacerbated by tightening English control, while a distinct, if varied, American civilisation began to emerge. New England was characterised by Puritan values, modified by commerce and the intellectual sophistication of the European Enlightenment, while in the plantation South the planter aristocracy developed a lavish way of life alongside influential adherents of Enlightenment ideals. Institutions of higher education such as Harvard and King's College (now Columbia University) flourished in this era, epitomised by the colonial common sense of Benjamin Franklin, and a rising egalitarian sentiment.

By the mid-1700s, however, the colonies were embroiled in the rivalry of their colonial masters in the worldwide **Seven Years' War** (1756–63), which saw France, Austria, Russia, Saxon, Sweden and Spain on one side engaged against Prussia, Great Britain and Hanover on the other. The main conflict in Europe, between Austria and Prussia over German supremacy, was preluded in America by the British fight against the French and their Native American allies, the Iroquois Confederacy, in the **French and Indian War** (1754–60). The war culminated in French defeat, with Britain gaining control of all Canada and the Great Lakes region, and French settlers driven out of Nova Scotia in a grand migration to Louisiana.

The costs of the war set in train the events that led to the American Revolution. Seven years of international warring had crippled most European economies, and Britain in particular began to re-examine the profitability of its colonies. With renewed insurrections by Native Americans increasing military costs in the American colonies, Britain tried to raise local taxes to pay for colonial defence. Without a tradition of taxation these duties were deeply unpopular and resentment widespread. The **Stamp Act** of 1765 was rapidly repealed following an outcry, but colonial political theorists, well-versed in Locke and French political philosophy, now had the bit between their teeth, asserting that any form of taxation without representation was tyranny.

The earliest phases of disgruntlement were marked by boycotts of British goods, ship-burnings and seizures, and episodic agitation. In one incident, in 1770, drunken sailors hurling snowballs at British troops were shot at; five became martyrs of the so-called **Boston Massacre**. In another, locals dressed as Native Americans to hurl an incoming cargo of tea from British vessels into the sea in protest at the tea tax, in what became known as the **Boston Tea Party** (1773). London's reaction was heavy-handed: it attempted to close the port of Boston and disbanded the Massachusetts government, which led colonists to prepare for war. Britain began to raid towns to seize weapons, but was met en route to an arms depot in Concord by guerrilla resistance at Lexington, which precipitated the **War of Independence** (known in America as the **Revolutionary War**). There were many pro-British loyalists at the outset, but Thomas Paine's 1776 pamphlet, *Common Sense*, swayed many to the patriot cause.

Independence

Working through the hot summer of 1776, a band of intellectuals including Benjamin Franklin, Thomas Jefferson and John Hancock gathered together to forge a **Declaration of Independence** to be signed by representatives from the Thirteen Colonies (4 July 1776). The document contained crucial passages on which a new nation would be founded, including 'all men are created equal…endowed…with certain unalienable Rights…among these are Life, Liberty and the pursuit of Happiness'. At the last moment pressure from the southern colonies caused anti-slavery passages to be cut, paving the way for future strife. The early divisions between the north, an intellectual and middle-class stronghold, and the south, the stronghold of what was effectively a landholding aristocracy, became clear.

The war against the British went poorly at first. Resistance to taxation meant American forces were poorly funded and, in the winter of 1777–8, on the brink of starvation. But at the same time the British were showing signs of weakness. With their supply lines to Britain severely stretched, and faced with American guerrilla tactics, they found it hard to assert effective control. The balance in the war was swung by the French and Spanish, who were quick to champion the colonists' cause as a means of weakening the British. French attacks on supplies travelling across the Atlantic made the British situation particularly difficult. Aside from providing troops and supplies to the colonists, they used their fleet to prevent reinforcements arriving at a crucial time, forcing the British surrender to George Washington at Yorktown in 1781.

The ensuing **Treaty of Paris** (1783) recognised American Independence, and the British finally left. The colonies began a period of competition and intense bickering under the too-loose Articles of Confederation (1781), which lasted until 1787, when a workable constitutional solution, based on a federation of states with a strong central government, was drafted. Within a complicated system of checks and balances, government would consist of three branches: a Congress of elected representatives, an Executive branch under the president, and a Supreme Court. An initial 10 amendments, called the **Bill of Rights**, outlined fundamental freedoms, including that of the press, religion and speech. Apparently straightforward in its principles, this Bill of Rights has been subjected to differing interpretations ever since. Most famously, it was used both to justify racial segregation in the 1890s and then to destroy the practice in the 1950s. Yet the main thrust of the American Constitution (ratified in 1789), the desire for just government, has remained intact.

The first president elected was hero of the Revolution George Washington, who was succeeded in 1797 by conservative Federalist John Adams. It was not until Democratic Republican Thomas Jefferson was swept to power in 1800 that a more consciously egalitarian style of government prevailed.

Expansion

The USA's staggering 19th-century progress was a defining era for the modern nation. It was a century of nation-building, both physically, as it extended from coast to coast, and ideologically, in the creation of one cohesive political unit. It was also a time of mass internal migration and immigration, surging population size, the virtual eradication of native peoples and European settlement throughout the continent, all mostly thanks to the development of an infrastructure built on a strong industrial base. The century includes some of the most bloody and sometimes unjust passages of American history, but by the end of the 19th century the USA had emerged as one of the world's richest and most powerful countries.

After independence, the first instinct of the new nation was to expand. For purposes of control it had suited the British to keep their colonies on the eastern side of the Appalachians; in 1800 almost 90 per cent of America's population of 5 million lived within 80km of the Atlantic. But it was the opportunities of western expansion that drove the new Americans.

One of the USA's first key deals was the **Louisiana Purchase** of 1803, which at the stroke of a pen doubled the land size of the nation for $15 million. Napoleon, fixated on his European ambitions, was keen to keep his armies in Europe and to sell his Louisiana colony – which ran between the Mississippi and the Rocky Mountains – to the USA. Most of this vast tract of land remained uncharted even at the time of the purchase, so that for President Jefferson it was a matter of urgency to find out what had actually been bought. Explorers Meriwether Lewis and William Clark headed west on their epic journey in order to find out.

One of the USA's next significant actions was to declare **war against the British**, in 1812. Officially this war was an objection to British attempts at an Atlantic blockade, primarily directed against Napoleon. But the war also served as a useful pretext to pick off Britain's remaining Native American allies around the Great Lakes, and to expand American power into these areas.

With much of the lower continent now in US hands, the east coast was soon awash with talk of a **Manifest Destiny** to spread the country from coast to coast. The realisation that the country had the capability of spreading across the whole continent became an almost religious, and certainly patriotic, duty. Wagon trains pounded the Oregon Trail heading to the west coast to fill what was still technically a British area with American settlers. The quasi-legendary status of the pioneering frontiersman was acquired at this time.

Aside from British interests in Canada, America's only major remaining obstacle to continental domination was now Mexico. The Mexicans had won their independence from Spain in 1821 and controlled Florida, Texas, the southwestern states and California. In 1836 Texas successfully ceded from Mexico, in a campaign that included the poignant battle at the **Alamo**. Texas then existed as an independent nation until 1845 when it asked to be let into the union. The **Mexican War** of the following year was a barefaced exercise in American aggression, which ultimately resulted in a forced purchase agreement. For the same price as the Louisiana Purchase, Mexico lost all its territorial interests north of its present-day border.

Meanwhile, a surprisingly amicable treaty with the British secured the **Canadian border** along the 49th parallel, as it already did in eastern Canada. This completed the coast-to-coast expansion of the USA in what became the lower 48 states, and the addition of Alaska, bought from a bankrupt Russian government in 1867, completed the expansion of the USA on the mainland.

Industrialisation

Fuelling and financing the USA's expansion was an industrial boom and an accompanying transport revolution, both of which hit their stride in the early 19th century. Particularly vital was the 1835 completion of the **Erie Canal** linking New York city with the raw materials of the Great Lakes. This cemented the role of New York as the country's commercial centre and brought new markets into range for the Great Lakes cities. The 1830s also witnessed a wider transport revolution as hundreds of miles of railroads linked remote, but potentially profitable, parts of the Midwest with markets along the east coast. Here on the plains and in the plantations of the South, agriculture also boomed, thanks to technology. The mechanical reaper made growing cereals viable in the Midwest, while southern plantations benefited from the invention of the cotton gin.

Civil War

Along with an intoxicating number of economic opportunities, the USA's rapid territorial expansion also raised fundamental questions within the federal government concerning how the new states should be governed. One particular sticking point was the question of **slavery** and whether this so-called 'peculiar institution' should be extended into new territory. Though the import of slaves from Africa had ended in 1808, slavery was still a core institution in the southern states, while in the northern states it tended to be ideologically unpopular, even though thousands here owned slaves too. While southerners upheld slavery as universally beneficial and biblically sanctioned, northerners were less able to endorse an institution alien to their individualistic and competitive society, and abolitionists saw themselves as Christian crusaders.

The government found itself deeply divided over the issue, with the north particularly opposed to the expansion of slavery west. In 1854, the **Republican Party** was founded on an anti-slavery platform, and in 1860 the party won power with the election of **Abraham Lincoln** as president. This result proved utterly divisive. None of the southern states had elected Lincoln, and it was only divisions within the **Democrat Party** that enabled him to gain power with just 39 per cent of the popular vote. The reaction of the southern states was to secede from the Union and its president, whom they had not voted for. Led by South Carolina, the states of Mississippi, Florida, Alabama, Georgia, Louisiana and Texas formed a **Confederacy** and a new nation.

While the issue of slavery would never have galvanised the north into war, this secession was considered a threat of the highest order to the fabric of the nation, prompting the north to wage war to save the Union. The **Civil War** began within weeks of the Confederacy's formation. Virginia, Arkansas, Tennessee and North Carolina sided with the Confederates. Despite having the more talented military leaders and far lower casualty figures, the Confederacy struggled to size up to the economic might of the Union. The subsequent Union success was aided by the reckless use of its superior numbers of troops, in a conflict where their dead outnumbered those of the Confederates six to one. In total, more than a million people were killed in a war made yet more bloody by the development of the machine gun.

Hostilities came to an end in 1865, but not before Atlanta was left a smouldering ruin and the South had been brought to its knees. The **Reconstruction** period that followed further crippled the South. Along with the weight of reparations, the South was also struggling with the loss of two-thirds of its pre-war wealth. The war had also brought the emancipation of slaves, rendering the plantation system – the South's lifeblood – inoperable. Yet emancipation did not mean equality for the southern African-American population. In many instances slavery was replaced by a barely preferable system of sharecropping, which gave labourers an often-measly portion of the crop and maintained an economic rather than legal subjection. White dominance, codified in segregation (Jim Crow) laws, was re-established as black people were denied the vote and an equal share in community life, affecting education, transport, hospitals, churches, housing and public facilities. As if this everyday discrimination were not enough, black people aso suffered intimidation and terror by racist organisations such as the Ku Klux Klan. The aftermath of the Civil War relegated the southern states to an economic backwater for almost a century, while the north prospered and expanded.

Opening up the West

In California, the discovery of **gold** in 1848 brought the rush of forty-niners, swelling the population, and the further discovery of goldfields in Colorado in the 1850s caused many to follow the call of newspaper man Horace Greeley to 'Go West, young man and grow with your country'. This steady stream of fortune-seekers and pioneering farmers exploded in volume after 1869 with the completion of the transcontinental railroad, starting a pattern of brisk regional expansion and settlement that was repeated time and again. The plains were still firmly in the hands of several powerful tribes of Plains Indians, so settlers would draw up agreements with Native Americans to share the land, before pushing them further west when the need for more land or discovery of gold made this economically useful. One major tactic used to force the Plains Indians to move on was to deprive them of their primary food source by encouraging the wholesale slaughter, often for little more than sport, of the vast herds of bison that roamed the plains. This brought the species to extinction and robbed the Native Americans of a way of life, while profligate farming practices rapidly exhausted the soil, pushing the ranchers ever westwards.

Soon the Native Americans learnt to distrust the promises of the 'forked-tongued' government and began to organise a resistance movement, under talented leaders like Sitting Bull, Crazy Horse and Geronimo. For 30 years a fairly one-sided war raged, with the benefits of defeating American forces, such as **Little Big Horn**'s defeat of General George Custer in 1876, short-lived. By the beginning of the 1890s all native opposition had been removed and the tribes confined to reservations. Many were confined to the poor lands of modern Oklahoma, joining other tribes who had been forcibly marched and corralled here when all the states east of the Mississippi were cleared of their native populations in the 1830s. The southwest region of the USA continues to be the centre of Native American culture today.

Immigration

With the USA stretching from coast to coast, the Civil War over, and the plains cleared of Native Americans, the opportunities of the USA again attracted waves of immigrants, who benefited from an **open immigration policy**. During the late 19th century tens of millions of immigrants flooded the country. The majority came from Europe, where industrialisation and overpopulation had created an impoverished underclass tempted to migrate in search of a new life. Immigrants tended to cluster into national or religious groups: Greek miners in southern Colorado; Basque shepherds in Idaho. Many of the newest immigrants eked out livelihoods in the ethnic neighbourhoods of the eastern cities, while the Great Lakes, the industrial hub of the nation, attracted workers en masse. Evidence of many of these communities survives today.

The cities of the northeast grew, too, from an influx of former slaves from the South who, together with the new immigrants, formed a supply of cheap labour that fuelled a rapid industrial and commercial expansion. A phenomenally wealthy class of industrialists emerged in this 'Gilded Age': **John D. Rockefeller** made his fortune in oil, **Andrew Carnegie** in steel, **J. P. Morgan** in finance. All built their empires at this time, on the backs of the toiling masses. Labour movements began to protest against gruelling factory conditions, but the opposition of business to unions was overpowering, aided and abetted by the governments of the time, which brutally suppressed strikes (Pullman, Illinois).

Identity and Imperialism

By the beginning of the 20th century the USA was an industrial powerhouse built on great mineral wealth and technological innovations, with an economy that ranked number one in the world. There were several epoch-defining moments in the early 1900s: in 1903 the **Wright brothers** achieved the first successful powered flight, and mass production and assembly line factories enabled **Ford** to produce volumes of cars at prices that were affordable enough to change people's lives and, ultimately, the landscape. In the arts, **Hollywood** acquired its first movie studio in 1911, while **jazz** spread from New Orleans and its origins among southern African-Americans to gain widespread popularity across the north, heightened by the exodus of musicians from the Storyville ghetto in 1917.

In the 1890s a new wave of expansionist sentiment drove US foreign policy, with attention directed towards the Caribbean and Pacific. The USA annexed the Hawaiian Islands in 1898, the same year that expansionist energy found vent in the **Spanish-American War**, which resulted in the US acquisition of Puerto Rico, the Philippine Islands and Guam, and the establishment of a quasi-protectorate over Cuba. Now a world power with interests in two oceans, the USA began a long history of intervention in Latin American affairs with its role in the Panama revolution. As President Theodore Roosevelt (1901–9) put it, 'speak softly and carry a big stick'. While he wielded his stick abroad, attracting criticism for his glorification of military strength and his patriotic fervour, the Republican Roosevelt championed progressive reform at home, denouncing 'malefactors of great wealth' and demanding a 'square deal' for labour. It took the 1913 Democratic reform government of Woodrow Wilson to turn Roosevelt's rhetoric into legislative reality, with Wilson's 'New Freedom'.

The World Wars

The USA attempted to stay neutral in the First World War, but old ties and important trade relations meant its sympathies lay with Britain and France. In 1917 it was finally dragged into the conflict on the side of the Allies by German U-boats sinking American ships. In the end, the vast death toll of the war – 10 million, including 130,174 Americans – shocked the nation and reaffirmed isolationist policies, especially after Wilson's **Fourteen Points** to ensure peace and democracy in Europe were thwarted at the post-war Treaty of Versailles. The USA was reluctant to join the **League of Nations** established at Versailles.

The war and Europe were quickly forgotten about in 1920s America, where the incipient consumer revolution brought cars, phones and radios to many households; manufacturing rocketed and the country boomed, enjoying new-found wealth and freedoms as fortunes were made on the stock exchange and in real-estate speculation. Women bared their shoulders and exposed their undergarments to dance the charleston, and enjoyed the right to vote, which the suffragists had squeezed out of politicians in 1920. A countervailing force in this upbeat era was the immensely unpopular **prohibition** of the sale and consumption of alcohol. Imposed to raise the country's moral tone, its main effect was quite the opposite: racketeering and organised crime proliferated, and street wars erupted between gangs controlling the profitable bootlegging industry. Al Capone and his cronies ruled Chicago, where, as in many cities, the corrupt police could be bought with bribes, blackmail and barefaced threats.

Yet the boom of the 1920s was built on the over-extension of credit in industry and finance, and bust came with a bang on 24 October 1929, 'Black Thursday', when the New York Stock Exchange crashed (the **Wall Street Crash**), bringing the **Great Depression**. The over-indulgence of the roaring 1920s seemed to devour most of the 1930s' good fortune; famine replaced feast. Before long up to half the workforce was unemployed, in an urbanised and mechanised age where workers could do little to help themselves. Families starved and the ripples of the disaster launched depressions in other countries worldwide.

The economy was slowly revived under the popular but controversial figure of Democratic president **Franklin D. Roosevelt** and his **New Deal** policies. These included social and welfare programmes hitherto unknown in America. US foreign policy remained isolationist. The Nazi rise in Germany, watched from afar, was largely ignored, although Roosevelt appealed to Hitler and Mussolini for peaceful settlement in 1939. Once the fighting started, American defence was strengthened to make the USA the 'arsenal of democracy', but it was only the surprise bombing of **Pearl Harbor** by the Japanese in 1941 that finally brought the country into the war. The American contribution was crucial to the eventual defeat of both Germany and Japan in 1945. The surrender of Japan was accelerated by the dropping of the first nuclear bombs on Hiroshima and Nagasaki, heralding a new age in warfare and international relations.

The Cold War and the 1950s

Roosevelt, Winston Churchill and Joseph Stalin had carved up Europe together at the 1945 **Yalta Conference**, with significant concessions to the Soviet Union, but at the end of the Second World War the USSR became, seemingly overnight, America's public enemy number one. In fact this scenario had already been envisaged. The USA and USSR were natural enemies, the two countries representing extremes in philosophy: democratic and capitalist America versus totalitarian and communist Soviet Union. The wealth and might of both, together with the proliferation of nuclear weapons, created half a century of tense tactical deadlock or Cold War. At the same time, America's post-war involvement in international affairs was striking: it backed the **United Nations**, helped Western Europe on the road to recovery with more than $12 billion of **Marshall Plan** aid, and played a leading role in the founding of **NATO**.

At the end of the war the USA found itself in a uniquely favourable position. Spared the devastation faced by much of Europe and Asia, it had secured for itself an unrivalled status as the world's dominant economic and military power. In the sheer relief of the post-war period, America celebrated its prosperity in new ways. A strong popular and youth culture emerged, through the media of long-playing records and television, and symbolised by the likes of Elvis Presley, Marlon Brando and James Dean. 'Lifestyle' became increasingly important to the masses, in the form of consumer durables bought as never before. The middle classes developed a near-obsession with modern comforts, and decamped to the suburbs; the result of cheap fuel and cars, extravagant road-building programmes and relaxed zoning laws, this migration began to create America's characteristic suburban sprawl.

Bland complacency may have typified some aspects of 1950s life, but important social changes began to take root too. The war years had disrupted the normal social order, with more women and ethnic minorities engaged in factory work and more workers moving around the country. Wartime social and geographical mobility had opened many people's eyes to previously unimagined opportunities, laying the foundations for the civil rights and women's movements of the 1950s and '60s. A new wave of African-Americans moved north, and massive numbers of all ethnic groups moved to California.

And while in some ways the nation relaxed, in others it became tense and paranoid, particularly with regard to communism. The **House Un-American Activities Committee**, led by **Senator Joseph McCarthy**, conducted witch hunts across the nation, with particular focus on writers, journalists and film-makers. The fear of communism also led to American military involvement in Asia.

The Soviet launch of Sputnik, the first artificial satellite, in 1957 rang alarm bells in the USA that the Eastern Bloc was technologically surpassing it. A decade after the successful Maoist revolution in China, the USA also feared the Domino Effect, a commonly held theory that one Asian country after another would topple and succumb to communism. These two fears led to the space race and the Vietnam War, which together formed the backdrop to 1960s America. A key event was the tense stand-off with Russia over the 1962 **Cuban Missile Crisis**, when US intelligence uncovered Soviet plans to station missiles on Cuba. For an incredibly tense moment the world seemed bound for all-out nuclear war, until the USSR backed down. Driven by its commitment to a policy of communist containment, the USA became involved in Vietnamese politics and the **Vietnam War**, fighting with the south against the communist regime in the north. As the war dragged on, with the terrible human cost mounting for both sides, and victory seemingly unobtainable, protests at home grew.

Activism and Protest

The cornerstone of the protest movement against the Vietnam War was the new generation. Born in the baby boom of the post-war years, these teenagers and young adults questioned the values of older generations. This was a generation that had not lived through depression or war. Less preoccupied by survival, young people could afford to challenge accepted mores, embracing new cultural forms – and recreational drugs in the process. The 1969 Woodstock Festival saw hippies roll in the mud shouting 'make love, not war'. The anti-war movement became part of campus life, and the shooting of protesters at Kent State University in 1970 a milestone of the white middle-class protest movement.

The same atmosphere nurtured more ground-breaking civil rights campaigns, most notably in the struggle for racial integration. A momentous 1954 Supreme

Court ruling (*Brown v. Board of Education*) paved the way for the desegregation of schools, by declaring segregation 'inherently unequal', although the order met with much resistance, sometimes violent. A successful bus boycott in Alabama in 1955–6, initiated by the defiance of Rosa Parks, and led by civil rights campaigner and advocate of passive resistance **Martin Luther King Jr** (*see* box, below), heralded the end of segregation on city buses. Freedom Riders challenged interstate bus segregation, and the segregation of restaurants, beaches and other public places was also tackled with increasing effect in the 1960s. The victories of the civil rights movement gained momentum in that decade with legislation prohibiting discrimination in voting, education, employment and housing. Militant black Muslim leader **Malcolm X** espoused African-American power through violent revolution until his assassination in 1965, inspiring the separatist **Black Panthers**.

A Dream That Changed a Nation

Born into a middle-class Atlanta neighbourhood on 15 January 1929, Martin Luther King Jr became a Baptist minister when he was 18, and went on to earn a PhD in Boston. While intending to live a quiet life teaching theology, circumstances found him thrust to the head of the civil rights movement. To this he brought many of the philosophies of Mahatma Gandhi, and it was through 10 years of largely non-violent protest that he effectively managed to end the statutory discrimination that had existed in the USA since the country's founding. His technique was to select a strongly segregated city and mobilise the African-American population to demonstrate or to boycott services, forcing the white authorities to negotiate or resort to violence. Media coverage of the latter would also create such a national outrage that in turn the federal government would be forced to act. In 1963 he delivered his most famous speech from the steps of the Lincoln Memorial in Washington:

> I have a dream that one day on the red hills of Georgia the sons of former slaves and the sons of former slave-owners will be able to sit down together at a table of brotherhood. I have a dream that one day even the state of Mississippi, a desert state, sweltering with the heat of injustice and oppression, will be transformed into an oasis of freedom and justice. I have a dream that my four children will one day live in a nation where they will not be judged by the color of their skin but by the content of their character. I have a dream today.

In 1964, aged 35, he became the youngest person ever to receive the Nobel Peace Prize. Just four years later he was assassinated, by one James Earl Ray, who claimed he was part of a larger conspiracy. The claim was never investigated at his trial, but conspiracy theorists still suspect that the FBI, who had branded him 'the most dangerous and effective Negro leader in the country', may have had some involvement in his death.

A new phase of **women's liberation** took off in the 1960s, as women sought equal pay and employment opportunities, day-care centres for children, and freedom from sexual harassment and stereotyping. The National Organisation for Women (NOW) led prominent campaigns for equality, while writer Betty Friedan galvanised a generation of women with *The Feminine Mystique*, an attack on the traditional notion that women could only find fulfilment in homemaking and childbearing. The birth control pill fuelled a sexual revolution, and in 1973 a Supreme Court ruling (*Roe v. Wade*) legalised abortion.

In a decade that saw the personal become political, significant liberal concessions were secured, but those volatile years also saw the shocking assassination of popular Democratic president **John F. Kennedy** (1963) and Martin Luther King (1968). Like the Vietnam War, this unstable atmosphere could not last, and the decade turned into the more peaceable 1970s.

The 1970s: Consumerism Unleashed

The 1970s began by quickly countering much of the work of the 1960s. Having dropped seven million tons of bombs – twice what it had done in the Second World War – and following the loss of 57,000 American lives, America withdrew its troops from Vietnam. A peace treaty was agreed in 1972 and the last of the troops left in 1975. On the home front there was disillusionment with the idealistic counter-culture of the previous decade. Instead America turned itself away from foreign affairs and debates to concentrate on creating the world's greatest consumer society. Platform shoes danced beneath flashing lights as polyester and disco took over. Fun was the goal.

In politics, too, there was a right-wing backlash against the era of protest with the election to the presidency of the cynical and manipulative Republican **Richard Nixon**. His term in office remains best known for his resignation over the 1972 **Watergate Affair**, which exposed a botched attempt to bug the Democratic offices, in which he was implicated. Liberal southerner **Jimmy Carter** replaced Nixon for a difficult spell in office plagued by a series of unfortunate events in the Middle East. The forming of the **OPEC** cartel of the oil-rich Arab countries caused an energy crisis that drove up fuel prices and plunged the USA (and the rest of the world) into a recession. The US embassy in Tehran was stormed and its staff kidnapped by Islamic revolutionaries. Carter's ineffectual attempts to resurrect the economy and secure the hostage release resulted in a swing back towards the simple, reactionary policies of the right.

The 1980s

The 1980s was a right-wing era of Republican domination, with **Ronald Reagan** masterminding a series of simple, successful but ultimately short-sighted policies. Reaganomics handed tax breaks to big business, spurred short-term consumption and deregulated markets, causing a temporary boom at the expense of an explosion of national debt. By the end of the decade, what had been a creditor nation in 1980 had become the world's largest debtor. One reason for this turnaround was Reagan's aggressively expanded military spending, which included not only a proliferation of nuclear weapons but also aid to right-wing guerrilla groups in countries such as Guatemala and Nicaragua, and to the mujaheddin in Afghanistan. Trying to keep up with this arms race effectively bankrupted the Soviets, and contributed to the withering away of the Soviet Union. Either way, the gradual demise of the USSR as a world power and the thaw in relations heralded the end of the Cold War and the start of a new world order.

Contemporary America

With the fall of the Iron Curtain and the final collapse of the USSR in 1991 along with the remainder of the Eastern Bloc, the 1990s saw America left all-powerful in a new world, where its enemies were hard to recognise or define. The 'end of history' was declared and the budgets of US defence and intelligence organisations slashed. **George Bush Sr** replaced Reagan and continued market liberalisation, although his hands were tied by debt. Having liberated Kuwait from an Iraqi invasion, his policies led the country into recession and handed power to the young Democrat **Bill Clinton**. The new president promised an era of government activism after more than 10 years of hard-line, forceful right-wing politics and *laissez-faire* rule.

Meanwhile, a hi-tech revolution exploded as military technology was commercialised. Personal computers, mobile phones, the Internet and e-mail became part of daily life for most Americans, revolutionising communications and stimulating a surge of financial interest in new technologies. The late 1990s were epitomised by a mad and fanciful scramble for online business opportunities, behind which the economy rallied with unbridled – although misplaced – optimism. With the economy booming, the public was in a forgiving mood, and a scandal about Bill Clinton's relationship with 24-year-old White House intern Monica Lewinsky managed to rock but not unseat the government. In 1998 terrorist attacks on US embassies in Dar-es-Salaam and Nairobi by a previously little-known Islamic terrorist organisation calling itself al-Qaeda (the base), orchestrated by a self-proclaimed Islamic jihadi called Osama bin Laden, went almost unnoticed.

Either Clinton's affairs or the dullness of Al Gore did just enough to unseat the Democratic government, however, as in 2000 the nation elected **George W. Bush** after a hard-fought electoral contest whose results were so close that they almost produced a constitutional crisis. This began another decade of predominantly Republican rule, which started badly as the overvalued hi-tech economy plunged on the stock market. Attention was soon distracted from the country's economic difficulties by the shock and horror of the September 11 2001 terrorist attacks on the World Trade Center and the Pentagon, which killed 2,986 civilians on American soil. Vowing to fight a 'crusade' against Islamic terror in the aftermath of 9/11, Bush launched attacks on Afghanistan, the suspected hide-out of Al-Qaeda leaders, and prepared for the invasion of Iraq, a plan already advanced by the right-wing 'hawks' of the administration before 9/11. *See also* **The USA Today**, pp.64–87.

Food and Drink

America is a country where bigger tends to be thought of as better, and nowhere is this more the case than with food. Effectively the national meal, it's burgers, fries and cola that spring to the minds of most foreigners when they think of American food. Indeed, given the geographical and cultural diversity within the USA, it is perhaps the only type of food that seems to be universally appreciated. The long and often antisocial hours that many Americans work leave them little time or energy left to prepare food – hence the reliance of much of the nation on fast-food outlets, amd one of the world's largest obesity problems. Ubiquitous menu staples include enormous steaks, burgers and piles of ribs or half-chickens all accompanied by a gigantic plate of salad or vegetables and bread. But fast food is only a small part of what is available.

But the nation's ethnic diversity means that there's also a wealth of imported cuisines to pick from in any of the major, and most minor, cities. Italian, Mexican and Chinese (usually Cantonese) restaurants and takeaways are almost everywhere, and Japanese food is common in bigger cities. Many of these come with a uniquely North American twist in their preparation. The quality of most

Vegetarian USA

Only about 2 per cent of Americans are vegetarian but almost two-thirds of Americans regularly choose to eat meat-free for health reasons. As a result, you should find vegetarian options on the menu almost everywhere. The exceptions to this are the fast-food places. Among them, only Taco Bell, the Tex-Mex fast-food chain, has much in the way of vegetarian choices, though the odd veggie burger is available on the menu at the burger places. You'll also find most college towns and larger cities have a vegetarian restaurant, while most of the others will generally have a selection of veggie choices.

Wherever you go, beware of meat and meat by-products creeping into dishes where you wouldn't expect it. Mexican restaurants often make tortillas and beans with lard, though will sometimes use vegetable oil if you request it. Thai and Vietnamese restaurants cook many of their dishes with fish sauce, but can use soy sauce if you ask them to. Lastly, it's worth double-checking that your vegetable soup or risotto is not based on chicken stock.

of this food is unwaveringly good, and the quantities typically large. Some of the very best food, however, is found in restaurants and eateries specialising in regional foods, which use local techniques and ingredients to prepare tasty and memorable dishes. Often these are among the most expensive, but in most cases meals cost well below what they do in the UK. With almost half of all American meals eaten in restaurants of one sort or another, eating out has been made cheap. Expect to pay $5–8 per person for breakfast, $5–12 for lunch and $10–25 for dinner (plus drinks).

Meals

The traditional American **breakfast** is a throwback to the country's agricultural past and involves hearty plates of bacon, eggs, fried potatoes, toast and pancakes, French toast or waffles, often slathered in maple syrup and all washed down with refills of coffee. These days it's mostly eaten as a special treat or at weekends – often one part of a lengthy and calorific **brunch**, typically as a self-service buffet. Otherwise, hardworking Americans are more likely to eat breakfast on the fly, often in their cars – which are universally equipped with cup-holding devices – on their frequently long commute. Less heavy options offered at most restaurants and cafés include fresh fruit, yogurt and cereal. A continental breakfast consists of juice, coffee or tea, bread or pastry.

Commonly, American **lunches** are quick affairs involving fast food or soups, salads or sandwiches. Those restaurants open for lunch may offer a limited selection of their full selection of main courses (entrées) and often more cheaply than in the evening.

The **evening meal** is most often the biggest meal of the day and the most likely to be a communal, sit-down affair in the home. Takeaway meals and eating out are popular and probably more common than home cooking.

Cafés, Bars and Restaurants

At the most basic level, **fast-food outlets** provide predictable around-the-clock snacks and are found everywhere. You'll generally find more interesting food in the **food courts** that are often found in malls and occasionally office buildings. Here an arrangement of booths provides good cafeteria food from a range of ethnic sources. It's cheap, quick and has the advantage that a group of people can select different styles of cuisine but share a table.

A long-standing cornerstone institution in the USA is the 24-hour **diner**, almost invariably decked out in 1950s décor. The retro appeal of Formica counters and vinyl booths in many of these is paralleled by the food, which usually consists of a large number of traditional home-cooked favourites. Diners are ideal for breakfast – usually available all day – and later a sit-down burger, sausage and mash or even a burrito.

Inspired by diners, the next notch up in the dining chain is the so-called '**family restaurant**'. These provide table service and a homey environment and foods. Often there'll be a good salad bar and a huge selection of sandwiches, soups and traditional larger meals, such as meatloaf dinners and roasts. Ice-cream sundaes are often good here, and kids' menus expansive. The chain Denny's is one of America's most successful family restaurants. Cafés also exist in the USA but rarely take the form they do in Europe, and the term can cover a range of places. Most tend to serve healthier fare and usually only serve snacks or light meals. Another casual dining option – popular in the evenings – is **bars and grills**. These can be good for steaks and hearty bar food like wings, burgers, pizzas and nachos. Many, particularly those attached to microbreweries, have a good range of beers on hand to help wash everything down and so are best in the evening. **Steakhouses** offer broadly similar food but are a little more upmarket and offer slower-paced meals in dimly lit, often mock-western surroundings. Bigger or more cosmopolitan cities will have more European-style restaurants with slow-paced sit-down service and a slightly more formal atmosphere, pricier menus and smaller portions.

Children are generally welcome at all but the snootiest venues; you might want to call steakhouses and the more formal big city restaurants in advance, since these are generally adult environments.

Regional Specialities

Each American region has some distinctive foods of its own, and local cuisine often has roots in the regional climate and growing season, the proximity to the sea and its ethnic heritage.

New England

The coastal towns in the northeastern USA have a rich tradition in seafood specialities, with clams in particular served up in every imaginable form. They're fried, steamed and even eaten raw but are most popular when served up as clam chowder. Many competing local chowder recipes exist, but most are creamy and have chunks of potato and onion. The clambake, a traditional Native American meal, has also had a recent revival. Here choice shellfish are mixed and cooked together – traditionally dug into a firepit – with corn, chicken and sausages. But the most nationally celebrated New England speciality is lobster, with Maine lobster popping up on menus throughout the continent and popular as a food for a special occasion.

New York

In New York you can hear half a dozen languages while walking a single block, so it's not surprising that the city contains enough variety in food for you to make a virtual journey around the world – sampling any cuisine from Afghan to Vietnamese. What is on offer is so varied that you can visit not just continents and countries but often also regions within them. Particularly worth seeking out are the Puerto Rican rice-and-beans places and Chinese dim sum, though the New York experience wouldn't be complete without picking up an unusual bagel from one of the many Jewish delis or a 'slice' from one of the many New York pizza parlours, with toppings that are considered meals in themselves elsewhere. New York is also the country's centre of *haute cuisine*, with fearsomely talented chefs, impeccable food and service, and prices to match.

The Mid-Atlantic

One standout speciality of the mid-Atlantic states is the Philly cheesesteak: a roll stuffed with beef, melted cheese and onions. But some of the region's best cooking comes from traditional Amish kitchens, known for a profusion of stews and pickles and particularly excellent sweet pies, like shoofly pie.

The Capital Region

In the Capital Region, the area around Chesapeake Bay is well known for its seafood specialities. Look out for oysters and local varieties of soft-shell crab, served highly spiced and eaten whole.

The Southern States

Southern cooking blends some of the best elements of European, Native American and African traditions. Meat inevitably forms the cornerstone of meals and whenever possible is barbecued and then slathered in mildly spicy sauces. Some traditional items like hogjaw (meat from the mouth of a pig) and chitterlings (innards of a pig) might make you feel a little queasy if you are unfamiliar with them, but are worth trying.

Accompanying the meat are items like biscuits, mashed potatoes, grits, collard greens and black-eyed peas and often a wonderful thick cornbread that's useful to soak up the thick gravy commonly poured over everything. Corn also often appears alongside fried fish in the form of hush puppies: fried corn-balls with herbs and chopped onions. Cobblers, pies and layered cakes provide the post-meal sugar rush.

Louisiana

Louisiana's Creole cuisine evolved from combined French, Spanish, African and Caribbean traditions. Rich and fragrant, and typically spicy, its key ingredients are red beans and rice and unusual local fish like crawfish or catfish.

The most famous dishes are probably gumbo – a stew of okra, chicken, shellfish and sausage – and jambalaya, where broadly the same ingredients are served mixed with rice as in a paella. An exotic regional meat is alligator, which frequently appears on menus throughout the region. A rum-laced bananas foster is the appropriate rich and gooey end to any full meal.

The Midwest and the Rocky Mountains

The Germans, Czechs, Poles and Scandinavians who peopled the plains in the 19th century brought with them hearty central and northern European cuisines that were ideally suited to hardworking outdoor lifestyles. Heavy potato dishes and beef predominate here, and the steaks are particularly famous.

The large cattle herds of the plains of Wyoming and eastern Colorado have helped develop a legendary steakhouse tradition, but be warned that the odd local delicacy of 'Rocky Mountain oysters' is actually calf or sheep testicles served with a spicy dip. Perfect to wash down all this hearty fare are the light lager beers born mostly out of the Czech and German brewing traditions. American versions of these are far lighter in flavour and body, with around 80 per cent of US output brewed in the Midwest.

Nothing is considered more American than apple pie, and the Midwest is also well known for making these and other great fruit pies.

The Southwest

That the southwest was for a long time in Mexican hands is evident in its dominant foods. Burritos, enchiladas and tacos, routinely smothered in spicy chilli sauces, can appear at any meal of the day. The cornerstones of Mexican food are rice and beans – the latter often pinto beans and served refried (boiled, mashed and fried) – and stuffed in or scattered around versions of the tortilla, a thin corndough or flour pancake. Soft and rolled, it's a burrito – which becomes an enchilada when baked in a sauce. If it's folded and fried hard it's deemed a taco; if fried flat and topped with the filling it is a tostada.

With the southwest being the country's Native American stronghold, this is also the place to explore the native foods, whose good breads are the highlight. In Texas, which is famous for its steaks and obsession with grilling, Mexican food is fused with its own cuisine, leading to what is called Tex-Mex. Be sure to look out for Santa Fe-style food, the local *nouvelle cuisine* that reflects the Spanish heritage of the southwest and emphasises the use of ultra-fresh and unusual local ingredients.

California and the Pacific Northwest

Contemporary Californian cuisine is loosely based on French *nouvelle cuisine*, playing on the benefits of eating high quality, fresh and locally grown ingredients in simple creations. The preoccupation with health as much as aesthetics means that portions are smaller than is normal for the USA, and the vegetables used are harvested before maturity and steamed to preserve

Menu Reader

A la mode – served with ice-cream

Biscuit – buttery roll

Blue plate – the daily special

Chicken-fried steak – thin steak battered and deep-fried like chicken

Chilli – generally a meat and bean stew spiced with chillies

Club sandwich – a three-layer sandwich including chicken, turkey, bacon, lettuce and tomato.

Cobbler – fruit pie, served with cream or ice cream

Collard greens – any sort of cabbage where the green leaves don't form a compact head, including, for example, spinach

Corn dog – hot dog on a stick and fried in cornmeal batter

Dressings – four universal types: blue cheese (creamy blue cheese), ranch (creamy and slightly tangy), Italian (just oil and vinegar) and French (sweet red dressing)

Eggs – fried over easy (fried then flipped); sunny side up (fried)

Eggs Benedict – poached eggs in a creamy hollandaise sauce

English muffins – crumpets

French toast – egg-dipped bread, fried and covered in maple syrup

Grits – white cornmeal made into porridge

Hash browns – shredded fried potatoes

Home fries – fried and seasoned potato wedges

Pickle – a gherkin

Sub – baguette-shaped sandwich with lots of mustard and mayonnaise and slices of deli meats, cheese and salad; typified by the sandwiches sold at Subway; regional names include *pickles grinder, hero, hoagie* and *po'boy*

Surf 'n' Turf – steak and seafood combined on a plate.

vitamins and flavour. Meat is generally organic and fish line-caught. But perhaps the most interesting contribution of Californian chefs has been their creativity in fusing different cuisines. Latin American and Asian flavours play a strong part in the creative process, and the resulting creations tend to command extravagant prices. In the damp and verdant Pacific Northwest, local chefs have capitalised on nature's bounty. The abundant wild king salmon and the oysters along the northern coast make up some of the key regional flavours and are wonderfully accompanied by local wild mushrooms, berries and fruits. Seattle is known for its dedication to coffee.

Drinking

It is difficult to generalise about the Americans' relationship with alcohol. On the one hand many of the original immigrants were Puritans whose traditions fired a temperance movement that saw alcohol outlawed during the Prohibition period. On the other hand drinking is as large a part of the culture, particularly urban culture, as it is anywhere in the western world.

Today, several states, notably Utah, and many counties within various states have tight or total restrictions on the sale of alcohol. In these areas restaurants may be unable to serve alcohol, so you will need to bring this in from a county that isn't 'dry'. Elsewhere you need to be 21 to buy or drink alcohol and ID is routinely checked in most bars in the country – a process often rigidly applied even to those who look old enough to be the parents of the person checking. The process of buying alcohol for private consumption varies immensely by state. Sometimes it's available from grocery or convenience stores along with off-licences (liquor stores); sometimes it's not available on Sundays. In most towns you are not allowed to drink in public places, like parks or beaches, even if drinking is part of an innocent family picnic. It's also usually against the law to carry an open container of alcohol in a car.

In the major cities it's easy to find *Cheers*-style boozing establishments, where punters are lined on bar stools or tucked away in booths. But in smaller towns bars are more often rather seedy and unwelcoming all-male establishments. If the **light beers** that are most common in the USA aren't to your taste, there are plenty of other **handcrafted ales** tucked away around the country, often as part of microbreweries with adjoining **brewpubs** – effectively bars on the premises of a tiny brewery. On the east coast, good beers to look out for are Boston-based Samuel Adams or New Amsterdam. In the Midwest try Pete's Wicked Ales, while in Texas the Lone Star brand has a loyal following, as do San Francisco-brewed Anchor Steam beer, and Red Sail Ale in northern California.

Cocktails too are popular, with many bars specialising in them; many Americans' knowledge of cocktail recipes is extensive. National creations include mint julep (bourbon, mint, sugar and crushed ice), martini (vermouth and gin) and the Bloody Mary (vodka, tomato juice, hot sauce).

The Honky-Tonk

Britain may have its pubs, Germany its beer gardens and Italy its cafés, but only America can lay claim to the dusty, hard-drinkin' honky-tonk. Known in different parts of the country as a juke-joint, a tavern or simply a 'dive', the honky-tonk is as much a part of American culture as fast food, Disney and endless kilometres of highways. The south and southwest regions can probably lay claim to the honky-tonks with the most pure DNA, though certified joints exist from Manhattan to San Diego.

The first step in finding a real honky-tonk is to locate the poor part of town: here the beer is cheaper and colder, the jukebox louder, and the locals more ready to let it rip. Sure, sanitised lounges are fine for an after-theatre martini, but sometimes you need a place with sawdust on the floor, crooked pool tables in the back room, and a country-and-western band rocking out in the corner – which is invariably what you'll find in a true, dyed-in-the-wool honky-tonk. Step into one in the mid-afternoon (you'll be able to identify it from the myriad neon beer and liquor signs) and let your eyes adjust from the bright sun outside to the cool, convivial gloom inside; you should eventually be able to make out a long, scarred wood bar, with a handful of regulars hunched over it, nursing longnecks of Budweiser. Step up to the bar, have a seat, and order a cold beer – ordering wine or fancy drinks at such places will get you eyed suspiciously at best. Hang around for a bit (by yourself works best), have a couple of drinks, and soon enough someone will surely strike up a conversation. When you stumble out hours later, you're likely to have made friends for life.

In **soft drinks**, too, America is the great innovator, with acquired tastes such as root beer alongside the world's most popular fizzy drink: cola.

Wine

America came of age as a wine-producing nation in the 1960s, and in the 1970s Californian vintages began to receive serious international recognition. Since then the industry has thrived there and elsewhere in the USA, making the country one of the industry's world leaders.

Of the many states in which wine is produced, the leader is California, whose wine-growing history stretches back over a century, to the days when 18th-century missionaries fermented grapes for communion wines. Today's harvest is still mostly based on grapes of the Old World species, *Vitis vinifera*, which has been developed using a variety of new technologies now commonly adopted in wine-making that were pioneered in this state. Some of the best wines come from the Napa Valley area north of San Francisco, where around 80 per cent of the workable land is under vines. Here, rich soil and balanced weather help produce wines in the French tradition. Distinguished wines from that region include cabernet sauvignon, chardonnay and zinfandel. Dry Creek and the

Russian River lands are another popular part of California for wine-growing, with the wines from these regions beginning to rival those of Napa. Abundant fog in these areas produces the soft, fruity wines.

Californian wine makes up around 90 per cent of the country's production but other areas of the USA also produce some interesting vintages. The Pacific Northwest uses its cooler and damper climate to copy age-old techniques and produce strong wines in the European tradition. Washington State's grapes are

Case Study: It's Not What You Know...

'In America it's not what you know, but who you know...and how much money you've got,' laughs Tom Beetson, age 28, from Lanarkshire, who met his American wife in Scotland in 1995 and moved over the following year. 'I'd had a series of odd jobs and was working in a warehouse just before I left Scotland, and so I arrived with no particular skill.' But that didn't seem to matter when it came to finding a job. 'Initially we moved to Arizona where my wife's family lives, but we soon relocated to San Francisco where I got a job in a bar, despite having almost no bar experience and not even a visa, through a recommendation of a friend of the family. Under any other circumstances, I wouldn't recommend working illegally, it's just not worth the hassle and the pay is abysmal. But I was lucky and soon realised that even with being married the whole process of getting a green card and permanent residency was still extremely tough. I also realised that this is a country of middle men and so I employed a lawyer to sort things out for me, which seems to have speeded things up considerably. But even once I was legal I stayed in the bar for quite a while, as the amount you earn in tips is amazing. Most of the other barmen had degrees, but couldn't financially justify moving on.'

Beetson eventually left to find a job with more sociable hours and eventually, this time through friends with whom he shared his hobby of motor cars, he ended up working as a mechanic.

'Americans are very friendly and don't seem to discriminate on the basis of your education or qualifications as much as in the UK. The opportunities are much better and you're judged more on what you have, not how you got it. I thrive on the Californian get-up-and-go but sometimes I also miss the easy familiarity of home. With my accent I have to speak much more slowly for Americans to understand me and their sense of humour is more slapstick and less ironic than the Scottish. I also get frustrated by American ignorance of the outside world, which is phenomenal but not surprising when you see what is in the newspapers here. On the other hand I also find people usually genuinely interested in hearing about Scotland.'

He says he's now firmly settled and wouldn't move from San Francisco: 'Though its expensive, there's lots going on and great countryside nearby. The food is also exceptional, as is the marijuana, which seems to be enjoyed by people from all walks of life.'

particularly good quality and its white wines the most celebrated, though you can also find some quality merlots and cabernets here. Idaho uses the high altitude of its vineyards to good effect, benefiting from the high sugar content of local grapes to produce good body and taste. The local reds are very light with a delicate fruity flavour. In the east most wines come from New York State – especially the Finger Lakes region – and were long made mainly from native grapes such as concords, catawbas and the southern scuppernong, although most of these have now been replaced by hybrids and Old World species.

Sports in America

Simply put, most Americans are passionate about sports. From the 'national pastime' of baseball to what's fast becoming the new national pastime of NASCAR (stock car racing), it can often seem as if everyone has a favourite sport and favourite team. There are many reasons for this, but one is that sports – specifically, talking about sports – cuts across class divides; a minimum wage-making gas station attendant might have nothing in common with a Wall Street stockbroker, but likely as not they both watched the Yankee (baseball) game the night before and both have a favourite shortstop. Women are, on the whole, less involved in the general sports mania than men, though this is changing as more and more young girls are brought up on a diet of 'soccer' and women's basketball. That said, whatever your gender or sports inclination, you really should make it a point to check out a game or two before making a judgement on the whole phenomenon. College (American) football games are positively infectious in their pageantry, NBA (the pro league) basketball games are a frenzy of sight and sound, NASCAR races are a wholesale immersion into middle-American values, and a baseball game – whether minor or major – feels like everything good you've ever heard about America.

Most major cities have a pro team in at least one of the big three sports – football, basketball, and baseball – while virtually all cities have some sort of minor league team; these minor league games often make for a more down-home and friendly (not to mention cheaper) experience. Prices for tickets range from $10 or so for major league baseball bleacher seats to hundreds of dollars for courtside NBA tickets. Check each sport's governing organisation's website for details of teams in your area: **www.mlb.com** for baseball, **www.nfl.com** for football, **www.nba.com** for basketball, **www.nhl.com** for hockey, **www.nascar.com** for car racing, and **www.mlsnet.com** for soccer – not yet very popular in the USA, but steadily growing

Profiles of the Regions

Such is the immense size of the USA that whatever you look for you're likely to find it somewhere – probably many times over and even within the majority of its states. The USA spans half a continent between the world's two biggest oceans and is a country defined by open spaces. It measures 9.1 million sq km, a figure that's hard to take on board, until you realise that the drive from New York on the east coast to San Francisco on the west is around 4,800km – roughly the distance between London and Cairo. On the drive – which typically takes around five days – you'll cross 20 state lines, each marking boundaries between different state laws, and pass through four time zones. The journey will also take in the whole spectrum of landscapes: the rocky, wooded northeast will give way to the windswept Great Lakes, which stretch out as the rolling, grain-laden plains whose abrupt end comes at the hulking snowcapped peaks of the Rocky Mountains. Travelling west of these, you'll need to pass through the sun-baked deserts of the southwest before arriving in fertile and densely populated California.

But, other than the absolute enormity of the distances involved, most striking – particularly to those who come from the relatively cramped and hugely varied Old World – is the cultural homogeneity of the country. Whereas in Europe a three-hour drive can typically take you through three or four linguistic zones and countries with different identities and histories, a three-hour drive in the USA may well not even take you out of one state – Texas is twice the size of Germany and Alaska twice the size of Texas. You can drive for days and the cultural landscape will hardly change much, for the uninformed observer.

The reasons for this relatively uniform cultural landscape stem from the USA's short history. By emerging to its current extent in a time of transport and telecommunications revolutions, the USA is a country whose regions were peopled and developed simultaneously, with many of the same cultural influences at work. This has given the nation a surprising cultural cohesion – especially considering the vast distances involved – and helped make it less regionally divided than it might otherwise have been.

Nevertheless, a good deal of subtle regional variety does exist, with much of it arising from the different early histories of the various regions and their particular climates (*see* **Getting to Know the USA**, pp.4–7, and **References**, 'Regional Climate Charts', pp.229–31).

Regional differences aside, many of the most extreme contrasts exist on a more local scale. One city neighbourhood can be radically different from an adjacent one, and the cultural difference between a big city, a small town and a rural district cannot be overestimated. The choice between these is likely to be as important as choosing between regions.

Similarly, Americans are an ethnically varied bunch, yet relatively few ethnic groupings concentrate themselves on a regional scale. Somehow many different nationalities have converged to create one vast culture. To some extent various immigrant groups have maintained old ways but perhaps more amazing is how, within a generation, elements of their traditional cultures have been discarded in favour of joining a hybrid yet distinctively American culture: one with its own distinctive etiquette and attitude underwritten by a consumer culture that is ubiquitous and far-reaching. Yet the American identity works only on the largest scale, and masks the sheer variety and ethnic mix that coexists. People are often loyal to their state and happy to take much of their identity from its traditional cultural nuances. And on the most local scale, ethnic splinter groups often lead entirely separate lives, with their own neighbourhoods, shops, clubs, newspapers, and TV and radio stations.

The following section should help identify which region might suit you best, though in the end, of course, where you settle may come down to job availability, or other ties. But bear in mind that wherever you end up, location doesn't matter as much as it does in other parts of the world. In a nation with some of the world's most advanced transport infrastructure and telecommunications systems, even vast distances can shrink.

No country has a bigger Internet presence than the USA, so it makes sense to use the web to find out about the country before you travel. Websites like **www.123relocation.com**, **www.relo-usa.com** and **www.craigslist.com** are particularly helpful in supplying practical local information, but one of the best ways to gain a virtual impression is to visit the official state tourism websites. City websites are also useful – even small communities will have one – and all are easily found using an Internet search engine like Google; for a list of major ones, *see* **References**, pp.251–4.

The Northeast

When Frank Sinatra crooned 'New York, New York' he wasn't just repeating the name of North America's liveliest, most cosmopolitan and streetwise city; he was referring to its location in New York State. New York State is at the centre of a vast urban belt – occasionally called the Great Eastern Megalopolis – that stretches up the east coast between Boston and Washington and inland as far as Philadelphia. This makes New York City the epicentre of the USA's most densely populated region. This population density and the familiar compact dimensions and arrangements of the landscape can help Europeans feel more at home here than in the vast open spaces out west. But even within the relatively compact northeast, there's a huge amount of geographical variety. Thanks in part to the presence of the Appalachians – which mark the western edge of the region – most of the USA's climatic zones are represented.

Culturally too, the northeast has a little of everything. Most of the immigrants arriving in the USA from Europe first landed in the northeast, and large numbers felt no need to head any further west to start a new life; work was easy to find in a region that was once the cradle of America's industrial revolution.

New York City

As the biggest city in the world's most influential country, New York considers itself the capital of the world. The presence of the United Nations Headquarters and the world's premier financial centre on Wall Street helps stake the claim. It was the doorstep to America for generations of immigrants, and many New York sights, like the Statue of Liberty and the Empire State Building, have certainly become icons of the modern age and made the city world-famous. But it's only once you arrive and see the city's mesmerising and addictive ethnic diversity that the claim seems entirely justified.

A panoply of cultures is represented here, with each making a distinctive contribution to the city's overabundance of food, music, theatre, art and literature. The pace is energetic and exhilarating, and many of the 8 million New Yorkers snappy, brash and often fiercely eccentric. The chaotic, cramped and often dirty city is a far cry from the wide spaces and polished urban areas that largely characterise much of the rest of the USA, which makes it a city unlike any other on the continent. In many ways it has more in common with Europe's biggest city, London, than with other US cities.

Settlement on the site of modern New York began in 1624 when the Dutch West Indies Company founded a trading colony on the southern tip of Manhattan Island at the mouth of the Hudson River. Two years later the island was bought for a handful of trinkets from Native Americans – a good deal on both sides, since the people in question were not even locals but simply passing through. The colony of 'New Amsterdam' then began to take shape here, administered by the Dutch hands for the first, fairly miserable 40 years. With alcohol banned and religious freedom limited, it was to some relief among its residents that the colony fell into British hands in 1664. Quickly renamed New York, it stayed staunchly loyal to the British, even into the 1770s, when it showed no real interest in joining the jockeying for independence.

At the end of the War of Independence – when the city witnessed the swearing in of George Washington as the republic's first president in 1789 – New York was a bustling and dirty seaport of around 33,000 people. From this point on New York entered into almost a century and a half of explosive growth. This was particularly encouraged by the 1825 completion of the Erie Canal, which connected it to the Great Lakes and made it the continent's largest port. By 1830 New Yorkers numbered 250,000; by 1850 this figure had doubled; and by 1880 it doubled again to more than 1 million. This was an era of tenement culture in the poorest areas, where problems were compounded by widespread corruption in public services. But elsewhere in the city, skyscrapers began to sprout, shaping the New York of today.

Yet all the immigration of the 19th century was as nothing compared to the final huge wave of European immigration in the early 20th century. The channelling of immigration into the continent through Ellis Island made New York the gateway to the continent and by 1930 the city's population had leapt up to 7 million. Throbbing with poor immigrant families, despite Depression-era struggles the city boomed. As groups struggled for survival in an uncertain and unfamiliar new world, close intra-community bonds gradually gave rise in some cases to a tight, ethnically defined criminal underclass.

Economic buoyancy in the 1950s then saw the introduction of yet more diversity, with a boom in the African-American population and a massive influx of Hispanic Americans. Many of these immigrants replaced groups who had previously been concentrated earlier in the centre of the city. From the 1950s to the 1970s American cities witnessed the flight of their middle classes to the suburbs, and nowhere was worse hit than central New York, which developed a reputation for deprivation and crime, well-illustrated by its unreliable, dangerous and graffiti-smothered subway.

The city slowly improved in the 1980s, during the financial boom of the Reagan era, but these short-term policies produced only a short-term reprieve. By the 1990s the city had regressed and was again suffering from its traditional problems: too little money, too many people and fierce racial tension. But the 1990s also saw the introduction of strict anti-street crime measures. Policies of 'zero tolerance' for even minor law infringements slowly brought misbehaving New Yorkers into line, so that the city managed to shake off its more notorious aspects of its reputation; today most districts feel fundamentally safe at most times of day.

Much of this was thanks to the hard-nosed policies of Major Rudy Giuliani, who will always be remembered for his firm leadership on and after the 9/11 terrorist attacks on the World Trade Center in 2001 (*see* box, p.65). Many of the 3,000 killed were firemen, police and rescue workers who entered the doomed towers shortly before they collapsed. Ever since this terrible episode, city security has been severely tightened, producing an even safer but at times tense atmosphere. Modern-day visitors entering the USA through the likes of Newark Airport can expect a tough grilling. But these days few will be able to afford a spot in Manhattan, where soaring property prices and an extremely competitive market push many into New York's other boroughs or over into New Jersey with its sea of highways and intersections.

The Mid-Atlantic States

Standing in the shadows of New York City, **New Jersey**, **Pennsylvania** and to some extent **New York State** are seen in the popular imagination as a densely populated and fairly grimy region, thought to be dominated by the smoke stacks of New Jersey and the coalfields and steel mills of Pennsylvania – the world's foremost steel producer in the 19th century. But much of the region's commitment to heavy industry is a thing of the past, and such is the size of this region that even the gritty post-industrial towns are interspersed with expanses of virtual wilderness and pockets of cultures where the way of life has remained unchanged for centuries.

Once hotly disputed by the Dutch, English and French, the region finally fell under control of the English in the mid-18th century. The native population, including the Iroquois, who had sided with the French in wars against the English, was confined to reservations. In places, though, relations were good, particularly under the leadership of British Quaker William Penn, who established Pennsylvania as a haven for religious tolerance. The area was rich in furs and, by the mid-18th century, Protestant sects such as the Quakers, Mennonites, Amish (*see* box, below) and Irish Presbyterians had pioneered successful farming communities in the region.

In the struggle for American independence the region became tactically vital. American control of the Hudson River could effectively isolate New England from Britain's other colonies, and consequently more than half the battles were fought in this region. After independence, heavy industry was established, with Eastern Pennsylvania powering the many mill towns along the rivers. Since then, and in line with the general decline of manufacturing and heavy industry in the western world, much of this activity has now ceased. Communities are now split between depending on tourism or as existing as commuter towns for the big cities. Success in both areas is based largely on the outdoor beauty of the quieter nooks in the area and their accessibility to the big cities. Particularly attractive areas include the Catskill and Adirondack Mountains, the Finger Lake region in upstate New York and the Niagara Falls on the Canadian border.

The Children of the Anabaptists

The so-called 'Pennsylvania Dutch' have nothing to do with the Netherlands. Their name is a bastardisation of 'Deutsch' or German, the traditional language of the Amish and Mennonites. Their forefathers were Anabaptists who fled here to escape their persecution in early-18th-century Switzerland. The corner-stone of Amish beliefs is a strict adherence to biblical codes, the interpretation of which famously leads them to reject machinery – travelling in horse-drawn buggies rather than cars and forgoing electricity – and to live by simple means. This principle extends to a very conservative dress code, with men wearing black trousers, braces, a straw hat and beard (but without a 'militaristic' moustache), women wearing simple, plain ankle-length dresses devoid of decoration (a definition that includes buttons), aprons and lace bonnets. Broadly speaking, Mennonite beliefs are a relaxed version of those of the Amish, which allows them greater integration in the modern world.

Many of the quiet, mid-sized and often quaint artsy towns that are scattered across the region, and particularly in upstate New York, are pleasant places to live. Among the larger places to consider are **Albany** and bohemian **Buffalo**. Of the region's big cities, both **Philadelphia** and **Pittsburgh** are likeable and energetic. **New Jersey** is much less attractive and divides largely between urban wasteland and sprawling suburbia. But if you look hard you'll find quiet and wealthy nooks even here, as well as all the benefits of being close to New York City.

New England

'Live free or Die!' proclaim the vehicle licence plates of **New Hampshire**, and certainly New England has a history of a fierce sense of justice and independence. The first shots in the American War of Independence were fired here, and New England abolitionists were vital in forcing a civil war against the South.

Today, New England likes to view itself as cradle of the nation and a repository of all things truly American. Nostalgia for a sometimes fictional past certainly plays a large part in this self-image, with many of the region's painfully pretty small towns conforming to an idyllic type. Here clapboard houses cluster around rolling greens and white spire churches. And within the homes is a deep sense of satisfaction that has fostered a white, Anglo-Saxon and Protestant (WASP) élite. The area has produced powerful families – including the Kennedy and Bush dynasties – who dominate the region's prestigious Ivy League colleges, which are widely considered among the country's best.

By American standards New Englanders are a little reserved, and tend towards a certain frugality of speech and in material goods, which can make them appear unfriendly. But, generally, this is just a more formal style and people are outgoing and hospitable enough. This is never more so than at the region's many unusual festivals. The annual pumpkin festival in **Keene**, New Hampshire, for example, celebrates the carving of thousands of different designs into the vegetable. Many festivals also have ethnic roots and the whole New England area is full of groups maintaining strong cultural connections with their homeland. **Boston** has a weighty Irish influence and tight Italian communities; **New Bedford** in Massachusetts and **East Providence** in Rhode Island are largely Portuguese; **Manchester** in New Hampshire and **Woonsocket**, Rhode Island both have large Francophone communities; and onion-shaped church domes announce Russian communities in many small places. Thanks to this ethnic mêlée, there is a good variety of food in the region, too – rivalled in the USA only by New York and California (*see* 'Regional Specialities', pp.27–31).

The first European contact with the region was made around AD 1000 when Vikings under Leif Eriksson began the settlement of Vinland the Good. Its location is unclear but it seems to have been somewhere between

Massachusetts and Newfoundland. Run-ins with fierce native Algonquin meant the settlement was soon abandoned, and it wasn't until the early 16th century that Europeans returned. Some fisherman began to migrate annually into the region, but it was only in the early 1600s that the French and British attempted to found permanent colonies. Aside from the bountiful waters for fishing, there was, however, little reason to colonise the area. Soils were thin and conditions harsh and unfamiliar. Consequently many of the first settlers here were refugees from religious intolerance seeking to found free religious communities, including those who famously came on the *Mayflower* (*see* **Getting to Know the USA**, 'European Settlement', pp.10–12).

These pioneers found thick forest, now famous for its autumnal (or fall) colours, extremely changeable weather and fiercely cold and often snowy winters that made survival a real trial. The region's thin soils and the settlers' lack of local agricultural know-how made life tough, but somehow, and often with the help of Native Americans, the colonies succeeded. By the end of the 16th century most of the Native Americans had been forced off their land – being defeated in the war of 1675–6. This paved the way for another burst of immigration, including a particularly big influx of Huguenots and Irish. This helped bring an end to the Puritan domination of society, which slowly emerged with a definite class structure and the establishment of the powerful élite which has survived to the present day.

New England prides itself as the birthplace of American Independence and it was certainly the stage for key events. These included the 1770 Boston Massacre and the 1773 Boston Tea Party; and in 1775 the first shots were fired at Lexington and Concord. Ironically, though, nationhood meant economic suffering for New England. Severed links with Britain made it a backwater and it was soon left in the shadow of Philadelphia, New York and the new capital, Washington. The region briefly came to the fore again in the 1790s by spearheading America's industrial revolution with its water-powered cotton-spinning mills. But soon it sank back to concentrating on its traditional strengths of education, commerce and medicine, which continue today.

Energetic and stimulating **Boston** is New England's biggest city and benefits from the strong university presence of Harvard University close by; it has become a popular place to settle for British expats. Many sizeable and pretty towns in the vicinity, including **Salem**, **Concord**, **Lexington**, **Province Town** and **Cape Cod**, have a strong visible history, but can also be a bit too touristy and crowded.

South of Massachusetts, the states of **Connecticut** and **Rhode Island** operate as New York's back door and are a far cry from their days as pioneer territories, being today largely determined by their rows of patrician homes, mansions and compounds of the rich élite. To the north of Massachusetts the towns thin, to be replaced by more appealing scenery of **New Hampshire** and **Vermont**, which presents an archetypal picture of small-town Yankee America, where small towns service ski resorts and a fairly traditional way of life. The area has attracted drop-outs, who live side by side here with die-hard conservatives. The largest and northernmost state, **Maine**, is known for rural life and a rural wilderness that can rival any other.

The Capital Region

It was no accident that the nation's capital, **Washington, DC**, was placed just where the north blends with the south. For northerners their capital feels southern; for southerners it has some distinctively northern traits. And much of the surrounding region has elements of both and is generally hard to pin down. Many of the contrasts and contradictions are particularly highlighted in Washington, where the corridors of power lie adjacent to inner-city poverty, but the region's extreme climatic patterns are just as schizophrenic. Cold, snowy winters lead into rainy springs and uncomfortably hot and humid summers, which make the cool, crisp autumnal weather a relief.

The British originally settled the region, beginning alongside the rich estuary of **Chesapeake Bay**, where tobacco quickly became the most lucrative crop, giving the region considerable colonial importance. The half of the population engaged in the backbreaking job of harvesting tobacco was made up of African slaves.

The fight for independence made the region vital, as many of the decisive battles were fought here and it later became the political birthplace of the nation. Less than a century afterwards, the region was also bloody with the battles of the Civil War as it decided the future course of US history. The capital of the Union – Washington, DC – and that of the Confederacy (see p.16) – Richmond, Virginia – are only 160km apart. Once differences were settled, the region became stronger than ever in steering the fate of the nation, a pivotal role it maintains to this day.

Considering that it is the capital of such a significant nation, Washington is rather sleepy and provincial, though the city's magnificent and monumental architecture of grand government buildings, historic sites and museums helps distract from this. Just as attractive is the quirky and engaging city of **Baltimore** an easy one-hour drive to the north. As the country's second-largest gateway for immigration, its multicultural roots are still very much in evidence.

Surrounding Washington, DC, and effectively serving it, is **Virginia**, a pleasant rural state with some hugely exclusive suburbs south of the capital, but which otherwise is best known for its plethora of historic sites. To the west, where the Allegheny Mountains rise, is sheltered West Virginia where mineral exploitation once ruled, creating inventive mining communities that spawned bluegrass music (see **The USA Today**, 'Bluegrass', p.97). Today, most of the employment in the mountains is in providing for outdoors enthusiasts.

To the north of the capital, **Maryland** is the hardest state to pin down. An eccentric northern outpost of the South, it is a far more attractive prospect than **Delaware**. In the latter overwhelmingly industrial and commercial state, companies thrive on permissive laws, and the absence of a sales tax pleases shoppers.

Many possibilities exist for finding and living an appealing small-town life in some of the region's minor cities. These include **Annapolis**, close to Washington, DC, and **Charlottesville** or **Fredericksburg**, a couple of hours' drive to the south. **Wilmington**, in northern Delaware, is another good option and close to Philadelphia.

The Midwest

West of the Appalachian mountain chain, the Midwest region of the United States centres on the western Great Lakes and the upper Mississippi valley. But this rather vague term also often includes the states of the Great Plains and so covers a vast tract of the country that includes the states of **Illinois**, **Indiana**, **Iowa**, **Kansas**, **Michigan**, **Minnesota**, **Missouri**, **Nebraska**, **North Dakota**, **Ohio**, **South Dakota** and **Wisconsin**. Generalisations over such a large area are difficult, but some common elements exist. These include its topography, which is generally flat with only occasional rolling hills, and the region's dependence on agriculture. As the country's breadbasket, the Midwest has some of the richest farming land in the world and is well known for its grains and cattle. The northern part of the region has also been the site of much of America's heavy industry, though with its decline many of the heavily industrialised parts of the Midwest have become dubbed the Rust Belt. Culturally, the Midwest is popularly characterised as conservative, isolationist, Protestant and predominantly white. This has some basis in reality, though it glosses over the variety of politics, religions and ethnic groups that coexist here – particularly in the big cities.

The Great Lakes

Ageing industry and great natural beauty lie side by side around the Great Lakes where rocky peninsulas and sluggish waters are fringed by the wharves of decaying ports – and both define the region in equal measure. But the region's centrepiece is undoubtedly its five Great Lakes, which, together with the tens of thousands of smaller bodies of water, constitute the largest body of fresh water in the world. Lake Superior is the largest, peppered with fleets of ocean-going tankers and extending over 480km from east to west, with its lengthy shoreline frequently experiencing high winds and sizeable waves. Together the lakes essentially determine the climate of the region. In summer lake breezes help cool the hot summers, though in winter they do little to help with the region's brutally cold weather; drops below −50°F are common.

The Great Lakes are also the region's lifeblood in a commercial sense, and it was their presence that excited the interest of early French explorers who sought the Northwest Passage – the fabled northerly sea route to China. The route never materialised but the French did proceed to lay the foundations of some modest colonial outposts in a network of forts and Jesuit missions along the crucial shipping routes. Local tribes, like the Huron, Iroquois and Algonquin, became close trading partners and allies. But the good fortunes of both the French and Native Americans largely came to an end with the loss of the French and Indian War (1754–60) to the British. The establishment of an independent America, local large-scale white settlement, and finally the Black Hawk War of 1832, put a final and bloody end to traditional ways of life.

During the same era waterways were created, which at once developed the region and made it the national transport hub. Routes linked the Great Lakes not only to each another and to the Gulf of Mexico (via the Mississippi River) but also to New York with the completion of the Erie Canal in 1825. Once established, this network enabled the region to power the USA's tremendous 19th-century rise in agricultural and industrial might. **Chicago**, with its gigantic stockyards and multiple railheads, developed into the 'Hog butcher to the world', as Carl Sandburg put it, and also the site of the world's biggest agricultural commodities market. Meanwhile, in the countryside, waves of immigrants developed agricultural smallholdings. **Wisconsin** and **Minnesota** particularly attracted Scandinavians and Germans, while Illinois and Indiana attracted southerners fleeing the Civil War.

The happy coincidence of abundant fuel and ores in the region coupled with the efficient water and rail transport allowed many regional cities to become industrial powerhouses. The iron and steel works of Cleveland benefited from their accessibility to shipping, as did **Detroit**, helping it become the capital of the world's car industry. The happy combination of a convenient location and good transport were equally vital to the success of Milwaukee's big breweries, which thrived on the doorstep of the region's rich grain fields.

The rocketing economy of the Great Lakes region required a vast workforce, and recruiters turned to the poor African-Americans in the South, who began to migrate en masse in search of jobs. The region's cities swelled and developed a new layer of multi-ethnic culture. Musical traditions came north with the migrants, and the jazz and blues of New Orleans soon mutated into new strains as it arrived on a grander stage and began to develop into a national art form.

By the early 20th century the Great Lakes had become the wealthiest part of the USA, the industrial powerhouse driving the country. This made it the obvious seat of power for the high-profile gangsters, like Al Capone, who thrived during the Prohibition era in the 1920s and '30s. Times have since changed: Prohibition and gangsters are things of the past, but so too is much of the region's industrial might. As in much of the developed world, heavy industry increasingly found itself losing out to overseas competition from less developed nations. The consequences of this global restructuring have in many cases been devastating in the region. Many of these old industrial cities have suffered inordinately from this decline, with deprivation and urban blight replacing their once proud prosperity. Subsequent clumsy management and poor city planning have made cities like Detroit notorious centres of civil unrest and unemployment. Yet some urban centres, particularly **Cleveland**, have begun successfully to battle back, finding ways in which to regenerate themselves and their economies. Despite this, prestigious and cosmopolitan Chicago remains the region's key and most attractive city. But that said, big city life forms only a small part of the region – which is essentially dominated by tiny communities fringing the smaller lakes.

The Great Plains

The massive gateway arch in St Louis is symbolically considered the beginning of the American West. Beyond here the land is dense with romantic associations that celebrate the myth of a wild frontier. Traders, explorers and pioneers forged their destinies here, but today this vast patchwork of grasses and grains is anchored to gigantic farms and occasional small, functional and largely unexciting communities.

The Great Plains – loosely all the northern USA west of the Mississippi and east of the Rocky Mountains – only really opened up in the 1870s after the American Civil War and the creation of the transcontinental railroad. Soon the awesome herds of bison – an estimated 60 million of them – were slaughtered to make way for ranches and cowboys. The slaughter was also part of an official strategy to starve the Native Americans off the land, and the era was marked by a series of worthless treaties that shunted Native Americans further and further west onto smaller and more economically worthless reservations. This process was completed by the late 1870s – but not before brilliant strategists like Sitting Bull and Crazy Horse had inflicted stinging defeats on the US Army – particularly at Little Bighorn, an event also known as Custer's Last Stand.

Although in the long term the plains have proved bountiful for farmers and ranchers, in the short term living in this region can be extremely hard and hazardous. Not only do the vast spaces create a sense of isolation and a necessity for self-reliance, but the weather offers a severe and hugely unpredictable force to contend with. Tornadoes, dust and lightning storms, freak blizzards and heavy flooding are a fact of life in the area. Droughts too are frequent, and in the past have taken their toll on its people, most famously during the Great Depression. Today, modern farming methods help to cushion climatic variation, while threatening local life by ushering in a trend of the corporate takeover of family farms; which has led to depopulation in many areas. Those left are predominantly white and the region as a whole is the heartland of conservative Middle American values. This and the dull landscape – celebrated almost exclusively for its 'big skies' – means the region is generally passed over by both relocating Americans and settling expats alike.

The Rocky Mountains

Spanning over a thousand kilometres from the Canadian border to the deserts of the southwest, the Rocky Mountain states of Colorado, Idaho, Montana and Wyoming encompass a wildly varied array of landscapes and wildlife, but a relatively sparse human population. But as the rest of the USA – whose taste for outdoor recreation continues to increase – wakes up to the wonders of the region, the population has been growing steadily in recent years, particularly in **Colorado**, whose largest city, Denver, doubled in population during the 1990s. In summer the region is an outdoor paradise, with all manner of trails and rivers to explore on foot or by mountain bike, raft or kayak. In winter the skiers, snowboarders and snowmobilers take over.

At the time of the white discovery of the Rocky Mountains the Native Americans in these lands were largely nomadic hunters. It was only after the Louisiana Purchase of 1803, followed by Lewis and Clark's expedition west, with the reports of abundant game, that the area really began to be opened up. This news fast filtered east, so that it was not long before the booming fur trade brought beavers close to extinction. Bust followed boom in the industry, establishing a pattern that the region witnessed time and again. The discovery of gold in 1858 near Denver rapidly attracted permanent settlers, who moved from one Colorado mountain town after another as they boomed with gold and silver. These all collapsed at much the same speed as they grew, but not before all the native peoples had been shunted out of the mountains. These mountains continue to hold the main treasures today, albeit in the form of remarkable opportunities for recreation in the great outdoors. In the last 20 or 30 years, it's these aspects that have begun to attract large numbers of vacationers, wealthy second home owners and telecommuters. Winter sports have become big business, with the mountain resorts of Colorado alone attracting over 12 million skiers and snowboarders every year.

Dynamic and sophisticated, **Denver** is by far the largest city in the region, with nothing bigger for 1,000km. Technology blossomed here in the 1990s, when ambitious companies realised it was easy to attract bright young graduates into the area. Denver lies on Interstate 70, one of the country's major east–west highways, and so acts as a gateway to much of mountainous Colorado. Easy accessibility along this road has buoyed a succession of old mining towns into fashionable communities with a certain rustic chic, the most successful, such as Aspen and Breckenridge, living off the cluster of ski resorts.

The northern Rocky Mountain States are much less on the beaten path, more sparsely populated and have considerable wilderness areas, particularly in Idaho, where some entirely unexplored pockets still exist. Fewer than half a million people live in **Wyoming**, although the **Yellowstone National Park** in the state is popular. The inaccessible northern areas of **Idaho** and **Montana** – areas first opened up by Lewis and Clark's famous expedition – are a big lure for radical non-conformists of all kinds ranging from white separatists to die-hard environmentalists.

Texas

Texas has a strong identity and mystique that no other state can match. Today it's as much a land of modern cosmopolitan cities with high-rises and hi-tech industries as it is a land of the open range dotted with longhorn cattle and nodding oil derricks. But no matter where you are in the state, pick-up trucks, cowboy boots, Stetsons and beef in all its many guises proliferate. And the Lone Star state is also famous for its feisty independence, immense pride and the warm hospitality of its people. Everything is bigger – and so better – in Texas, and certainly its geography bears this out. The state is 1,300km wide and nearly 1,600km north to south, thus encompassing a huge geographical diversity.

In the 1600s the region's generally nomadic native peoples found themselves beginning to compete with the Spanish, who had begun to explore the area in search of gold. This turned out to be a fruitless exercise, but nevertheless the newcomers established missions and forts here in order to secure the land from the French, who might otherwise have been tempted to spread west from Louisiana. In 1821 Texas found itself becoming part of a newly independent Mexico as it severed its links with Spain. A strong Hispanic influence continues in the state to this day, not least in its food.

Mexico encouraged the settlement of the land, and soon numerous Anglo-American colonies became established in the territory. Frictions stemming from restrictions on settlers led to the Texan Revolution of 1835–6, of which the legendary Battle of the Alamo was a part. The battle saw all 189 Texans defending the Alamo Fort die – but at the cost of 1,600 Mexicans. Just six weeks after the Alamo fell, Texas won its independence from Mexico at the Battle of San Jacinto, where the Texan soldiers (shouting, 'Remember the Alamo!') killed several hundred Mexicans, while losing only nine of their own. From 1836 until 1845 Texas stayed an independent nation and only joined the American Union under the proviso that it could secede whenever it wanted – a clause still written into its present-day state constitution.

Houston is Texas' largest city, with a population of around 2 million; it is hot and humid, in the swampy east of the state, and has a similar climate to that of Louisiana. Every bit as cosmopolitan and brash, though not quite as large, is

Dallas in the northern part of the state. It shares its airport with the smaller city of **Fort Worth**, a quintessential Western place. The state's third major city, **San Antonio**, is unlike the other two, with a long history of considerable Mexican influence and population. Lying between the three major cities, **Austin** is an artsy, intellectual and liberal enclave in an otherwise deeply conservative state. The north and west of the state is more lightly populated, with a more mountainous and drier geography that merges into the deserts of the southwest.

The Southwest

Wedged between America's two most populous states – Texas and California – are the four extremely sparsely populated states of **Arizona**, **Nevada**, **New Mexico** and **Utah**. These largely occupy a russet-red desert landscape of baked-earth rock monoliths and yawning canyons, making up a land of fierce temperatures, sudden thunderstorms, flash floods and forest fires. This visually enchanting virtual moonscape also comes with many irresistible vestiges of the Old West, not least thanks to its relatively large Native American population, whose culture maintains a strong presence throughout the region. The region is particularly known for its native crafts, elegant traditional pottery and kachina figures. Woven Navaho rugs decorate adobe dwellings with an interior terracotta look, and the local silver and turquoise jewellery is widely exported. Hispanic connections are strong, too. Up until just over 150 years ago the region was in Mexican hands, and today Spanish-speakers are as ubiquitous as the spicy Mexican food.

Archaeological records of the region tell of fascinating cultures like the Hohokam, Mogollon and Ancestral Puebloans (formerly called Anasazi), who occupied parts of the area from 300 BC to around 1500. Records are sketchy, but Ancestral Puebloans appear to have had a strong and sophisticated culture, and they have left evidence of complex cliff palaces and cities, along with signs of extensive astrological know-how. Their descendants, the Pueblo peoples of New Mexico and the Hopi of Arizona, ended up competing with less sedentary tribes such as the Navaho and Apache who migrated into the area from the 14th century. Europeans finally arrived on the scene in 1540 when Spanish explorers entered the fray, looking for mythical cities of gold. Around 1600, Spanish colonists founded the state of New Mexico, which stretched into California and Colorado, and became a neglected backwater of Mexico, before being forcibly taken over by the USA in 1848. This coincided with a gold rush era and a period of ongoing conflict between Native Americans and the US army, in which warrior chiefs like Geronimo fought extended campaigns.

The native tribes eventually lost their cause and were moved off all economically useful land and on to designated reservations in the west. Many of these were in the southwestern region, where the awkward terrain and harsh climate meant few settlers would be able to make a go of it. Today, one-third of Arizona remains under the control of Native Americans.

One exception to the minimal success of pioneers in settling across the region were the Mormons (*see* box, p.74) who fled from religious persecution in the eastern USA to **Utah**. Here their determination, co-operation and sheer hard work allowed them to build what amounted to a separate country. Today 70 per cent of the state's population remains Mormon and the bulk of local resources and political control still remain in Mormon hands.

Of the four states, **New Mexico** bears the most obvious traces of Spanish heritage, particularly evident in colonial style towns like Albuquerque, Santa Fe and Taos. **Nevada** is the most desolate of the four states, scenically perhaps the least attractive, but, as the location of the world's premier gambling city **Las Vegas**, it has completely different concerns.

California

Named after an imaginary island inhabited by Amazons in a Spanish novel, California is the stuff of fantasy and the USA writ large. Vast, glitzy cities face on to sea, sand and surf, backed by high mountain ranges, and contain ethnic groups of every type and political persuasion. The state has the largest population (over 35 million) and agricultural output of any state and is an economic powerhouse. If it were a country, its economy would rank sixth in the world. But its power and influence go even beyond its bountiful natural resources and economy. Through its inventiveness and imagination it has become the cornerstone of the world's most influential industries, many of which are headquartered here. Its film industry and music business together define western popular culture; its computers and hi-tech innovations drive major sectors of the modern economy.

While California is certainly a trendsetter, it is full of contradictions. As the home of counter-cultural movements from the beat of the 1950s, the hippies of the 1960s and radical political and ecological movements ever since, it has cultivated strong liberal values. These have put it at the forefront of environ-mental awareness, let it embrace gay culture and allowed for a permissiveness that makes it the US capital of a $12 billion-per-year pornography industry. But at the same time it is the home of reactionary politics, spawning Ronald Reagan, Richard Nixon and now Arnold Schwarzenegger. Somewhere out of this odd combination, California has become a cultural think-tank. This is where traditions and etiquette are quickly broken – and then reinvented. From dress-down days and plastic surgery to extreme health-consciousness, Californian values have done much to shape the modern USA. Many of these values are clearly faddish, but none is more precarious than the state's long-term fate, as it perches on the San Andreas faultline. A massive and possibly cataclysmic earthquake is expected at any time.

California has always been one of the most densely populated parts of North America. Searching for gold in the 1540s, Spanish explorers found a series of peaceable tribes living along the coast with almost no history of conflict. With no obvious evidence of local riches, the Spanish only began to colonise the area in the late 18th century, with the 1769 establishment of a fort at San Diego becoming the first of a chain of missions – a day's walk from one another – up the coast.

The territory of present-day California became part of Mexico in 1821, as the country gained its independence from Spain. But, thanks to an influx of Anglo-American settlers and the USA's manoeuvrings, California fell into American hands in 1848. Gold was discovered in the same year, and the gold rush that followed caused a population explosion in San Francisco; in these wild 49er days its population rose to 90,000. And although most of the gold fields were played out within 15 years, this became the start of a trend during which California's population doubled every decade for a century. Vital in stimulating this was the 1869 completion of the coast-to-coast railroad, which brought California to within five days' travel of New York, at a time when a one-way ticket was an affordable $1. Much of this railroad was built by Chinese labourers, with some 15,000 brought into state for the purpose. The conditions of their existence were poor and, once the line was completed, they suffered a wave of discriminatory legislation. But even so, most stayed on, becoming one of California's largest ethnic groups. Strong Asian influences are present, as befits a state on the Pacific rim of North America. But even stronger than the Asian influence in modern California is that of the Hispanic community. Spanish now outweighs English as the first language in the state, and the state continues to attract more immigrants from the South. The Hispanic community now makes up the vast majority of California's foreign-born residents – which add up to a quarter of its population. Tensions among and between immigrants and the poor led – as they once did in New York – to the formation of numerous street gangs, with racial tension and a spate of violence a feature of Los Angeles life in the 1990s.

California's two biggest cities, Los Angeles and San Francisco, could barely be more different. **San Francisco**, the smaller of the two, spreads its wooden houses, densely clustered, over a series of steep hills, and has the advantage of a stunning setting beside a large bay. The city system actually spreads all around the bay, with **Oakland** in the east tightly incorporated. **Silicon Valley**, famed for its cluster of hi-tech corporations, lies to the south. From here, a series of pleasant small towns spreads along the coast. These include **Santa Cruz**, **Monterey** and **Santa Barbara**, stretching to Los Angeles, an easy day's drive from San Francisco. As you head south, the climate progressively improves. Around San Francisco, the coast is regularly chilly and overcast, with drizzly conditions common throughout the winter. But by the time you reach LA you have the benefits of the southern Californian climate, which is sunny all year round.

Most Europeans are left overwhelmed and yet at the same time under-impressed by **Los Angeles**. A hopeless sprawl of freeways and suburbs, it has no real centre and is hard to come to grips with. The city's notorious smog is also unappealing, and at its worst during the height of the summer. A more pleasant, outgoing and manageable city is laid-back **San Diego**, hard by the Mexican border, which has a strong Hispanic feel. The city is also a right-wing enclave, thanks in part to its important role as a military base.

The South

Margaret Mitchell's *Gone With the Wind* would have us believe the American South to be a delicate and romantic landscape swathed in Spanish moss, and peopled by well-mannered, heroic men and frail débutantes. Yet this alluring portrait misrepresents the South as much as the stereotypes in countless other fictional representations that have blighted it. Many outsiders have come to think of the region as one peopled by hillbillies, rednecks, racists and dirt-poor, underprivileged African Americans, where reactionary politics and evangelical religious fanaticism run wild. Elements of all these exist, but the combined effect is a wildly inaccurate caricature. The region is equally remarkable for the southern drawl in speech and a matching slow-paced tempo in life as well as the all-embracing, polite and charming southern hospitality.

Its colonial history helps explain the separate path the South has taken from the rest of the country. Plantation agriculture made the region prosperous, under the guiding hand of a landed gentry with their legions of black slaves. That situation created two classes and exceptional inequality, much of which remains to this day. And in the southernmost parts of the region a Spanish or French colonial heritage has also left its mark on the culture and people.

As its main transport hub, **Atlanta** acts as a gateway city to the South. A successful hi-tech and thoroughly modern city, it is surrounded by the southern heartland, much of which is a relatively poor backwater.

Culturally, one of the most stimulating place before the devastation wreaked by Hurricane Katrina in 2005 was **New Orleans**, where a Cajun influence in language, and culture gave us fine spicy seafood concoctions and great jazz. The historic French quarter was relatively undamaged, but it remains to be seen how long the reconstruction of the city will take.

Florida, although in the South, has a very different character from the rest of the region, peopled as it is mainly by retiring northerners and expat Cubans. Even its moody tropical climate is different from the rest of the South. But the hot sticky summer is common to the whole region, and makes living an active life without air-conditioning unthinkable.

The Southern Heartland

The Southern Heartland, which comprises the states of **North Carolina**, **South Carolina**, **Georgia**, **Kentucky**, **Tennessee**, **Alabama**, **Mississippi** and **Arkansas**, has a bad reputation among liberals, which dates back to the Civil War days (*see* pp.16–17). Since then, the activities of the Ku Klux Klan and the suffering and bloodshed of the civil rights movement in the 1950s and '60s have only served to reaffirm preconceptions.

Yet the South has never been as uniform nor is it as extreme as is often thought. Even during the Civil War there were pockets of weighty Union support, particularly in the mountains. And today the make-up of the overwhelmingly African-American cotton belt is markedly different from the white hill-farming regions in Kentucky and Tennessee and the hi-tech belt of North Carolina and Northern Alabama, and a far cry from the rural backwaters of southern Georgia. The region is equally geographically diverse. While the Appalachians rise in the Tennessee, Kentucky and North Carolina, the Atlantic and Gulf coasts are known for subtropical beaches and peaceful barrier islands.

Historically the region developed along with its plantations. The area became a vital point in the triangular trade across the Atlantic, with African slaves making the gruesome journey to the Americas to toil in the baking heat of the plantations supplying British cotton mills and tobacco factories. The success of the plantations demanded more land for expansion, so that the largely peaceful and agrarian Native American tribes were soon moved on to Oklahoma to make way for farming. Yet, despite the immense profitability and wealth of the region, its economy was severely one-sided. Concentrating entirely on agriculture, the South was content merely to supply the northern factories that monopolised the lucrative manufacturing industry. This weakness was laid bare during the Civil War and subsequent reconstruction period. Not only did the manufacturing might of the north help the Union win the war, but the resulting forced abolition of slavery made plantations far less profitable and effectively dismantled the economy of the southern heartland.

Changes in the wake of the Civil War not only spelt the end of a way of life in practical terms; it also effectively made the southern heartland a backwater for the following century. As the plantations broke down, huge numbers of former slaves became unemployed, which triggered mass migrations to cities like Memphis and Atlanta, but also the north. Meanwhile, in a backlash against the equality that the north tried to enforce, various segregation laws that disenfranchised, forced out of office and persecuted virtually all African-Americans were passed, and there was a surge in Ku Klux Klan activity. Only the protracted and courageous actions of many ordinary citizens during the Civil Rights campaign of the 1950s and '60s – led by Martin Luther King Jr (*see* box, p.22) – finally ensured a basic level of equality.

The Big Muddy

By draining the Great Lakes into the Gulf of Mexico, the Mississippi has become America's most significant river. Its ability to carry freight between north and south has made it vital, but its ability to link the two extends well beyond this and not least in the popular consciousness. It has also become the unofficial boundary between east and west USA.

Though one of the world's busiest commercial waterways, the river has become romanticised, in part by the novels of Mark Twain who was raised on its waters and spent four years as a riverboat pilot. These romantic associations are at their most potent and evocative in the South where chugging along on a steamboat – out of Memphis, St Louis and it is to be hoped once again one day New Orleans – remains the classic way to explore. It is also particularly in the South that the Mississippi winds and meanders – 'the crookedest river in the world' in Mark Twain's words – over a broad, flat floodplain where it continually shapes and reshapes itself. These nutrient-rich alluvial floodplains have resulted in a productive farming belt. But farmers are only a small proportion of the millions along the river whose lives are fundamentally shaped by it and who have affectionately given it the title of Old Man River.

Yet the river is not entirely benevolent. Floods have been disastrous – today almost the entire length of the river is lined by flood banks or levees, which famously broke in 2005 at New Orleans – and in the South, the river's waters help create an unpleasant humidity. Nor is the river particularly attractive. At points the Mississippi is over a mile wide – the name means 'big river' in an Algonquin language – but is described as accurately by its nickname 'The Big Muddy'; its earthy-brown waters drag 1lb of dirt along in every 500lb of water.

Former slaves often said that they had sung in the cotton fields when they were at their most miserable, and somehow the musical traditions of the South are reflected in this. Out of deprivation and oppression, talented African American musicians developed new and exciting musical styles that have reverberated around the world and informed many modern musical traditions. Among these are blues, jazz and gospel, and in general the southern heartland, and particularly Tennessee continues to be a musical stronghold. Nashville and Memphis – erstwhile stomping grounds for Elvis Presley, Dolly Parton, Otis Redding and Hank Williams – are particularly notable for country and blues respectively. Understandably tourism is also big business in these towns, with both seemingly centred around fairly wild strips of bars.

Tourism also helps keep afloat the stylish coastal cities of **Charleston**, South Carolina and **Savannah**, Georgia or the historic ports towns of Natchez and Vicksburg in Mississippi. Elsewhere, college towns like **Athens**, Georgia, and **Chapel Hill**, South Carolina are youthful vibrant communities, while **Asheville**, North Carolina, tucked in the shadow of the Smoky Mountains, is one of the region's few liberal and less religiously fundamentalist communities.

But to find the South at its most modern and dynamic you need to travel to **Atlanta**. The so-called Sun Belt, which stretches from here to Phoenix, Arizona, is particularly well developed around Atlanta. Hi-tech industries have flocked into the area and helped fund a revival that helped improve the region's racial relations. Atlanta's hosting of the 1996 Olympics was considered a real landmark in launching the city onto the world stage. Politically, too, the South has been coming out of the shadows of the north, producing soft-spoken and relatively liberal political leaders in the form of Jimmy Carter and Bill Clinton.

Yet the South continues to be generally poorer than the north and huge inequalities and poverty remain. These are perhaps at their most extreme in Mississippi, once the fifth-richest state in the Union, where the demise of slavery and cotton has left shocking inequality and poverty. This is mainly among the African-American population, who in many cases lead entirely separate lives from the whites.

Florida

Around 700 people per day move to Florida, the self-proclaimed 'Sunshine State'. This pattern has existed since the 1960s, and in the last 40 years the state's population has tripled. Most of those arriving are retirees but all are lured by the absence of winter and the thousand miles of sandy beaches that have made it the country's premium vacation land – something capitalised on and encouraged by the creation of Walt Disney World™ Resort, which sprawls over 27,500 acres of central Florida.

But Florida is not just tanned flesh and a cartoon mouse. It also has strong Hispanic ties and a dynamic Cuban and Caribbean community, whose calypso and reggae sounds dominate many of the city bars. The pancake-flat state also has natural delights in the form of forests, rivers deserted beaches, coral reefs, mangrove swamps and abundant wildlife. The climate, too, is also more like that of the Caribbean than the rest of the USA. Summers (May to September) are often muggy, with regular afternoon storms.

John Cabot first sighted Florida in 1498, just six years after Columbus' first foray to the Americas. A 1513 mandate from the Spanish crown, urged by unfounded rumours of gold, saw the territory quickly conquered and colonised, while most of indigenous population died from new diseases to which they had no natural immunity. The first permanent settlement in the USA, **St Augustine**, took shape here. Though the territory had a spell under British rule, this was short-lived and the Spanish got the territory back following American independence. But not for long. In 1814 the USA began fighting against the Seminoles – fugitive Native Americans and former African slaves arriving from the west – who put up stiff resistance to American forces and were driven out of the fertile lands of central Florida and into the Everglades. In 1819, Spain ceded the territory to the USA, in return for the cancellation of debt, and the

Learn Seminole

The Seminole Indians have two languages still in use today, neither of which is traditionally written. Muscogee (Creek) and Miccosukee are related but not mutually intelligible. Both languages contain sentence structures and sounds that do not exist in English and are difficult to pronounce for the English tongue. With some words the two languages seem to mirror each other; and sometimes the two are quite different. For example, the English word for bread would be pronounced '*tak-la-eek-i*' in the Muscogee dialect and '*pa-les-tee*' in Miccosukee. 'Dog' is '*ef-fa*' in Creek, '*ee-fe*' in Miccosukee. 'Cow' is '*wa-ka*' in Creek '*waa-ke*' in Miccosukee. Many Seminoles are fluent in both languages; some only speak one or the other.

The names of many Florida cities, counties, places, rivers and lakes are taken from Seminole words, both Creek and Miccosukee.

Apalachicola	place of the ruling people
Chattahoochee	marked stones
Immokalee	my camp
Miami	that place
Ocala	spring
Palatka	ferry crossing
Yeehaw	wolf
Pahokee	grassy water
Okeechobee	big water

A Few Seminole Words

ee-cho	deer
ya-laahe	orange
o-pa	owl
hen-le	squirrel
sho-ke	pig
laa-le	fish
yok-che	turtle
chen-te	snake
ke-hay-ke	hawk
nak-ne	man
coo-wah-chobee	big cat

first American governor was sworn in. Agriculture, particularly beef and citrus fruits, helped develop the state, but only in the latter half of the 20th century, with the development of mass tourism, was it put firmly on the map.

Far and away the state's major and most lively city, the bilingual and half-Hispanic (specifically Cuban) town of **Miami** is an enthralling place, but as a key location in the drug trade, and a place where racial tensions often surface, it presents anything but an image of perfect social or interracial harmony. More idyllic communities can be found in the small towns up and down the coast. In the far south the **Florida Keys** are a 100-mile string of islands, ideal for fishing and diving, that centre on **Key West**, a funky, anything-goes sort of place. The east coast north of Miami is fairly solidly urbanised, thanks in part to the hundreds of miles of beaches running alongside the major settlements of **Fort Lauderdale**, **Boca Raton** or the millionaires' playground of **Palm Beach** – all attractive seaside towns.

Louisiana

Louisiana has a multinational history and a Creole culture that sets it apart from the rest of the USA. Its French and Spanish ancestry is writ large and it's the only state whose laws are still based on the Napoleonic legal system. It is also famed for celebrating pirates, voodoo, and above all Mardi Gras with gusto. But the swamps of Louisiana are a hard place to make a living, and many of its residents are among the poorest in the nation, a fact painfully revealed in the aftermath of the Hurricane Katrina disdaster in 2005.

Present-day Louisiana was first settled by the French in 1682, who braved the swamps to harvest the abundant cypress. Later it moved between British and Spanish ownership, but it always seemed to attract fugitive groups. French royalists escaped here from the French revolution; Spaniards came from the impoverished Canary Islands; former black slaves from the West Indies. But one of the biggest groups to influence the area was the Acadians – French Canadian refugees forced out of Nova Scotia by the British in the 18th century – who traversed the continent in search of a new life in a wildly different climate: their direct descendants today are the French-speaking Cajuns. The mix of ethnic groups has also combined to form an entirely new group: Creoles. This confusing term is used to refer to people of either French or Spanish parentage, but today to all things native to Louisiana and particularly African-Americans.

Mardi Gras: Carnival Louisiana-style

The local tradition of bingeing on the fun just before the start of Lent goes back to the earliest French colonial times. Of all the towns where it's formally celebrated, it has always been done with the most zest in New Orleans. Here spectacular parades, masked balls, drunkenness and debauchery go on for a full week before the final blow-out on 'fat Tuesday' (literally Mardi Gras in French). In the last decade or so, the thousands of out-of-towners who headed here for the party have changed the atmosphere somewhat, but much of it is still authentic and it's definitely still good fun. In late 2005, the news is that the festival will still go ahead – for news check out **http://mardigrasneworleans. com;** the site has fascinating historical links and enables the online purchase of costumes and grandstand seats – and even video streams of the parades.

Louisiana came into US hands in the Louisiana Purchase. For $15 million Napoleon I handed over all French lands between Canada and Mexico, the Mississippi and the Rockies. In 1861 the state seceded from the Union to become part of the Confederacy, even though its Black Code assured slaves of far better treatment than elsewhere in the South, including giving them the right to meet socially, take Sundays off and marry. The Civil War and particularly the following period of reconstruction crippled the economy of Louisiana, and only recently had tourism begun to turn things around, a process which may well be reversed since the 2005 hurricanes wrecked most of its principal town.

The Pacific Northwest

Geographically, the Pacific Northwest region spreads over international borders, incorporating not only the states of **Washington** and **Oregon** but also a large part of Canada's province of British Columbia. These three have much in common, in terms of climate, topography and liberal politics, with many people, particularly in Washington, regularly crossing the Canadian border to work or play in and around Vancouver.

The white presence in the area first became significant in the 19th century, as traders and explorers searched for the fabled Northwest Passage – an ice-free route between the Pacific and Atlantic. But there was little in the way of permanent settlement, as Russians from the north and the British from the east began to compete in the area for fur trade profits. Large-scale settlement began in the 1840s, as a surge of American settlers along the Oregon Trail, following in the footsteps of Lewis and Clark, whose expedition of exploration was the first to cross the interior of the continent. Thousands of settlers coaxed their ox-pulled covered wagons across more than 3,000 kilometres of pristine, rivers, forests and mountains, relying on their self-sufficiency and their ability to trade and negotiate with natives in what has since become the classic American migration. Though the route was treacherous, most survived the trek, and pretty soon the volume of American settlers in present-day Washington and Oregon gave the USA *de facto* control of the area. The situation was ratified in the 1846 agreement with Britain: all lands south of the 49th parallel became American, those above Canadian.

The bulk of the settlement in both states is along the Pacific coast, location of both **Seattle** and **Portland**. The prevailing weather patterns arrive here from the west, driving in all manner of stormy and rainy conditions, which are effectively trapped on the western side of both states by the north–south band of the hulking **Cascade Mountains**. Vegetation thrives in these damp conditions, with atmospheric, misty and moss-laden forests abounding. The maritime climate also keeps winter temperatures mild, although high up in the mountains record snowfalls are regularly seen. While trapping moisture in the west, the Cascades create a rain shadow in the east. Consequently the eastern parts of both states are given over to arid, sparsely populated agricultural plains. The rather dull city of **Spokane** is the major regional hub here.

Topographic and climatic similarities aside, Washington and Oregon are two hugely contrasting states. Washington is far more dynamic and business-orientated, its packed freeways serving important military bases and the headquarters of Microsoft. Its main city, Seattle, is a busy place with a vibrant coffee house culture and buoyant musical scene that's known for both jazz and grunge. Oregon has been strictly protected from this kind of development and so has a far more laid-back feel.

Alaska

Larger and wilder than any other state, Alaska is the USA's final frontier. It is a land of enormous ice fields, endless tundra, carved glacial valleys, dense rainforests and magical fjords. And in it the wildlife roams free, with bears, moose and wolves common and gigantic salmon fairly choking many of its rivers. The sheer size of the state is hard to grasp. Measuring 1,518,775 sq km, it's roughly the combined size of Germany, France, Spain and the UK. It has 17 of the USA's 20 highest peaks and its largest glacier is twice the size of Wales. Yet the state is peopled by only around 600,000, which makes for endless undeveloped space and gives relative freedom for pioneers to stake their claim and make a go of it.

The long dark winters, fierce weather and the isolation of much of the land mean it is not a place to be trifled with. It may not be as cold as commonly thought, but the weather in the state is also hugely unpredictable. Average temperatures range from around −7 to 18°C (19−64°F) in **Anchorage**, where it rains more than it snows. Possibly more off-putting than the weather, though, are the mosquitoes that choke the air in the summer months, and are jokingly dubbed the state bird.

Alaska is thought to have been the first area in North America to be populated when, around 14,000 years ago, nomadic tribes crossed a land bridge that's now submerged beneath the Bering Sea. These peoples set up hunter-gatherer communities, which successfully expanded to fill much of the continent in the following centuries. But it wasn't until 1741 that their lives became intertwined with the outside world, when Danish explorer Vitus Bering, funded by the Tsar of Russia, became the first to set foot on the peninsula and claimed the land for Russia. At this time a number of tribes inhabited modern-day Alaska, including the Aleut, Athabasca, Tlingit, Yupik and Inupiat. All lived a subsistence existence, based on fishing and the hunting of marine mammals. Once the knowledge of the abundance of fur seals and sea otters here filtered back to Europe, there was a flurry of interest from Russian, British and Spanish pelt-hunters. In 1799 Russia

Case Study: A Rep's Guide to the Regions

Graham Smith, 38, works as a sales rep for an engineering company and gets to travel more than most. So, since emigrating from England 15 years ago, he's seen a good deal more of the USA than most Americans.

'The USA is far more diverse than most Brits give it credit for. I'm based in Florida, which has people from all over the US and is also the premier European holiday destination. But holidaymakers who base their impression of the entire country on this region and what you see on the telly – which many seem to do – are simply wrong.'

Smith explains that his frequent business travel to different parts of the country has helped him unravel some of the differences. 'The northeast around Boston and New York is the most fast-paced and perhaps most European. People are friendly enough, but tend to keep themselves to themselves. In the South the attitude is absolutely different. People will readily strike up conversations with strangers, yet are perhaps more suspicious of outsiders.' Smith continues. 'I don't know if it's down to the heat or not, but the pace is far more relaxed. People appear less stressed and have more time for idle chit-chat'. This, he says, translates into absolutely vital differences in business matters. 'People expect more face-to-face contact and deals are often done on the basis of trust and codes of conduct. There's also far more polite etiquette to observe and whatever you do, don't swear in the Bible Belt!' But Smith admits that even these are sweeping generalisations. 'Even the South is hardly uniform. Texans can be quite brash, while those in the Carolinas are often softly spoken. Go to places near Mexico, like San Antonio or San Diego, and it's sometimes hard to find someone who speaks English.'

Smith also considers east–west differences to only be slightly less significant than north–south contrasts. 'Californians can be rather prissy and are often seen by other American's as particularly eccentric in a demanding way. Mid-westerners are at the other end of the scale and typically highly conservative. Their lack of exposure to the wider world seems to make them distrust everybody and particularly change.' But Smith also believes that you can find places you'll like anywhere in the USA, though he strongly suggests that, initially at least, small town life should be avoided unless you want to embrace parochial American values. 'They may be friendly but the situation can easily become claustrophobic and exceptionally boring. If you're not close to a major city and airport you'll likely feel cut off from the world.'

established the first colony, at present day **Sitka**, which formed a base to allow pelt-hunting to extend all the way down the coast as far as California. But by the early 19th century returns from pelts were beginning to wane, as was Russia's interest in the colony. Given its debts from the Crimean War, Russia elected to sell the land to the USA, in what became one of the biggest land deals ever brokered, although the land went for a mere two cents per acre. Most

Americans initially thought little of the 1867 deal, but this judgement was reversed around 15 years later as the first gold was struck. Logging and commercial fishing also proved lucrative, at least for a while, but the area's real wealth lay in Alaska's immense oil and natural gas reserves.

Recent rises in the price of oil have encouraged exploitation in Alaska, and the possibility of drilling in the Arctic National Wildlife Refuge (AWNR) could create another economic boom. Hotly debated and environmentally heavily criticised, these proposals were rejected by Senate by only a single vote in 2003, but have now been passed. Tourism has also begun to play a large part in today's economy, with many of the most attractive and relatively accessible areas now reliant on this source of income.

Hawaii

The easygoing Hawaiian Islands boast fine beaches, excellent year-round weather and world-class surfing, windsurfing, kayaking, diving and snorkelling, making them a born holiday destination. But if you're looking for a quiet and idyllic island paradise, think again. As the Canary Islands of the Pacific, this archipelago annually attracts around seven million package tourists; and despite its isolated position in the middle of the North Pacific ocean – 2,600km from mainland USA – Hawaii is still recognisably and commercially American.

The Hawaiian island chain was formed by repeated volcanic activity above a stationary hotspot beneath the earth's crust. Each volcanic episode thrust up material on a massive scale to create an island and as – over thousands of years – the crust moved, these islands became a chain. The first humans to colonise the islands were the Polynesians, who arrived somewhere between AD 500 and 700. The societies they established here flourished for around 300 years, before Tahitians conquered the islands, introducing cannibalism and strict social taboos in the process. By the time Captain Cook chanced on the islands in 1778, the culture had long ago lost contact with the outside world, but had thrived on the verdant islands, growing to a population of around one million. Contact brought widespread disease that drastically reduced the population and began a reshaping of the island and traditional culture.

The first of several boom-and-bust cycles to hit the islands was the frenzied exploitation of their forests. The logging of sandalwood brought so much wealth that traditional farming and fishing methods lapsed and the islands began to become dependent on imports for virtually everything – a pattern that continues to this day.

At around the same time, Hawaiian society was in some moral chaos as its traditional taboo system was being dismantled by its royalty. This offered fertile ground for the New England missionaries that arrived in the 1820s and quickly moved into positions of power in government, and whose offspring became the most powerful class. They were quick to realise the economic potential of the fertile volcanic soils and fine weather, with the result that soon Hawaii was overcome by a wave of sugar plantations – a labour-intensive industry that required workers to be recruited from overseas. Soon immigrants began to outnumber natives.

The success of sugar production in Hawaii drew it closely into the economy of the USA. So tightly were the two bound that it began to be in America's interest to control the island government firmly, and annexation became almost inevitable. The process started with a group of white businessmen putting themselves in control, in a process enforced by the US military. Even at the time, the event was not universally condoned in the USA, and the American actions were the subject of a formal apology by President Clinton 100 years later.

After its formal annexation in 1898, Hawaii grew to be of vital strategic importance to the USA, which soon built large army and navy bases here. One such was at Pearl Harbor, which the Japanese attacked in 1941, effectively bringing the USA into the Second World War. It was only years after the war, in 1959, that Hawaii became a state, a move supported by the overwhelming majority of islanders, though many of the 8,000 pureblood descendants of the native islanders remained vociferous opponents.

Today the production of sugar and pineapples is a dwindling part of the economy, which is dominated by resort tourism. **Oahu** is the main tourist island and location of **Honolulu**, the capital and largest city. Mass tourism is also widespread on **Maui** and **Kauai**, while **Molokai** (the smallest island) and **Big Island** (the biggest, also confusingly called Hawaii) are much less developed. The geographical pattern on most of the islands is similar, though: the northeast coasts are lusher and damper, while the southeast coasts are dry and almost barren, making them the perfect location for big resorts.

The cost of living in Hawaii is high – around 20 per cent more than in the mainland USA, with the cost of housing particularly steep. But, despite the problems of overdevelopment at the larger resorts, these culturally diverse and climatically wonderful islands, where easygoing friendliness and a warm-hearted spirit of hospitality is the norm, can be a great place to live.

The USA Today

The terrorist attacks of September 11, 2001 may not have changed the world, as the press at the time would have liked us to believe, but it certainly changed the American view of the world and its own priorities. Today, twice as many Americans as in the 1990s say that they are paying attention to national and international affairs, when they used to care more about local stories. While media attention and political strategies have undoubtedly played a large part in leading the country's values, the ongoing threat of foreign terrorism has clearly joined the USA's economic woes as a big issue for most people. The country's five-year-long economic downturn has yet to show signs of lasting improvement.

But the attacks have not just switched America's focus; they have also appeared to accentuate America's characteristic traits. Strong patriotism defines the country more than ever, and its current government is more nationalistic than previous administrations. It also openly appeals to resurgent fundamentalist Christian and family values. Yet because America is profoundly heterogeneous, vast numbers of people do not share these values and politics, creating deep divisions within the nation. The emergence of two distinct and ideologically divided groups can be seen particularly in the closely fought presidential election of 2004, but also affects every American issue, and the resulting tensions are played out in the strong biases of media organisations.

America's current politics have also widened differences between it and the rest of the world. For much of its history the USA has had an active and confident role as a standard-bearer of universal values such as democracy and human rights. These have been based on deep convictions of institutional superiority, economic primacy and self-belief in the USA as a place apart from other nations. This has never sat entirely well with some of the rest of the world, and recently it has experienced increasing disapproval in the global community. In a world that can't seem to get enough of American pop culture and brands, there is at the same time a growing criticism of American foreign policy.

Politics

The United States is a federal republic whose **constitution** is the world's oldest and best-known, and is the glue that holds together a uniquely diverse nation of peoples who stem from every corner of the globe. Drawn up in 1787, the constitution runs to just a few thousand words, but it is a concise and measured document, which provides a careful system of checks and balances to ensure power is spread. Over its history it has – with several relatively minor hiccups – remained remarkably resilient in practice, and effective in creating a stable democracy. The constitution balances collective power between three branches

9/11

On September 11, 2001, terrorist attacks on the World Trade Center and Pentagon killed more than 3,000 people and caused all Americans to re-appraise their relationship with the outside world. Suddenly, and as at Pearl Harbor, the horrors of international struggles were brought onto American soil.

The destruction of the World Trade Center was particularly potent because of the symbolism of the towers. In their 28-year lifespan they had became the focal point of New York City's skyline and a symbol of the city's success. Yet on a cool, crisp autumn morning, as many people were starting their working day, two hijacked planes crashed into the towers within 20 minutes. Rescue workers raced to evacuate the buildings, but largely to no avail. Many of those on the upper floors jumped to their deaths. Then, as the towers finally swayed and crumbled, hundreds of fire-fighters, police officers and rescue workers became further victims of the tragedy, losing their lives among the debris and incredible clouds of dust as the towers collapsed. These events unfolded live around the world thanks to the tight media coverage.

Manhattan's skyline now looks gap-toothed. And though the wounds will heal and a project to redevelop the World Trade Center site with a glass spire that reaches to the height of the former towers is in progress, a visible scar will remain.

of central government – the executive, legislature and judiciary. Individual states have their own separate constitutions and government – in most cases organised according to the same pattern. The vast majority of institutional posts – including judges in some states – are filled through election rather than appointment, which gives the USA more elected offices than any other country: in a four-year cycle there are around a million elections. Perhaps under-standably, this set-up also produces one of the world's lowest voter turnouts.

The System of Federal Government

The three main federal (central) government branches are the executive (the presidency and affiliated offices) the legislature (Congress) and the judiciary (the Supreme Court and federal courts). An unusual feature of the system is that the executive and legislature are elected and housed separately, and that their co-operation is vital to the passage of good government. The president can veto acts of Congress – though this can be overruled by a two-thirds vote in both houses. The House of Representatives can impeach the president for treason, bribery, or 'other high crimes and misdemeanors', in which instance the Senate could remove him from office with a two-thirds majority.

The federal government deals with all aspects of foreign affairs, national defence, maintenance of the currency and the regulation of interstate commerce. State governments deal with all other areas. US nationals over the age of 18 have the right to vote – unless they have a criminal conviction, in which case their right is lost unless they receive a rare pardon from their state governor. The many millions of immigrants with green cards who are effectively permanent residents of the USA have no right to vote – an ironic case of 'taxation without representation'.

The Executive

The president is the US head of state, elected via an electoral college representing the states, and serves for a maximum of two four-year terms; the president must be born a US citizen, be at least 35 years old and have been a US resident for at least 14 years. Presidential elections are held every leap year on the Tuesday after the first Monday in November. The current US president, George W. Bush, is now in his second term, which will end in January 2009.

Presidential election campaigns concentrate on simple, well-used, powerful themes of patriotism, defence, crime, the family and taxes. The most popular presidents have been those with a talent for connecting with ordinary people and summing up their message clearly and succinctly – qualities attributed to Franklin D. Roosevelt, Ronald Reagan and Bill Clinton.

Although virtually all the attention focuses on the presidential candidate himself – particularly on television, which plays a key part in the modern voting process – a presidential election results in the appointment of an entire administration. Unlike in the UK, members of this cabinet are not appointments generally from among those elected by the people, but are simply presidential appointments. All appointments face a confirmation hearing by the elected Senate. This process amounts to making around 2,000 appointments. At the top of the hierarchy are the cabinet secretaries who are based in the White House and head the government departments, which collectively make up the national administration. The most important of these are the Department of State, responsible for foreign policy; the Treasury; and the Defence Department. Other government departments include those with responsibility for agriculture, commerce, education, energy, health and human services, homeland security, housing and urban development, interior justice, labour and transport.

The Legislative Branch

The US Congress is the legislative branch of government that debates and creates legislation. It divides into a Senate and House of Representatives in a bicameral system (a governmental system that divides the legislative function between two chambers).

Senate's 100 members are elected on a plurality (first-past-the-post) system for a six-year term, two for each state, with one-third of its members retiring every two years. The House of Representatives' 435 members are also elected on a plurality basis, but for two-year terms. The number of representatives elected by each state is determined by quota fixed by population sizes. The largest states, like California or Texas, elect more than 20 representatives each, while tiny Montana elects only two.

The role of the Senate is to deal with all bills except those involving revenue and provide its 'advise and consent' for all foreign treaties. The Senate also has the power to confirm or reject presidential appointments, including the cabinet. The House of Representatives has the sole right to propose revenue bills, though these may be amended or rejected by the Senate.

The Judiciary

Questions of federal law are decided by the judiciary, which consists of the Supreme Court, the US courts of appeal and US district courts. The Supreme Court is the highest court of appeal and consists of nine judges who are appointed for life by the president – with approval from the Senate. Its decisions are final and legally binding on all parties. When deciding cases, the Supreme Court can review the activities of both state and federal governments and can rule that their laws are unconstitutional. In so doing the Supreme Court has nullified laws and delivered momentous judgements on issues like racial segregation, abortion and capital punishment.

Below the Supreme Court sits a hierarchy of lower federal courts. These deal with cases arising under the US constitution or any law or treaty. Federal courts often hear cases of disputes between citizens resident in different states.

Civil courts are clearly distinct from criminal courts. The former cover disputes between parties, while the latter prosecute those who break the law. Minor crimes are categorised as 'misdemeanors', while serious violations of the law – like robbery, murder, rape and drug-dealing – are 'felonies'. Only felonies usually require an arrest and an appearance in court; misdemeanours are dealt with by a summons and a fine. If you are arrested you will be frisked for weapons, handcuffed and read your rights. These include the right to remain silent. Following arrest you are advised to wait to have a lawyer present during questioning; your right to a phone call should be used to enlist the help of one – via an embassy or consulate if you are a foreign national.

An unfamilar part of the American legal system is the accepted practice of plea bargaining, which involves an agreement that if the defendant agrees to plead guilty to a lesser charge then their case will be speeded up and their sentence reduced. Another unusual aspect is that American lawyers are allowed to work on a contingency 'no win, no fee' basis, which means that in civil cases they will fight hard to win and take on any case where rewards are high – their fees are usually calculated as a percentage of damages awarded. This encourages a rather more litigious society than in the UK and Europe, driven by lawyers who are offered insanely high rewards for their services. If you find yourself either side of the litigation process, beware of the minefield that exists and be sure not to say anything to anyone connected with a case without a lawyer present. Many social services provide free legal assistance to immigrants.

State Legislature

Each state has certain fiscal and legal rights and powers to make its own laws, and a large degree of autonomy to control its own affairs and set its own taxes. Areas where control is most conspicuously exercised include trade and commerce, education, transport, marriage and divorce, weapons and social services, wages and criminal justice. All the states except Nebraska (which has a unicameral system) have a bicameral legislature that follows the model of the federal legislature. Each state has its own flag, seal, song, motto, flower, bird and tree.

States are subdivided into counties, municipalities, towns and districts, each with its own form of administrative government. Municipalities include all urban areas, large and small, and in the largest the local government will consist of a mayor and city council. Mayors have considerable and broad powers (in contrast with their largely ceremonial role in the UK), while counties are governed by a council, usually with a head, whose powers vary widely.

Local government looks after education, police, fire and ambulance services, libraries, health and welfare, public transport, parks and recreation, waste disposal, highways and road safety, and trading standards. Local laws determine many things in everyday life – for example what restrictions are placed on the sale and consumption of alcohol.

Political Parties

The political system in the USA is strongly two-party. Power is either held by the **Democrats**, who were formed at the beginning of the 19th century, or the **Republicans** (originally called the Grand Old Party) – whose founding in the mid-19th century was built on a strong anti-slavery platform. Though both are among the oldest parties in the world, a member's affiliation to party policy is not as strictly adhered to as in most other countries, and members of both parties encompass a wide variety of ideological and regional interests. Democratic socialism, of the type strong in Europe, barely registers electoral support, so party differences are small – only minimally larger than those within parties – and it is not uncommon for politicians to change parties.

Though their policies have more in common than not, the two parties have strong separate images: the Democrats are seen to be liberal and somewhat more left-wing than the right-wing Republicans. Generally the Democrats favour higher levels of public spending and taxation to stimulate the economy

Photo essay
by Christian Williams

1 Streetcar, New Orleans

2 Skyscrapers, Chicago
3 Patriots' Day parade, Boston

4 Prairies, North Dakota
5 Statue of Liberty
6 Cowboy boots, Nashville, Tennessee

5

7

8

7 Miami Beach, Florida
8 Grand Canyon

9

10

11

9 Mississippi steamer
10 Kennedy Space Center, Florida
11 Savannah, Georgia

12 Grand Central Station, New York
13 Swamps, South Carolina
14 Snowboarder, Copper Mountain, Colorado

13

16

15 Colorado
16 Kayaking, North Carolina

18

19

17 Central Park, New York
18 Busker, Central Park
19 Vietnam Veterans' Memorial, Washington, DC

21 Apartment block, Boston

and increase welfare. As a result, their electoral base tends to include blue-collar workers, ethnic and religious minorities and educated professionals. The Republicans favour a more conservative and *laissez-faire* approach to government, as usually championed by big business and private enterprise, farmers and all those unlikely ever to require a welfare net – particularly America's large middle class.

Independents can have a strong support in political rallying, and personality politics can be vital, particularly in local politics, as can stances on single issues such as abortion and homosexuality, which are often far more important than party allegiance. Minor parties like the **Green Party** also exist, yet, in the absence of proportional representation in the USA, they have only the tiniest toehold in government and are effectively excluded from the political system.

The System in Operation

The first stages of the presidential campaign are the **primaries**, in which candidates from the same party run against one another to determine who will represent the party at the presidential election. Campaigns for these often begin two years before the election itself and costs always add up to many millions of dollars. Parties often contain substantial and numerous factions; among the best known are Jesse Jackson's Rainbow Coalition and the Christian Coalition, a powerful conservative lobby of those on the evangelical right-wing. The series of primaries and **caucuses** serves to decide who will stand for the post of president for each party. On the Tuesday after the first Monday in November in a leap year, Americans vote in the **presidential election** itself. Their votes go through an **electoral college system**, which balances each state's voting power with its populace. Voters cast their votes for electors (not the presidential candidate) who are pledged to one party and its candidate on the ballot. Each state has as many electors as it does senators and representatives combined – a total of 538 (100 senators, 435 representatives and 3 votes for the District of Columbia). All of each state's votes go to the party polling the most votes, and the party with the majority of the 538 votes nationally has their elected leader become president.

Once in power, the style of a president's governance is partly determined by the power of his influence and party in Congress. Congress can sometimes be swayed by a strong president, but if the opposition party exists in any numbers, it can be extremely hard to get legislation passed. This system frequently acts to thwart the president – with President Clinton famously hamstrung by the Republican control of Congress for his entire eight-year administration, thus preventing his restructuring of the American healthcare system.

Yet despite these tendencies for the system to be controlled by party politics, it is a much less rigid system than in the UK, where executive authority depends on party adherence and discipline. Congressmen and senators are more independent figures who are as likely to build coalitions according to regional interests and personal ideologies as along party lines. However, since the 1970s there has been an increasing trend towards toeing the party line – particularly among Republicans, but also among Democrats.

Yet, no matter who is in power, they are hugely influenced by the thousands of lobbyists and pressure groups residing in Washington. Many of these have considerable influence, particularly those supporting commercial or business interests. Most powerful corporations or wealthy special interest groups employ huge staffs of professional lobbyists to put their case, and financial support is targeted to key members of Congress. This is, however, an accepted and traditional part of American politics, with the result that it is practically impossible for Congress to try to enact legislation that goes against the interests of the richest and most powerful lobby groups.

Ultimately, the main way in which the two parties vary in governance is often in the way they choose to practise federalism. Democrats typically favour 'co-operative federalism', offering to subsidise welfare, education and various other programmes in return for following nationally led policies. Republicans tend to favour a more hands-off approach, leaving the two streams of government to their own devices as far as revenue and government is concerned.

Ideology

Unlike most countries, the notion of being an American is not just about being tied to particular piece of land but is also a state of mind. This helps explain the country's extraordinary capacity to attract and absorb immigrants, but also the country's unity and attitude to the rest of the world – since it must necessarily define its values in opposition to this. In practical terms the idea of being American translates into a belief in personal freedom and strength and hard work; the importance of patriotism and overpowering military strength to defend your values. Yet, simple as all these principles at first glance appear to be, there is also a considerable breadth of interpretation available. An ardent supporter of the 2004–5 Iraq war will probably claim to defend it for patriotic reasons, while a strong opponent such as Michael Moore in his film *Fahrenheit 9/11* will claim to oppose the war – also for patriotic reasons. Either way, patriotism is clearly a positive buzzword to American people, yet deep divisions in the debate about what this means threaten the cohesiveness of the nation. This national split into two broad camps is considered in the section 'Internal Issues' on pp.80–87; this section considers those beliefs that apply more or less universally.

Personal Freedom

In the American constitution every individual has the right to **'life, liberty and the pursuit of happiness'** and one central premise of American government is every individual's right to personal freedom. Much of this is enshrined in the **Bill of Rights**, which protects citizens from government abuse and lists a series of liberties to which individuals have a right – which famously includes the right to bear arms. While the overwhelming focus on rights and the protection of freedoms is highly laudable, it has also helped create a litigious society. The USA has more lawyers per head than any other country, and rights are frequently upheld at the expense of personal responsibility.

Distrust of Government

Another central strand of most people's relationship with politics is a deep distrust of government, particularly federal government. The sharing of power between federal and state government is an ongoing concern, even though the constitution demarcates the limits of the power of each. Similarly a tension exists concerning the balance of power between local communities and the wider state. The tension was most horrifyingly demonstrated in the blowing up of federal government offices in Oklahoma in 1995, at the cost of 166 lives. One of the most contentious strands of the relationship between the individual and the state is in taxation – levels of which have always been kept low throughout the USA. Resistance to taxation was a key element in the USA War of Independence. Promises to cut taxes are almost always a vote-winner.

The Pioneering History

Another key to understanding present-day American politics is the legacy of its pioneering history. Escaping ties and persecution by fighting and working hard to build a new life has left its imprint on the psyche of the nation. It has underwritten the nobility and importance of self-reliance as well as ensuring a belief that opportunities should be allowed to be as bountiful as possible, in order to ensure the American way to flourish. Generally, Americans are more worried about the protection of their personal freedom than the existence of a social safety net – in contrast with Europe, where it is the other way around. As a result the US welfare state is comparatively flimsy and guns proliferate – there are around 212 million handguns in the country.

America's pioneering history and comparatively recent struggle to build a nation has given rise to a high level of patriotism. A belief exists that Americans have collectively carved the most successful and powerful country in the world, by overcoming the odds of a virgin territory and the Old World order. This has produced a sense of a unique destiny – of being the chosen country.

In many senses this embodies much the same attitude as that of the 12th-century Crusaders. And though Americans don't share quite the same strength of religious conviction, Christianity is one of several traditional values that drive US patriotism. Every US coin and note bears the inscription 'In God we trust'. Traditional family ties also predominate. Whereas in Europe religion tends to be a personal, optional matter, and patriotism not a big concern; in the USA it is broadly the opposite. While Europe's growing wealth has been translated into values of self-expression and a celebration of ideological diversity, in the USA it has strengthened what many consider the sources of the country's success.

Current Policy Themes

President George W. Bush came into office in 2000 on the basis of a slender and hotly contested victory. The main problem he initially faced was getting the US economy back on track after its dive into recession, but soon after the World Trade Center attacks this goal took second place to asserting US power and declared values in the world.

The absence of a tangible enemy in the form of a country saw the Bush administration engage in a difficult game of shadow-boxing. Hunts for terrorist leaders of the Al Qaeda terrorist network – particularly Osama Bin Laden – in countries like Afghanistan saw no real success. Instead the government chose to pursue an old and more tangible enemy in the form of Saddam Hussein in Iraq. Many commentators see this war as using Iraq as a scapegoat to give the patriotically fuelled, post-9/11 Americans a tangible result. Other critics of the was maintain that a desire to retain some control over Middle East oil supplies played a part. Importantly, the USA's circumventing of the United Nations, proceeding with many allies including Britain but without a UN mandate, could have far-reaching effects on the strength of that organisation and the way in which the international community operates.

Bush was able to use the USA's success in the Iraq war to his advantage to keep power for a second term in the next election in 2004. The gap in popularity between him and his opponent, John Kerry, narrowed, as things were going badly in Iraq, but ultimately the American public seemed to feel it better not to change leadership in the middle of a war. In his second term President Bush has a much firmer base in Congress, which will give him far more opportunity to introduce necessary swingeing economic (see 'Boosting the Economy', p.78) and social reforms – particularly a major overhaul of the state healthcare system.

Foreign Policy

American foreign policy has always been torn between isolationism and involvement. Generally the American people have believed that the country should keep out of international affairs, particularly major conflicts like world wars, where involvement always costs thousands of American lives. Governments have taken a very different view: that global political involvement is essential to America's power, influence and wealth. And certainly America plays such a vital role in the world economy and geopolitics that a large degree of involvement is justified. In consequence, presidents have frequently spent considerable amounts of time cajoling their countrymen to sanction a greater overseas role. In the wake of the 9/11 terrorism, permission to be more proactive in foreign policy has been easier for the government to obtain. Amid national fears of continued terrorism and of a spread of weapons of mass destruction, the American government has waged a 'war on terror', during which it has actively engaged in formally deposing oppressive regimes in both Afghanistan and Iraq. In so doing, they have not only entrenched US resentment in the Arab world but have also distanced themselves from many of their traditional allies. With a similar degree of wealth and a dominance of Christianity, Europe is America's natural ally. Yet, excluding Britain, the relationship between America and Europe is something of an uneasy one on both sides, and a shift away from Europe is occurring within the USA administration, as increasing numbers of those in the government are drawn from the deeply American west of the country rather than from the European-friendly northeast.

An integral part of the USA's foreign policy strategy has always been the maintenance of dominant military power. The USA spends more on defence than the next dozen countries combined. The notion that American dominance be not even challenged, let alone surpassed, was vital to its national security strategy of 2002 and was the core reason for the revival of its nuclear weapons programme.

Extending the State

Another theme of the Bush administration has been the extension and intervention of the state into people's lives, though this is perhaps more a side effect of other policies. A combination of fear and a call to American patriotism was used to push through a number of uncompromising and otherwise highly controversial policies with little opposition. The **Patriot Act** was one such piece of legislation. It came into force in 2001 and is due to expire at the end of 2005, when it is likely to be replaced with similar, and permanent, legislation. This act expanded the government's search and surveillance powers and its ability to detain foreigners. On some levels the act seems to balance the country's security against civil liberties, but it has also been asserted that the principles threaten to rob the personal freedoms and right to privacy that have long been thought cornerstones of American life.

Another way in which the government reacted to the heightening of the perceived threat of terrorism was to tighten security at the country's borders and increase monitoring of foreign visitors. To administer this process, a new federal bureau, the Department of Homeland Security, was created.

But it is not just in the realm of national security that Bush has sought to extend federal powers. He is also interested in healthcare and education, exemplified by the 'no child left behind' policy requiring the testing of students – traditionally state responsibilities.

Religion

The USA is fairly evenly balanced between those who are devout and those who are entirely secular, and some 141 million Americans – around half of the population – are church members. This is unusual for a developed country, since elsewhere in the world a growth in wealth and modernisation has been accompanied by the development of a more secular culture. Instead, 60 per cent of Americans say religion plays a very important part in their lives (Allensbach Opinion Research Institute, 2002) compared with just over 30 per cent in the UK. Furthermore, many of those actively engaged in religion are involved in fundamentalist faiths: 39 per cent of Americans describe themselves as born-again Christians, with the result that three times as many Americans believe in the virgin birth as believe in evolution.

The Many Religions

Freedom of religious expression is a cornerstone of the US constitution, and in the absence of a unifying national church this has helped minor churches and small sects to proliferate throughout the country.

Despite there not being an official state religion, the USA is an overwhelmingly Christian country. Around half the country's population are Protestant. The Protestant church divides into numerous denominations, the

Mormons

The Church of Jesus Christ of the Latter-day Saints, better known as the Mormon faith, was founded in 1830 by Joseph Smith. He claimed to have discovered a set of golden tablets in upstate New York from which he transcribed the Book of Mormon, subsequently considered by his followers to be a distilled and purer form of the Bible. Smith's successor, Brigham Young, set up colonies in the northeast of the USA, but life in these was made difficult by the mainstream religions that dominated local governments. Eventually, and after a skirmish in St Louis, Young led his flock to the Salt Lake basin where they established the city of the same name and a semi-autonomous territory of what has become Utah.

This state remains heavily dominated by Mormons, with the vast majority of positions of power and influence filled by adherents to the faith. Many of the state's laws, particularly governing alcohol, reflect this Mormon heritage and devotion to clean living, yet the Mormon faith is one of the least understood of all Christian faiths – in part because their services are strictly reserved for church members. The Mormon belief in polygamy similarly led to the faith's being shrouded in mystery. However, though Brigham Young may have had 55 wives, the practice has been banned in the church for over a century.

largest of which are the Baptists, followed by (in size order) the Methodists, Lutherans, Presbyterians and Episcopalians. About a quarter of America's population is Roman Catholic, while the largest single other grouping – around 15 per cent of the population – is made up of non-believers. The remainder of the population – around 10 per cent – worship from among the entire range of world religions, including around 6 million Jews, 4 million Muslims and a sizeable population of Hindus.

Though overall not numerically significant, the USA has also sprouted a number of home-grown religions, of which the Mormons (see box) have been the most successful. Others include the Shakers, who survive in small numbers in Maine, the Amish (see box, 'The Children of the Anabaptists', p.40), the Christian Scientists, the Seventh-Day Adventists and Jehovah's Witnesses. America, particularly California, is also well known for sprouting a wealth of cults, which include the Rajneeshies, the 'Moonies', Scientology and Transcendental Meditation. Many of these incorporate oriental philosophies into their faiths, and most require extreme commitment and involvement by their members – which may include donating a large proportion of their wealth. The country has over a thousand TV and radio stations devoted to religious preaching and discussion – usually incorporating regular requests for monetary pledges.

Patterns of Religion

Though there are isolated believers of virtually every faith scattered in most parts of the USA, the pattern of belief in the country has a distinct geography and social profile. If you are secular you are more likely to live in the north or on the coast and be single, male, Democrat and have a college degree. If you are deeply religious you are more likely to live in the south, vote Republican, lack a college degree, be married and be female.

Of all of these patterns, the most distinct is the geography of fundamentalist religious belief. Evangelical churches are most popular in the South, where the Baptist church is particularly strong in an area of the South often referred to as the Bible Belt. This vague term is generally used to refer to the southeastern quarter of the USA: territory stretching from Texas north to Kansas, east to Virginia, and south to northern Florida. It is in this region where so-called mega-churches – churches that hold over 2,000 people – are particularly popular, and some are large enough for a congregation of 6,000. These aren't traditional churches, though, and are set up for PowerPoint sermons that are projected onto video screens visible from outdoor cafés within the church complex, so you can sip a cappuccino during the service.

Religion in Government

The strong, persistent and uncompromising voice of Christian funda-mentalists in the USA causes those who are secular cause for concern.

Certainly religious groups are some of the country's most socially active and organised associations, and they are perhaps more likely to be vocal and busy in politics – and less apathetic – than the rest of the populace. This has given the Christian-Right considerable strength in politics at every level, and signs exist that the influence of Church in government is growing both in its acceptability and prevalence. The Bush administration is itself openly religious: White House staff arrange Bible study classes; Bush calls Jesus his favourite philosopher; and increasingly religious leaders are flown to Washington to discuss social policy. This trend has profound consequences for several ethical debates, particularly about issues concerning homosexuality, abortion and stem cell research (*see* 'Internal Issues', pp.85–6).

The Family and the Role of Women

America has long been distinguished by its large and relatively homogenous middle class, which emerged in its present-day, and generally suburban, form in the 1950s. Half the American population lives in suburbia and it is the natural environment for the nuclear family, where two parents and two kids share a house, car, pet and annual vacation. Despite the well-publicised break-ups and constant reshaping of many families – only half of American children live with both their biological parents – three-quarters of American families are headed by a married couple, and two-thirds own their own home.

Within these statistics is buried a vast diversity of family structures. Some households – particularly Catholic and Mormon ones – have lots of children; many of the most recent immigrants live in multi-generational families under one roof; and generally there's a pattern of marrying later, with less haste to establish yourself as part of a nuclear family – particularly among the educated middle classes.

The role and status of women in the USA is similar to that in Europe. While pockets of opinion – adding up to around 20 per cent of the population (down from 30 per cent in 1980s opinion polls) – still hold that women should return to their traditional roles, it is generally understood that sexual equality should exist and be promoted where possible. In practice, women in small-town America are still more likely than men to devote themselves full-time to a household and family; in the bigger towns and cities women are as likely to be in full-time work and pursuing a career. Legislation prohibits discrimination on the basis of sex and, by and large, women in America have much the same opportunities as men. That said, the proportion of women in heavy industry, in boardrooms and in politics continues to be considerably smaller. America has yet to have a female president, although women were given the vote in 1920.

The Economy

The USA is without question the largest, most technologically advanced economy in the world. With only 5 per cent of the world's population, it produces 25 per cent of its economic output. Its economy is generally strong, resilient, diversified and self-sufficient in most things, with the crucial exception of oil – of which 40 per cent is imported. The importance of exports to America's economy is comparatively low – as a percentage of GDP this hovers around the 10 per cent mark.

The economy is overwhelmingly service-based, with 80 per cent of its population employed in sectors such as media and entertainment, distribution, real estate, transport, finance, healthcare and business services. Manufacturing only employs 18 per cent of the working population, and its output has been in steady decline for around a decade – now amounting to around 14 per cent of GDP in 2001 (down from 17 per cent in the mid-1990s). Leading sectors here include motor vehicles, aerospace, telecommunications, pharmaceuticals, chemicals, electronics and computers. However, this low figure partially obscures the importance of the new economy (information technology) since this is driven by information and communications sectors that increasingly defy classification in terms of services or manufacturing.

The USA's extremely productive agricultural sector employs only 2 per cent of the population, yet thanks to sophisticated biological and technological techniques it produces high yields with minimal manpower. Cereals, cotton and tobacco are the most important crops.

The Boom of the 1990s

An era of restructuring began at the end of the Cold War, when spending on arms was suddenly cut and many industrial sectors suffered. The diversification of companies and retraining of staff followed, and some areas showed adaptability by embracing new technology and increasing productivity. But other sectors, such as steel, collapsed in the face of new foreign imports. The overall trend, though, was that from 1992 the American economy expanded at a furious pace, with massive takeovers and giant mergers commonplace.

The government actively encouraged the process of globalisation. The lowering of trade tariffs, particularly, supported the growth of multinational companies, and the formation of the **North American Free Trading Area (NAFTA)**, which includes Mexico and Canada, helped stimulate intracontinental industrial growth. The establishment of this trading area is widely considered one of president Bill Clinton's most significant achievements.

Economic Downturn

Economically, the new millennium started badly for the USA as the dot-com bubble burst, reducing the stock of many high-tech companies to pennies and precipitating a sharp decline in the stock market. At a rate unprecedented since the Great Depression, this heralded a period of economic recession, which ended nine years of robust growth.

The onset of recession was compounded by the 9/11 attacks in 2001, which almost immediately caused a loss of around 200,000 jobs in the travel industry. The economy then suffered accounting and insider-trading stock scandals – most notably that involving Enron in 2002 – which shook investor confidence. Federal government predictions of a $1.5 trillion budget surplus between 2003 and 2008 suddenly crumbled into a $1 trillion deficit over the same period. At the same time, state governments also struggled financially, with California's woes particularly chronic: its Silicon Valley having risen meteorically during the boom, it had furthest to fall in the bust.

Boosting the Economy

Given the economic climate, the first 100 days in office saw the new president, George W. Bush, try to stimulate the economy in traditional right-wing ways. Bush sought to apply many of the same Republican strategies as Ronald Reagan to turn the economy around, including lowering taxes, increasing defence spending and allowing for immense deficits. But the strategy was different from Reaganomics in one crucial way. While Ronald Reagan thought government was the problem and sought to dismantle that, Bush saw taxation as the problem and continually lowered it throughout his terms in government. The hope is that by decreasing the amount of taxes paid by every income tax payer and corporation, greater investment and growth will result, creating more jobs and tax revenue. At the same time Bush increased government spending – by 21 per cent in his first three years of government. These dual strategies saw the country quickly move from being one of the world's greatest creditor nations to becoming one of its worst debtors. Not surprisingly, US confidence in this strategy was deeply divided, and many commentators saw the embracing of such a large deficit a short-term solution that would worsen the country's long-term economic malaise.

One crucial strand of Bush's strategy to galvanise the economy has been to encourage energy consumption. Car manufacturers were not encouraged to improve the fuel efficiency of their vehicles and the USA has declined to sign the Kyoto Protocol limiting greenhouse gases, for fear of slowing the economy. Pressure has also been increased to allow wilderness areas to be opened up to resource extraction – particularly the Alaskan oil fields, which look set soon to be drilled.

Another crucial – and also internationally unpopular – strand of US economic policy has been the creation of protectionist barriers for its flagging steel industry. The weakening of the US dollar – from around $1.30 to the UK pound in 2001 to an artificially low level of around $1.80 by 2005 – can also be interpreted as another way in which the USA sought to limit imports – which are made far more expensive in the face of domestic US competition.

Outlook

Superficially at least, the signs in 2005 were that the US economy was on the up. An increase in military spending, combined with tax cuts and crude economic stimuli such as a weak dollar, resulted in growth in 2003 and 2004, during which time there was some recovery in the jobs market. Official unemployment figures slowly began to drop, though (contrary to conservative ideals) new jobs had not been created in the private sector but were instead largely the result of a growth in the federal government.

Somehow, the American economy became cautiously optimistic, even though nothing really delivered the promise of long-term improvement. In contrast, strong signs of long-term trouble persist, with the high price of oil fuelling inflation, reducing consumer spending, depressing sales and so discouraging expansion and hiring. In the short term the economy is expected to pick up, but in the long term the problem of sustaining both its huge trade and budget deficits remains.

Furthermore, there are signs that the lot of the average American is in a long-term decline. Even in the much-celebrated boom years of the 1990s the quality of life of the average American worker worsened. Today Americans work around 300 hours per year more than Europeans – though in 1982 the amounts had been about level. Additionally, the average number of people required to work to keep a family has been increasing. In the 1950s one breadwinner could keep an average family in comfort; today it generally requires two, and older people have extended their working lives out of necessity. At the very bottom of the economic ladder, a fifth of the homeless are thought to have work of some sort – yet this is clearly not enough to keep them off the street.

Regional Trends

In the century following the Civil War, the South became America's economic backwater, while the north firmly continued to develop as its industrial stronghold. But beginning in the 1970s, industry has begun to migrate from the north of the country to the south. This trend has been linked to both a decline in manufacturing industries and a boom in light industry and technology. This broad national trend is complicated by a myriad regional trends, however, and local economies vary drastically both within and between states.

California is the most prosperous state and known for its hi-tech industries, particularly around San Francisco, and for the entertainment-based industries around Los Angeles. Hurt by the closure of various military bases and the volatility of the technology sector, its economy has nevertheless suffered recent decline, and has been losing out to the bordering states of Oregon and Arizona, which have a lower tax burden.

The USA's other outstandingly wealthy states are Florida, Illinois, New York, Pennsylvania and Texas. However, this statistic is misleading since these are also some of the largest. In fact, the growth rate of some of the poorer, less populous states – like Arizona, Colorado, Idaho, Montana, Nevada, New Mexico, Utah and Wyoming – is currently far greater. While continued healthy growth in land-locked states is expected, of the biggest states Texas is perhaps the most promising. This has successfully diversified its economy from oil into technology and computers, and stands to benefit in a whole host of ways by its proximity to Mexico as cross-border trade increases. In contrast, prospects are relatively dim for the area that has suffered the biggest recent decline: the so-called Rust Belt stretching from Pennsylvania to Iowa. Elsewhere in the northeast, New England's computer boom, particularly in Boston, has helped offset problems elsewhere.

Internal Issues

Virtually all the USA's internal debates have their origins in the character and composition of the nation. On the most basic level, the country's history informs its basic points of view. Many traits appear directly descended from the kinds of values and priorities that come from carving out a fortune in a strange and not entirely hospitable land and away from the restrictive social order of the Old World. These include elements like a belief in freedom, the importance of self-reliance, hard work, individualism, practical creativity, disregard for social convention and mistrust of authority. This background produces a number of contradictions, but overall, and compared with Europeans, Americans do tend to be more conservative in social opinions – more likely to disapprove of divorce, abortion and homosexuality – but generally more accepting of cultural variety.

Yet these generalisations mask the true division in American society: the sum of the parts in no way hints at how deeply divided the populace is. This divide partly has its origins in the country's immigration history, particularly the population explosion at the turn of the 20th century. From a population of around 40 million in the 1860s the USA increased to over 100 million by the First World War. This new generation of immigrants, and particularly their children, created a new, materially prosperous, brash and buoyant society in big multicultural, liberal and relatively secular cities. This was at odds with the more established, socially conservative, ethnically narrow and devout rural America with its small-town values – particularly in the Midwest and Bible Belt. These two factions have been vying for control ever since, with the latter group consistently fighting change and being responsible for outlawing alcohol (Prohibition) and voting to end further large-scale mass immigration.

There is every sign that these gaps are currently widening, polarising the populace into two main groups, which appear to be in no way determined by personal wealth or income. These two sides usually oppose one another in a debate over any issue: one group is broadly religious, family-centred, somewhat conformist, predominantly married and Republican; the other is tolerant, progressive, secular, hedonistic, predominantly single and Democrat. This division has a well-defined geography, with the seaboards (excepting the south) tending to be Democrat (blue states), whereas the central and southern states tend to be Republican (red states). The ideological battleground for these two groups is suburbia – one of the least noticed phenomena in the USA, but vital to understanding the country.

Poverty and the Polarisation of Wealth

One of the USA's best-known ironies is that, despite being one of the world's richest countries, it has a disproportionate number of people living in poverty. Compared with other industrialised countries, the gulf between rich and poor is vast. The incidence of infant mortality is unusually high, it has the highest number of uninsured citizens, yet its public welfare and health systems are all comparatively poor.

The wealthy can afford to opt out of the system, and this is being made increasingly easier as the gap between rich and poor grows. Since the mid-1970s virtually all economic growth has disproportionally benefited the richest 20 per cent. This fifth of the population now earns more than half the nation's national income and owns over 80 per cent of its wealth. Meanwhile the poorest 40 per cent of households earn only 10 per cent of the income and own only one per cent of the wealth. Around 12 per cent of the US population is considered to live in poverty – defined as having an annual income of less than $9,000 per person, or $16,000 for a family of three.

Being in the position of earning little is particularly difficult in America, with its requirements for individuals to support themselves. This makes it easy for increasing numbers to fall through the net, yet welfare and public services remain less supportive thsa in Europe, largely because there is a strong aversion to more taxes and federal intrusions into the private sphere.

Health

Perhaps the single hardest aspect of the system to cope with if you are poor in the USA is the health system. Oddly, despite the country's having some of the world's best healthcare, it is fiercely expensive and remains financially out of reach for increasing numbers of Americans. If you are without private insurance you can expect only the most rudimentary attention. The spiralling cost of healthcare in the USA is only one part of the problem, though, as such factors as the ageing of the American population and the growth of obesity put more pressure on the system.

The USA does not have a national healthcare system or system of socialised medicine, although programmes such as Medicare and Medicaid provide basic health insurance to elderly and poor residents respectively. For most US residents, health insurance is provided as an employee benefit, leaving unemployed, self-employed and part-time workers to pay for their own insurance. In 2004, 45 million people in the United States (15.6 per cent of the US population), including 8.7 million children, had no health insurance coverage. An estimated 18,000 people per year die prematurely as a result of being uninsured. This is partly because the unemployed slip through the net. But the problem is also caused by a combination of the greed of the extra-ordinarily profitable pharmaceutical industries; the litigious state of America, which forces up practitioners' fees; and the insurers themselves, who take a large slice of contributions.

Those losing their jobs in the USA can usually continue their employer-based health insurance plans, though at a rate that is up to double the rate the employee paid while employed. When an employer-insured person loses their job due to illness and does not have sufficient resources to continue to pay for health insurance, he or she also loses his or her coverage. Consequentially, a recent Harvard University study found that medical bills are a leading cause of bankruptcy in the USA. The study found that many declaring bankruptcy were part of the middle class and were employed before they became ill but had lost their health insurance by the time they declared bankruptcy.

Efforts to provide universal healthcare in the 1960s and early 1990s foundered on widespread opposition, particularly by more conservative politicians who objected to government control of medicine, and business groups that did not want to experience a loss of profits with the increase of government bureaucracy in the healthcare and insurance industries. Despite a general agreement, enforced in law, that emergency care must be provided to all, there is no consensus in the USA that the availability of broader healthcare should be considered a right, nor that this service should be paid for by the state.

Apart from the growing number of elderly in the American populace, a key healthcare problem faced by all developed nations, the USA also has the developing problem of obesity to deal with. The number of chronically overweight adults in the country is great, and rate increases in the last decade mean that currently two-thirds of adults are overweight or obese. Children are particularly affected, their rates having more than doubled in the last decade as they devour a diet of TV dinners and fast food. Weight problems are now partly to blame for around 250,000 Americans every year. Many of the issues were highlighted by the popular film *Super Size Me* (2004), which examined the health risks of the American devotion to fast and junk food.

Education

Another basic area in which America has similar problems to the UK is in the provision of a high standard of education to all. Inequalities in this system are as rampant as anywhere in the developed world, with Ivy League universities being among the world's best while US public schools – which serve 47 million children – are of inconsistent standard. The quality of education is highly variable between regions and schools – in part because much of their funding comes from local sources and so reflects the wealth of the local community. In affluent communities, especially those with large numbers of childbearing families, the educational system tends to be more heavily funded per student and tends to be more effective. Communities that are less affluent or have a lower percentage of childbearing families generally spend less money per child. Statistical information has repeatedly demonstrated the general correlation between money spent per child and academic success. The disparity in public resources is matched by a disparity in private resources as well: affluent parents are able to spend much more money on books, software, tutoring and education-related travel than are other parents.

State governments, since the 1990s have grappled with these issues of educational equity. In some states, most prominently New Jersey, courts have ordered dramatically increased funding in lower income areas. In other states, legislatures have acted on their own initiative to equalise somewhat the funding available. In still other states, less action has been taken.

Nationally, the No Child Left Behind Act of 2001 has attempted to improve the quality control of schools, with mechanisms for testing schools, teachers and pupils; these are balanced with federal grants for compliance with the system, but effectively the Act increases control and intervention in manners that may not be considered locally appropriate.

For details on schools and colleges, *see* **Living in the USA**, pp.174–80.

Racism and Affirmative Action

The American annual calendar bristles with colourful ethnic celebrations drawn from all the world's great cultural traditions – St Patrick's Day, Chinese New Year, Cinco de Mayo and Carnival – yet race and ethnicity is a hot potato in the USA, and the country is arguably split more along racial lines than it is by class, gender, age or politics. Decades of struggle have at least created legal equality. Positive discrimination ('affirmative action') is also helping. This now carries the sanction of the Supreme Court and allows organisations to discriminate positively towards minority groups that have traditionally suffered exclusion. The logic is that by giving preferential access to education, employment, healthcare or social welfare, this action can help undo past wrongs. Yet deep divisions exist, not just between black and white, but also between Native Americans, Hispanics, Asians and every other American ethnicity. This harks back to an era where whites felt superior to other races. And even today the bulk of the country's power, wealth and control are overwhelmingly still in Caucasian hands. Unemployment rates are twice as high for African-Americans as for whites, and Hispanics fare only slightly better; 22 per cent of both groups are considered below the poverty line – compared with the national average of 12 per cent.

Crime, Prisons and Guns

The **crime rate** in the USA is legendary with, for example, four times as many murders per head of population as the UK. Punishment seems to offer little deterrent, since the US prison population is the highest of any country – both in absolute and relative numbers – and the USA is second only to China in the number of death sentences passed. Part of the problem may be argued to be the American gun culture, see below – but there is strong opposition to removing this freedom.

A substantial percentage of people behind bars are **drug offenders**, due to the so-called 'war on drugs', a stiff policy against the selling of recreational drugs. Long sentences became particularly common in the 1990s, leading to the passage of strict minimum sentencing guidelines in many states, and the 'three strikes' laws, which led to automatic incarceration for life after three felonies have been committed. Special provisions are given in the case of possession of crack cocaine, where there is a mandatory minimum sentence of five years. This penalty, the harshest of any drug law, primarily affects African-Americans. In 2002, the Honorable Charles J. Hynes (District Attorney of Kings County, New York), testified before the United States Senate Committee on the Judiciary that the sentencing disparity between crack cocaine convictees and powdered cocaine convictees was 100 to 1; powdered cocaine is far more commonly associated with wealthier Caucasian users.

However, the debate concerning **capital punishment** in the USA is more highly charged than that concerning its overcrowded prisons or its legal system. The death sentence is officially sanctioned by 38 US states, as well as by the federal government, though it exercises its right to use capital punishment infrequently. Each state practising capital punishment has different laws regarding its methods, age limits and qualifying crimes. Between 1973 and 2002, 7,254 death sentences were issued in the USA. These led to 820 executions, 3,557 prisoners on death row, 176 whose sentences were commuted by governors or state pardon boards, and 2,403 who were released, retried or resentenced by the courts. There were 59 executions in 2004.

Violent crimes, particularly, attract the death sentence in many states, and the high incidence of shootings and murder in the USA have also led fierce debate over the wisdom of America's **gun laws**. In 35 states, practically any non-felon can obtain a licence to carry a gun – and throughout the country felons find it easy to source firearms illegally. The massacre at Columbine, a Denver high school in 1999, when two students attacked their classmates and teachers with an arsenal of weapons, caused a public outcry for tougher gun laws.

The degree to which firearms can or should be regulated has, however, long been debated in the United States. Disagreements range from the practical (does gun ownership cause or prevent crime?) to the constitutional – particularly the interpretation of the second amendment. This states 'A well regulated militia, being necessary to the security of a free state, the right of the people to keep and bear arms, shall not be infringed' and is variously used to confirm that everyone has a right to a gun or that this is only in context of being part of a militia – depending largely on the person's stance on the gun issue.

Certainly the issue is considered too contentious for either political party to propose a ban. Democrats deliberations over guns are considered to have cost them the 2000 election. Surveys indicated that a perception of Democrats as 'anti-gun' contributed to Al Gore's loss in West Virginia, Arkansas and Tennessee. Winning any one of those states would have put him in the White House.

For more details on crime and the police, *see* **Living in the USA**, pp.172–4.

Abortion and Stem Cell Research

Since its legalisation in 1973, the issue of abortion has been a highly divisive one and one that sees the two political parties firmly at odds with one another. The Republicans generally support the view that the unborn foetus has a right to life, even in cases of rape and incest, while the Democrats generally believe a woman should have the right to choose. Currently polls suggest that 55 per cent of Americans take some middle ground on abortion rights – either supporting them with exceptions or opposing them with exceptions. Most disagree with their party's platform. Six in ten Democrats would outlaw abortion in some cases; nearly seven in ten Republicans would allow abortion in some cases.

Conneccted to the same fundamental principles as the abortion issue is the idea of government support for stem cell research – the cloning of human cells taken from aborted embryos, which promises ultimately to provide cures for many debilitating diseases. Those who oppose the principle of abortion as the unwarranted destruction of human life cannot simultaneously then encourage medical research or the government support of such activities.

President Bush limited federal funding to 78 existing stem cell lines when he set his policy on 9 August 2001. That policy has led to a patchwork of initiatives that scientists, patients and some lawmakers say has stunted progress on finding cures for diabetes, Alzheimer's and other diseases. Congress is in the process of trying to change this policy.

Homosexuality

While Americans are statistically less likely to approve of homosexuality than Europeans, tolerance is on the increase and some of the world's most openly gay communities are in the USA – particularly in New York and San Francisco. Overall, 90 per cent of Americans believe gay men and lesbians should have equal rights in job opportunities.

In 2003 the Supreme Court struck down a Texas sodomy law and in so doing declared that gay Americans have a constitutional right to privacy and equality. This might just be the start of a wave of gay rights legislation that creates equality in some of the ways that the 1960s civil rights legislation did.

One of the first issues that this process will have to embrace is the question of same-sex marriages. The first same-sex couples were wed in Massachusetts in May 2004, following a decision by the state's highest court that legalised gay marriages. Yet Massachusetts remains the only state in the nation where same-sex marriages are legal and in the past year, more than 6,100 same-sex couples married there – comprising one in six marriage licences issued in the state. Among the same-sex weddings, about two-thirds are female couples.

But the national debate over whether such marriages should be allowed is as fierce today as it was after the Massachusetts court ruling in November 2003 – and 18 states have adopted state constitutional amendments *against* same-sex marriages. A May 2005 poll, however, showed a significant drop in those against gay marriage – to 56 per cent of the population. The same poll showed support for gay marriage at 39 per cent.

Illegal Immigration

Immigration has always played a key part in US history and even today, given the much tighter controls, around 10 per cent of the US population is foreign-born. One consequence of laws restricting the number and ethnicity of persons entering the USA is a phenomenon referred to as illegal immigration, in which persons enter a country and obtain work without legal sanction. In some cases, this is accomplished by entering the country legally with a visa, and then simply choosing not to leave on expiration of the visa. In other cases people enter the country surreptitiously without ever obtaining a visa. Often, people entering in this fashion are economic refugees – a class of refugee not recognised by the US Citizenship and Immigration Services; these persons have left their home country in a desperate bid to provide financial support for themselves and/or their families. This is particularly true in cases where the minimum wage in the USA is several times what the average labourer earns in a given country; such immigrants often send large portions of their income to their countries and families of origin.

While this cheap workforce helps keep down the cost of many goods and services across the country, it also drives down the price of labour generally. The number of illegal workers in the USA is a major concern. Calls are being made to change the 14th Amendment of the constitution that requires that citizenship be granted to all children born in the country. Thus, if a child is born in the USA, his or her family is likely to be allowed to stay, as the child is a citizen and cannot be deported. These children of families with mixed immigration status are sometimes referred to as 'anchor babies'.

One of the latest and most vociferous groups to campaign against illegal immigration is the Minuteman Project – a group of private citizens who monitor the US–Mexican border in Arizona for illegal immigrants. Participants in the project, which began in April 2005, alert the US Border Patrol when they find illegal immigrants. Organisers suggest that over 1,000 volunteers will patrol the Arizona–Sonora border. Law enforcement officials fear vigilante violence.

Major Media

The media are perhaps the most powerful social force in USA, bombarding the populace from a growing number of angles – print, television, radio and Internet – and infiltrating every aspect of the American lifestyle. Television is the most powerful and all-pervasive medium, with the average American viewing around 1,500 hours per year. Reading occupies less than a tenth of this time in the lifestyle of the typical American, yet magazine and newspaper circulations and book sales remain healthy. This has been despite some powerful and rapid changes in the media over the last decade or so. On the one hand, the number of media outlets has exploded, thanks largely to the expanding presence of the Internet, while at the same time media ownership is being rapidly, and controversially, consolidated.

Ownership of the Media

The proliferation of the media has to some extent led to its consolidation, with the **Federal Communications Commission (FCC)** using the abundance of media as a reason for deregulating its ownership. Most of the subsequent media merging and concentration has benefited the big players, since the smaller ones will find it hard to compete, rather than the consumer, who may end up with less choice.

In 1996 radio was deregulated with the result that one company, Clear Channel, now dominates the industry, owning around half the nation's stations. The corporation's ownership of concert venues and ticket agencies gives it a strong influence on the music industry.

FCC rulings in 2001 allowed similar deregulation among the TV networks, although the biggest are still not allowed to merge. The companies that already dominate US media ownership are News Corp (Fox), Walt Disney Corp (ABC), General Electric (NBC), AOL Time Warner and Viacom (CBS). These conglomerates also own most of the nation's big magazines and movie studios.

In 2003 the FCC weakened rules governing the concentration of media ownership, allowing one company to own and run different forms of media in the same market. The result may well be that one company could own a local TV station, daily newspaper and several radio stations – thereby giving the major corporations more power and greater potential to manipulate the population.

Television

The USA's 220 million TVs are a feature in 99 per cent of its homes, churning out a brand of television that is characteristically inoffensive and anodyne, undemanding and easily consumed, but above all highly commercial. Advertising proliferates on TV in the USA, to the point where it often overwhelms the programming and even literally interrupts live sports. All these traits can largely be linked back to the history of the medium. Unlike other media, TV has always been almost solely corporate-run, with its success depending on attracting the widest possible audience for advertisers.

The proliferation of cable and satellite TV stations means that consumers have hundreds of channels to choose from, but six national networks – ABC, CBS, NBC, Fox, UPN and WB) dominate proceedings. **Prime time** on US TV is 8–11pm and dominated by dramas, with some reality TV shows. The rest of the time is devoted to a mix of soap operas and talk shows and sport on the main channels, but there is also a raft of other channels, including a range of special interest channels, like the **Discovery Channel** and **MTV**, 24hr news channels, weather channels and shopping channels to choose from. The content of all these mainstream channels is heavily censored, bare breasts are carefully

Super Bowl Madness

The grand finale of the professional American Football season, the late-January Super Bowl, has reached the status of an unofficial holiday. Life in the USA stops on Super Bowl Sunday as families gather to watch the climax of one of the country's most violent and complicated sports. Up to 140 million viewers tune in for the match, which, including commercial breaks and an extravagant and splashy half-time show, will easily last four hours. But as anyone who has been to a Super Bowl party will agree, it's the half-time show and the commercials that are more likely to stop conversation and attract attention, rather than the football itself. The commercials are considered treats: they are usually the first run of a TV commercial that has been months in the making at a cost of millions of dollars – a 30-second slot during the Super Bowl itself is worth well over a million. It's the ads, too, not the football, that people are more likely to talk about after the game – which at this level is often dominated by defences who block the aspirations of the nervous playmakers, to create low-scoring games.

hidden, swear words bleeped out – though showing scenes of violence is considered acceptable.

A large number of channels available through cable TV are subscription channels, which charge fees by the month for a block of time. **Home Box Office (HBO)** is one of the most popular channels and offers recently released movies. Other programmes attracting extra cost are high-profile sports events and pornography.

One channel that is a little different from the rest is the **Public Broadcasting Station (PBS)**, a commercial-free station, funded by viewer contributions and various grants. Its mixed programme sometimes includes British TV shows, rare on most of the other main channels.

Otherwise some of the best-quality TV can be found in long-running shows like *Saturday Night Live* (NBC), a long-running comedy show, and primetime news magazines like *60 Minutes*, (CBS), *Dateline* (NBC) and *20/20* (ABC).

Print Media

Despite the development of a strong TV culture and the proliferation of the Internet, newspapers and magazines continue to play a role in the USA. The highest-profile daily **newspapers** include the *New York Times* and the *Washington Post*, and can be found nationally, though every city will have at least one major daily paper as well. *USA Today* is another national, more lowbrow daily. *National Enquirer* is one of the most successful sensationalist tabloid.

Special interest **magazines** exist for pretty much every subject in the USA, but several are particular popular. These include *Cosmopolitan* and *Maxim*, for style fashion and lifestyle content, and the *New Yorker* and *Harper's* for stories and essays. Entertainment magazines include *People* for gossip, *Rolling Stone* devoted to the music industry and *Sports Illustrated* for coverage of the whole swath of sports popular in America.

Radio

Radio used to dominate American culture in much the same way as TV does today, but has since been reduced to something that just accompanies people on their commute – admittedly a considerable amount of time for many Americans. Hundreds of stations are scattered across both the AM and FM wavebands, but almost none broadcasts nationally. AM radio is usually dominated by talk radio, while FM is reserved mostly for music. Each transmitter has a four-letter call-name, which starts with a W for those located east of the Mississippi, and K to those west of the river.

One of the few radio stations with a truly national audience is National Public Radio (NPR), a station that mixes discussion shows with classical music and magazine programmes on investigating specific topics.

As with TV, most radio stations – with the notable exception of NPR – have a high advertising content. Recently, subscriber-funded satellite stations have become popular, partly due to the absence of advertising on them: some vehicles have satellite receivers fitted as standard.

The Presence of UK Media

Finding British newspapers in the largest US cities is possible, but often the expense and difficulty means you are better off perusing their on-line edition. The Internet will likely prove itself an indispensable source of UK (and world) news since most US media are fairly parochial in their coverage. If you have a high-speed Internet connection you will even find some programmes and sporting events (on, for example, **www.sportingstreams.com**) such as cricket and premiership football available as streams on the web.

The BBC has a presence in the USA in the form of the BBC World Service (**www. bbc.co.uk/worldservice/americas**) on short-wave radio, and it's usually possible to get reasonable reception in most parts of the USA. You may also stumble across the BBC news channel on some cable TV networks and occasional British programmes on the PBS channel.

Culture and Art

Culture and art in all forms have shown a strong relationship to the passage of history in the USA. Initially, US arts continued many age-old European traditions, but from the 19th century onwards American arts began to find their own style. Literature and painting came to terms with the new environment by using Old World techniques and media to explore its savage beauty and opportunity. Meanwhile the toiling African slaves were producing blues music, a melancholy rendition of traditional African rhythms.

In the 20th century, American culture became truly distinctive. Since then the USA has established itself time and again as a major innovator in the creative arts, putting itself at the forefront of modern movements in literature, film, music, performance, dance, architecture and painting. All the arts have been driven in some part by the economy and reflected the atmosphere of the times: vibrancy in the 1920s, the Depression in the 1930s, technological innovations in the 1940s, Cold War anxiety in the 1950s. At this time a mass-market pop culture established itself, which meant there was real money to be made in art and entertainment, leading to a surge in production within the industry. The protest era of the 1960s in part questioned this unbridled commercialism, as well as adding new layers of style and setting new boundaries for artistic freedom and expression. The era spanning from the 1970s to the present day has seen the emergence of technologies profoundly affecting culture and art. The hi-tech revolution has brought down costs for minor players and is having a radical democratising effect on the music, film and publishing industries. At the same time, the combination of a transport revolution, which has shrunk the world for the richest nations, and a broadening of the immigrant mix in the USA has created a love affair with fusion: styles in all art forms are repeatedly being forced together, often hybridising into new styles at a phenomenal rate.

But while the fringes of the arts have never been more active and dynamic, the mainstream is struggling. Many arts organisations have been feeling the pinch of economic recession, with funding cuts across the board. Some have even gone bankrupt. At the same time, media concentration within several conglomerate companies has tended to favour arts with the widest appeal – encouraging a mass of rather bland performances and limiting diversity – particularly in the fields of literature, film and music.

Literature

The first enduring classics of American literature were written in the early 19th century and featured strong, yet innocent and humble, individuals negotiating the raw American landscape, and often drawing spiritual lessons through their relationship with the wilderness, essentially producing salt-of-the-earth characters who were more popular and immediate to readers than refined European protagonists. Drawing on a specifically American experience that eluded European writers, James Fenimore Cooper wrote *The Pioneers* (1823), broadly considered the first truly American novel, then *Last of the Mohicans* (1826). The next great wave in American literature, again inspired by nature, was that of the New England Transcendentalists like Ralph Waldo Emerson and later David Thoreau, who both promoted an anti-materialism through focusing on self-reflection and a retreat into nature, and propounding the idea that nature was in fact an extension of God. Other great novels responded to these ideas; Herman Melville's *Moby-Dick* (1851), a cautionary tale warned of the mistakes of this philosophy, while Nathaniel Hawthorne's *The Scarlet Letter* (1850) examined the unpleasant side of Puritan New England.

Not part of this dialogue was Edgar Allen Poe, who wrote his gruesome short stories around this time and is credited with inventing several literary categories including the horror story, detective story and science fiction – which have since all became hallmark American genres.

Later in the 19th century, Mark Twain emerged, to become America's all-time best-loved storyteller, while at the same time using his self-consciously anti-intellectual work to express social criticism. *Huckleberry Finn* (1884) is considered a landmark and one of the all-time greatest influences on American literature. And social criticism was also the theme of Harriet Beecher Stowe's *Uncle Tom's Cabin* (1852), an exposé of slavery which helped fire the Civil War. The 1850s also produced the poems of Walt Whitman, a man ahead of his time, whose rebellious informal free verse would inspire a generation of poets.

The early 20th century was at first a time of great economic prosperity, in a period when the self-reflective movement still thrived in American literature. This coming together produced F. Scott Fitzgerald's *The Great Gatsby* (1925), which explores characters who are unfulfilled despite their overwhelming conspicuous consumption. At this time of rampant consumerism, many writers, such as Ernest Hemingway, T. S. Eliot, ee cummings and Ezra Pound, chose to move abroad. African-American literary creativity also came to the fore, fed by the excitement of the Jazz Age through the work of Langston Hughes, Nella Larsen and Zora Neale Hurston.

America's economic downturn in the 1930s also produced great novels that grew out of the decade's economic decay. William Faulkner wrote about the rural South, while John Steinbeck is best known for his Nobel Prize-winning *The Grapes of Wrath* (1939), charting the fortunes of a family fleeing the Oklahoma dustbowl to seek their fortunes in California. In his plays, Tennessee Williams also looked at the family dynamics of uprooted working-class southerners.

In the same decade, the detective story was almost single-handedly being turned into a hard-nosed urban realist genre of *noir* by Raymond Chandler (*The Big Sleep*, 1939).

The end of the Second World War ushered in a period of smug conformism in America, which literature sought to challenge head-on. Arthur Miller explored the frailty of the American Dream in *Death of a Salesman* (1949), while African-American writing suddenly grew in stature. Ralph Ellison's *Invisible Man* (1952) investigated the distinguishing features of black and white identities. Pulitzer

Prize-winner Gwendolyn Brooks published work that highlighted abortion, gangs and drop-outs. J. D. Salinger (*The Catcher in the Rye*, 1951) captured ironic dissatisfaction with American life. And a Russian immigrant, Vladimir Nabokov, told the controversial story of unconventional love (*Lolita*, 1955), while at the same time redefining English prose style for a coming generation of authors who overturned social and literary conventions in their writing. The post-war era also brought a generation of Beat authors, whose wild and freewheeling heroes paved the way for an era of hippies. Spearheading the movement were Jack Kerouac (*On the Road*, 1957), Allen Ginsberg (*Howl*, 1956) and William S. Burroughs (*Naked Lunch*, 1959). Women writers helped galvanise this attitude with a raft of feminist literature that accompanied a decade of great social movements. Much of it was tortured by personal anguish, as was the case with the writings of Anne Sexton and Sylvia Plath. The civil rights movement also sparked a series of dynamic and weighty writings, including those of James Baldwin (*The Fire Next Time*, 1963), who warned of the consequences of racial hatred, and Flannery O'Connor, who looked at inequality in the South.

Tensions between gender, ethnic and cultural identities have continued to be themes for recent writers such as Pulitzer Prize-winer Alice Walker (*The Color Purple*, 1983) and Pulitzer and Nobel Prize-winner Toni Morrison (*Beloved* 1987). Other contemporary writers are Jay McInerney, who in *Bright Lights, Big City* (1987) looked at 1980s Wall Street life, while David Mamet in his play *Glengarry Glen Ross* (1984) picks up where Arther Miller left off in his exploration of sales culture. Philip Roth also continues to deconstruct the American Dream. The trend in the most recent wave of literature has tended to favour a host of American writers with strong ethnic identities, including Native American Barbara Kingsolver, Chinese American Amy Tan, Cuban-American Oscar Hijuelos and Indian-American Bharati Mukherjee.

Film

With the most money to spend, the USA has been the world's major innovator on the silver screen. Based in Hollywood in Los Angeles for the vast majority of its life, the American film industry has employed an assembly-line method of film production, which has nevertheless brought us many great classics along with countless cookie-cutter duds. The USA also has a strong independent cinema, which has shown strong dissenting themes and used cutting edge experimental techniques, though this art form hasn't been exported nearly as well as the mainstream. The global success of these mainstream movies has come to define not only cinema but also the way in which America sees itself, and the way the world identifies America. The industry has been vitally important in cementing cultural stereotypes – cowboys, gangsters, chorus girls – and made millions around the world familiar with the prairies, open highways and glitzy, neon-lit skyscraper cities and their bland but wealthy suburbia.

Hollywood first emerged as the centre of the movie world in the 1920s, thanks to its previous prominence as a theatre hub, its sunny climate, its photogenic terrain and the emergence of a monopolistic studio system in New York City. Cinema started simply, with slapstick routines dominating the silent films, but soon after the First World War, actors like Charlie Chaplin, Buster Keaton and Mary Pickford became household names. These early artists were playful, exuberant and innovative.

But the silent films that dominated the 1920s were quickly phased out, as sound was added towards the end of the decade. In the early 1930s there was an explosion of daring filmmaking, with unrivalled artistic freedom that enabled the introduction of sex, violence and brash humour. Free-spirited times were summed up by films like *Freaks*, *Scarface* and *Morocco*.

But this era came to an abrupt end as two powerful forces combined to change the course of American cinema. While the introduction of the moral Production Code in 1934 toned down the raciness of cinema big business, studios like Paramount, MGM and Warner began to take control. The injection of money in particular allowed for a golden age where Hollywood blossomed, with the creation of glossy epics like *Gone with the Wind* (1939), the intricate *Citizen Kane* (1941), romance in *Casablanca* (1942), and touching morality tales like *It's a Wonderful Life* (1946) and the child-pleasing animated *Snow White* (1937) and *The Wizard of Oz* (1939) – all classics to this day. This golden age was also the era of the musical, with Fred Astaire and Ginger Rogers at their peak.

The 1950s was an era in which political paranoia saw the blacklisting of any artists with suspected, or even rumoured, ties to communism. This restricted the industry to a smaller pool of talent, and competition from television was affecting box office sales. At the same time, federal authorities broke up Hollywood's monopoly on distribution and exhibition. Picking up the themes of the time – anxiety over communism and nuclear weapons and a developing interest in space travel – an era of science fiction movies like *The Incredible Shrinking Man* and *Invasion of the Body Snatchers*, and mighty westerns like *High Noon* and *The Searchers*, brought audiences back to the movie theatres. The emergence of mass popular culture in the 1950s also began to make glamorous stars out of actors. Marilyn Monroe, Elizabeth Taylor, Audrey Hepburn, James Dean, Rock Hudson and Marlon Brando began to fill theatres with sex appeal alone.

The 1960s was a difficult period of transition for the movie industry, as it grappled to get to grips with the free-thinking demands of the era and the financial problems from the 1950s. In response, the industry cut studio costs, ended actor contracts and sold off departments; yet still it struggled. Finally it took a risk on a new generation of anti-establishment film-makers, partly made possible by the lifting of censorship and its replacement with a movie ratings system. The introduction of foreign film-makers also helped. The industry finally hit its stride in the late 1960s with Dennis Hopper's *Easy Rider* (1969) portraying youth rebellion and counter-culture in a way that fashion demanded. With the emergence of the 1970s came a series of more serious movies like Stanley Kubrick's *A Clockwork Orange* (1971), Martin Scorsese's *Taxi Driver* and Francis Ford Coppola's *The Godfather*, all exploring the darker side of human nature and interaction.

In the 1970s there was a reinvention of the blockbuster, driven by the financial possibilities of global distribution, such as George Lucas' *Star Wars* trilogy (1977–82) and Steven Spielberg's many films including *ET* (1982). These films began to make special effects centre stage, often at the expense of storyline, but their global financial success secured the global primacy of the American film industry.

While blockbusters dominated the emerging multiplex screens of the country, a strong independent film movement also began to take shape. Rob Reiner's *This is Spinal Tap* sent up rock music, while David Lynch's *Blue Velvet* dug beneath the surface of suburbia.

These dual trends continued into the 1990s when ever-increasing blockbuster budgets brought realistic dinosaurs and disasters, in the form of *Jurassic Park* and *Titanic* respectively, to millions in cinemas worldwide. At the same time the independent cinema was going from strength to strength, with the Coen Brothers creating a series of offbeat movies with cult potential like *Fargo* (1996) and *The Big Lebowski*, while the undeniably cult, if slick and violent, films of Quentin Tarantino (*Reservoir Dogs*, *Pulp Fiction*, 1994) created stylised portraits of violence in America.

Today's movie industry nets around $30 billion from theatres, and film rentals and digital era technology is economically rejuvenating and reinventing the art form at every level, from low-budget independents to big-money studios' special effects.

Music

Over its entire history the USA has been a breeding ground for unique musical styles fostered by immigrant communities, which have been imaginatively fused with other local styles to produce sounds that are now heard on stereo systems throughout the world. Since the mid-20th century American musical styles have extended their influence – particularly as blues, jazz, rock 'n' roll and hip-hop – in more corners of the world than any other. Many American musical styles can trace their origins to the South, although their popularity only grew rapidly when these reached northern audiences and a rich and powerful music industry developed in Chicago and Los Angeles.

Blues, Gospel and Soul

The 19th-century cotton trade produced not only the blood, sweat and tears of the harvesting slaves but also a rich spiritual mourning music. Based on African rhythms, the new sounds reflected the experiences of these labourers in America, developing into a unique American form of art. These traditional mournful sounds of the South, once fused with black Christian choral music, became gospel, then soul. These in turn evolved into rhythm and blues, jazz and funk – and even rock 'n' roll and hip-hop can trace their roots to blues, making it the grandaddy of American music.

Blues began to receive widespread popularity through travelling musicians likeW. C. Handy, whose 'St Louis Blues' is an enduring classic. But the musical form really evolved into a powerful style with migration of blacks to northern cities in the early 20th century. Here, voices such as that of Bessie Smith found new audiences, and after the Second World War musicians like Muddy Waters, Bo Diddley and John Lee Hooker became widely popular.

Jazz

America's classical music emerged largely in New Orleans, where its unique mix of cultures and upbeat atmosphere readily encouraged the development of a musical style that was essentially a fusion of ragtime, blues and military brass. The art of fusion has remained a core element of jazz in the form of an emphasis on improvisation, which, along with its tonal and harmonic rules, makes it a unique genre – one that has gone on to help shape the work of classical composers and orchestras.

Jazz began with ragtime, a form of piano music based on African rhythms fused with classical European style, considerably popularised by Scott Joplin. When combined with the blues music of the South and the celebratory military brass bands of New Orleans, a distinct musical style began to develop. But, as with blues, it was the migration of jazz to northern cities that really boosted the art form. Many musicians, including all-time jazz greats, the likes of Louis Armstrong, also migrated north, to huge audiences in Chicago. This ushered in an important and formative era of jazz in the form of swing, a big-band style of jazz, which soon swept the country in the 1920s and '30s. Duke Ellington and the swing orchestra of Glenn Miller reigned supreme, Count Basie was considered one of the great innovators, and Billie Holiday and Ella Fitzgerald added magnificent voices.

After the Second World War, bebop emerged as a reaction against the organised rhythms of swing. This has since been fused and refused with various types of jazz and other genres, and today all forms have some popular revival -- no one form dominates.

Bluegrass

Born in Appalachia as the child of Irish and Scottish folk music, bluegrass is characterised by fast-picking of banjos, mandolins and fiddles and high-pitched wailing. The first bluegrass musicians were coalminers and farmers in Virginia, West Virginia, Kentucky and Tennessee, but the distinctive style that prevails today was bred in the 1940s, largely by Bill Monroe. Like blues, elements of this indigenous musical form were used to make rock 'n' roll and so it can count itself as one of the parents of modern rock. Bluegrass remains popular folk music, particularly in the region where it originated, where catching an energetic gig is highly recommended.

Country

Like bluegrass, country music also has its roots in the Appalachians and among poor rural whites who built on the traditions of European folk to create sentimental lyrics and simple melodies. Although the style has developed considerably since, these elements are still essential, as evidenced by the work of two of country music's classic performers: Hank Williams with his air of tragedy, and Johnny Cash with his brazen honesty.

The major landmark in the development of country music was its fusion with western music in the 1920s. The latter was characterised by steel guitars and larger bands and added a distinctive twang to the genre. In the 1950s country had a deep influence on the development of rock music and rock 'n' roll, particularly in a fusion known as rockabilly. Such was the popularity of country that by the 1970s and '80s it had became big business, with musicians like Garth Brooks notching up record music sales. Today country and western is America's most popular form of music. Particularly in the west the airwaves are crammed with country stations, and artists like Willie Nelson and Emmylou Harris have enduring appeal.

Folk

American folk music has often embraced political and social activism, with direct lyrics and an honest spirit attacking the status quo. This activism was at its height in the 1960s, which was the golden era for American folk, although its popularity and influence before and since has also been substantial. Woody Guthrie picked on elements of patriotism in a time of depression with commentaries on union labour organisation. Pete Seeger then preserved American folk traditions in 1940s and '50s with his political comment that drew the attentions of the House Un-American Activities Committee. But it was in the 1960s that folk became the soundtrack of the times, as Bob Dylan and Joan Baez epitomised the climate of social protest, as did Arno Guthrie with his unlikely 18-minute-long but catchy hit 'Alice's Restaurant'. This song became a flag-bearer of the anti-war movement. Later in the 1960s the band The Grateful Dead grew out of folk and bluegrass traditions, to spearhead a lifestyle movement that celebrated drugs and counter-culture for a generation of the fans – so-called dead-heads.

Rock

Of all the American styles, perhaps the most enduring has been rock. Most early American styles contributed the formation of the genre, though some of the clearest links are in gospel and rhythm and blues (which developed in the 1940s out of swing). What is disputed, though, is when and where rock in its earliest form – as rock 'n' roll – started.

Certainly, the biggest early names in the sound were Chuck Berry and Jerry Lee Lewis, and Bill Haley and the Comets, who together laid the soundtrack for an era of poodle skirts and slicked-back hair. Elvis Presley famously built on this and caught the optimistic mood of the post-Second World War era, which effectively gave birth to teen culture and the need of the young to express a distinctive taste and style. The timing of the creation of rock 'n' roll was crucial; it developed out of a period when the target audience was teenagers and young adults, so making it the voice of a generation and championing their values. Their rebellious attitude of the 1950s and '60s was captured in the foot-tapping rhythms and introduction of electrical instruments.

Since its first creation, rock has morphed continuously, moving through the upbeat tunes of the Beach Boys and Buddy Holly to the 1970s when the Doors gave it a new edge and the Ramones created a unique brand of back-to-basics punk. In the 1980s Pink Floyd experimented with psychedelic influences while Bruce Springsteen reasserted the genre's blue-collar origins. Heavy metal particularly separated itself from the rest of the rock world in the 1980s, with provocatively dressed glam-rock bands such as Aerosmith and Guns 'n' Roses becoming huge commercial successes. The fast and edgy sound of Metallica all but created a new branch of music, that the band were not afraid to fuse with classical music in collaborative work with the San Francisco symphony orchestra. The 1990s rock scene virtually grew out of its repulsion with the false and stylistically excessive 1980s. A new form of rock, called grunge, involved a moody back-to-basics approach epitomised and popularised by Nirvana and Pearl Jam. Following this grunge wave has been an American reinvention of punk rock with bands like Blink-182 producing short, snappy songs. But more innovative was the approach of Linkin Park, who have fused rock and punk traditions with hip-hop to create a well-rounded commercial sound.

Soul, Disco and Pop

As music underwent important transitional phases in the 1960s and '70s, including the enormous body of work produced on the Motown label in the

1960s, pop began to become a distinct form of music, more approachable and with easily digested music and lyrics. Popular attention turned in particular to disco, a music that accompanied a lifestyle that celebrated dancing, kitsch and hedonistic excesses of all kinds. Gloria Gaynor ('I Will Survive') and bands like Parliament Funkadelic ('Tear The Roof Off The Sucker – Give Up The Funk') dominated the scene.

The 1980s saw disco fade as pop changed to fit the accompanying mood of the time. Madonna, who has become famous for successfully moving with the times, creating popular contemporary music over three decades, first became popular at this time and ushered in a new era of raunchiness and commercial ambition as explained in her song 'Material Girl'.

Little has changed in the world of pop since the 1980s, although the 1990s saw the creation of a new, demanding and ever-younger generation of consumer-orientated teens with unsophisticated palates who have sustained the popularity of undemanding but fiercely style-conscious performers such as Britney Spears.

Rap and Hip-hop

While disco foundered, rock became introverted and pop grew bland, a new wave of music called rap began to appear in the 1980s. With roots in the black and Hispanic street culture of New York's Bronx in the 1970s, it essentially began as the remixing of disco with the added 'scratching' of records by DJs and the development of a distinctive rhythmic lyrical style. Early stars like Run-DMC, Public Enemy and Tone Loc and the Beastie Boys effectively spawned a whole new musical genre. This has since evolved and grown in popularity at an amazing rate, with rap – now just the term for the lyrical chanting – fostering the musical form of hip-hop. Some of the earliest protagonists of the musical art form were part of a genre that has since been labelled gangsta rap. Bands like NWA ('Niggers With Attitude'), Dr Dre, Snoop Doggy Dogg and Ice-T captured and perhaps encouraged the early 1990s anger in black ghettos. Since these early days, hip-hop has been fused with more or less every other available musical style and evolved into a slightly less aggressive but no less misogynistic and commercially hugely successful form. As the first major white artist in the hip-hop scene, Eminem has given it a more mainstream face and firmly entrenched it among the white kids in the suburbs.

Painting

In comparison with cinema and music, painting has nt always been an art at the forefront of America's cultural self-expression. Yet despite this lack of everyday mass appreciation, many of the world's greatest private and public collections and museums are in the USA.

America's first truly indigenous art was that of the many Native American tribes. This mainly revolved around the adornment of everyday objects and around personal ornaments, though some tribes developed strong traditions of more public works. In the Pacific Northwest, totem poles and religious masks created evocative representations of earthly creatures fused with deities. Southwestern tribes became skilled at abstract art and as skilful potters worked many of these into clay. The Navaho also successfully combined art with craft by reworking Spanish techniques to produce rugs and silver jewellery.

Having copied and reproduced European styles for some years, the white American population finally began to develop its own distinctive style from around 1820s. These early-19th-century painters concentrated on grandiose depictions of the raw beauty of the landscape and sense of frontier. Perhaps the two greatest proponents of Western art were Frederick Remington and Charles Russell. Both were preoccupied with glorious and adventurous cowboys, and savage (and mythic) depictions of Indians that fleshed out the notion of the American West. Later in the 19th century, nature was looked on with new eyes with the 1880s powerful watercolours of the sea by Winslow Homer and the American Impressionist Childe Hassam. Meanwhile American portrait-painters were beginning to make their mark, with Charles Wilson Peale, John Singleton Copley and Gilbert Stewart flourishing – in part by painting rousing likenesses of revolutionary figures.

The 20th century heralded an era of stylistic experimentation and of realism. The Ashcan school and Robert Henri brought a sense of realism to the depiction of urban life, and the theme was picked up and played on during the Depression by Edward Hopper with his bleak urban landscapes of the 1930s and '40s. Broadly similar realist techniques, which in some senses began to compete, copy and play on the thriving photographic medium, also became popular as a way of portraying a cosy and idealised America, as evidenced for example by the enormous success of Norman Rockwell's magazine illustrations.

With the end of the Second World War, themes of Cold War insecurity were picked up by a development of abstract expressionism originating in 1940s Europe. Overconfidence is mixed with insecurity in the work of Jackson Pollock and Mark Rothko. These works fostered an age of pop art, in which high art was fused with popular culture. Andy Warhol famously bastardised mass-produced images of American icons to produce art and social comment. This has broadly continued to be the theme in modern American contemporary art, where the mix of media has become a vital part of art. The fusion of film, sculpture, photography, painting and video imaging has become common in a process that is constantly seeking to redefine its boundaries – or perhaps demonstrate that there is none.

Photography

Since its invention, photography has always played a powerful role in the USA. This has gone well beyond its usefulness as a record of public and private events, and has become both an important tool for influencing public opinion and a vehicle for artistic expression. It has particularly proved itself as a medium with a social conscience, by often conveying a powerful and thought-provoking, yet nonetheless impartial, message. Lewis Hine and Jakob Riis shot the urban poor, while Walker Evans and Dorothea Lange – particularly her evocative breadline photos – communicated the plight of the rural poor in the great Depression. The photographic medium in American hands has also produced some of the most powerful images of the 20th century: a first fragile image of the Earth taken from space; powerful war images by photographers like Robert Capa; the 1960s social commentary by Robert Frank; and the development of glamorous fashion photography.

Although photography was invented in the first half of the 19th century, it wasn't until the 1920s that photographs made their way into all aspects of contemporary life. Hand-held cameras suddenly gave ordinary Americans the opportunity to create their own visual images. Suddenly pictures were everywhere: on passports, in the press, in science. First World War photographs had helped convince America of its stake in a distant war. Advertisers, particularly, embraced photography for its ability to create plausible dreams.

In the 1930s, mass media based on photographs exploded, and popular magazines like *Life* and *Look* were dedicated to photographic journalism. An Associated Press 'wirephoto' could be sent instantaneously, and suddenly millions of people were seeing the same pictures. Sombre images from the Depression and then the Second World War were brought into American living rooms long before vivid images of glorious life drove a consumer frenzy in the 1950s.

Despite competition from television and elsewhere, photographs continued to be a powerful medium in the second half of the 20th century, a central facet of the pop culture that took root in America, and a vital tool for marketeers and image-builders, who can now increase their control over the medium using computer technology.

Architecture

America came of age architecturally in the 20th century when it no longer relied on resurrecting European styles, and perhaps its greatest contribution to architecture has been the skyscraper, whose bold, thrusting lines have come to symbolise the USA's grand aspirations and technical achievements and industrious commerce. The skyscraper was made possible by new construction techniques – particularly the development of iron-framed buildings, which made supporting walls unnecessary – and by the invention of the elevator. The first skyscraper went up in Chicago, Illinois in 1884.

Chicago was also the birthplace for much of the nation's architectural inventiveness. Some of the most graceful early towers were designed by Louis Sullivan (1856–1924), America's first great modern architect. His most talented student was Frank Lloyd Wright (1867–1959), who spent much of his career designing private residences characterised by strong horizontal lines, matching furniture and generous use of open space. Space was allowed to flow between rooms rather than being broken up, and textures were derived from undecorated materials. Opportunities offered by materials like steel, glass and concrete were instrumental in creating new shapes, patterns and design, and his angular aesthetic inspired a generation of 20th-century design.

From the mid 1920s on, Wright's designs became fused with Art Deco, so that the main design elements became the horizontal and vertical lines of the structural grid. Examples include the Empire State building in New York. But it was the European architects who emigrated to the United States before the Second World War who launched what became a dominant movement in architecture: the International Style. Perhaps the most influential of these immigrants were Ludwig Mies van der Rohe (1886–1969) and Walter Gropius (1883–1969), both former directors of Germany's famous design school, the Bauhaus. Based on geometric form, they hung glass curtains around steel frames to produce abstract shapes that doubled as buildings. A response to this stark style has been a growth in postmodernism among younger American architects such as Michael Graves (1945–). They have rejected the austere, boxy look in favour of striking contours and bold decoration reminiscent of historical styles of architecture.

First Steps

The immigrant path to the USA is a well-worn one and over the centuries millions of Europeans have crossed the Atlantic to seek new fortunes. And while the original lure of religious freedom and the driving need to escape economic hardships may have lessened for many Europeans, the image of the USA as a glamorous and cutting-edge land of opportunity persists. This novel and exciting draw continues despite – perhaps because of – the increasing spread of American culture into Britain over the past century, which has served to make its landscapes and culture very familiar.

As a result, most people will have fairly clear reasons why they might want to move to the USA. And the close links between Britain and the USA mean that arranging a flight between the two could barely be easier.

Why Live and Work in the USA?

Hackneyed though it is, the term 'American Dream' still best sums up why you would want to live and work in the USA. This conveys the possibility of forging your own destiny and gaining individual economic success through hard work, irrespective of your background.

Earning money is certainly the all-important part of this, but other elements can also provide a powerful draw. The pilgrims came to establish religious freedom, and the USA continues to constitutionally safeguard the rights and freedoms of its many minority groups.

Language and Familiarity

These days the USA has perhaps deeper ethnic roots in Africa, Latin America or even Asia than Britain, yet the status of English as the de facto national language gives the British and Irish a head start in the country. The way the English language is used on either side of the pond certainly has its obvious differences, and there is a minefield of nuances that can impede subtle communication, but, on the surface at least, complex communication is easy, and language itself will impose no limit on the level in which you can integrate in the society.

Similarly, although American culture has evolved well beyond early influences from the UK or Ireland, some customs, practices and manners are still shared. In fact, since America's growing cultural dominance of the western world, the amount of culture that is effectively shared has steadily grown. The bulk of modern pop culture, in particular, can be traced to the USA. In many senses, living in the UK forms the ideal groundwork for those keen on heading to the USA to live and work.

Opportunity and Independence

A shared language and the cultural familiarity are both particularly helpful in unlocking the fabled opportunities in the USA. For many British businesses the USA represents a dream market, the key to fantastical profits. The sheer scale of the place and its consumption is part of what makes the USA the most attractive destination in the world to those of entrepreneurial bent, who are encouraged by its straightforward business regulations, the ease of setting up, the positive environment and the network of support – which crucially includes light taxation. The American Dream is particularly suitable for those who wish to start their own business or be self-employed.

Centres of Excellence

Even if you are not an entrepreneur, America is likely to draw you, since in almost every field – from the academic to the commercial – the USA has conspicuous centres of international excellence. In this sense there really is something that will appeal to everyone, and in many cases, to perform at the pinnacle of your chosen field, you may in fact have no choice but to live and work in the USA.

Standard of Living

The rewards for success in the USA are as high as anywhere in the world and consequently so is the general standard of living. This is as high as anywhere in Europe and delivered with an almost mind-numbing convenience. And, while wages are relatively high, the cost of living generally isn't. Yet at the same time it's worth bearing in mind that there are fewer guarantees and safety nets in the USA, so a large portion of your costs will go towards ensuring your own security through insurance. Moreover, financial success often comes at the expense of your quality of life. The American work ethic can be gruellingly hard, and the existence of tensions between rich and poor can compromise the quality of your life if they mean that you have little time to enjoy your wealth and live in fear.

The Outdoors

If you can take time from your job you will find the USA a scenically stunning place, where spending time in the outdoors is rarely anything but unbridled pleasure. Images like the Grand Canyon or the New England, autumn colours are postcard classics, but wherever you live you are unlikely to be a long drive away from beautiful and unspoilt natural areas. And rarely will you be more than a day's drive from some true wilderness. It is an understatement to say that a lifetime of trips wouldn't exhaust the potential for outdoor adventure,

The American Dream

The origins of term 'American Dream' are uncertain, but what is clear is that it was during the deepening gloom of the Depression that the concept really caught on by offering encouragement to the impoverished. The first published use of the term was certainly in the 1930s and was defined by one commentator – historian James Truslow Adams – as a 'dream of a land in which life should be better and richer and fuller for every man, with opportunity for each according to his ability or achievement'. By the end of the Second World War it had become part of the national vocabulary.

The American Dream has always been defined quite loosely, with this definition certainly changing through time and being adapted to mean different things to different groups. However, as a promise of opportunity, abundance, equality and personal happiness, it has always been at the heart of reasons to migrate to the USA.

and the country is a place of pilgrimage for the likes of skiers, snowboarders, mountain bikers, hikers, climbers and kayakers. If you fall into any of these categories, a second home in the USA could well be a dream home.

Culture

The USA has one of the most distinctive modern cultures and one that is based on diversity. True, most Americans have little appreciation or knowledge of high culture, yet many have a good appreciation of the habits and customs of the many ethnic groups that they live beside. This multiculturalism can be a highly stimulating environment, and in that sense you can travel more within the USA without leaving it than anywhere else in the world. This diversity extends well beyond ethnic boundaries and also creates extraordinary differences between rich and poor, urban and rural, north and south. All this produces not only food for thought but also a fertile seedbed for all manner of innovations and trends. The cutting edge of global trends, be they in microcomputers or in hip- hop, is often in the USA. And it can be a delight to live among them.

Freedom

Underlying the notion of an American Dream is the concept of personal freedom. It is bound up with the hopes and dreams of the very first immigrants who left the restrictive Old World in the hope of living in ways they chose, by their own religious and moral codes. This theme was picked up, formalised and expanded in the Declaration of Independence. Thomas Jefferson's idea of 'life, liberty, and the pursuit of happiness' encompassed a belief that the fundamental goodness of humanity held out the optimistic promise of a social order built on the concepts of democracy, liberty, justice and equal opportunity, not on birth or inherited position. Much later this notion was again picked up by Martin Luther King, who appealed to the notion of the American Dream to justify equality between the races.

Striking it Rich

Crucially, the idea of freedom was not just a philosophical concept to ensure egalitarianism and personal choice. It also translated into economic freedom and particularly allowed individuals the possibility of amassing great wealth and translating this into dramatic upward social mobility – freedom from the restrictive social codes of the Old World. Leaving behind the post-feudal economies of western Europe – based on high levels of taxation, which it was believed stymied development – the American economy became a symbol of freedom from constraint. The notion that the system really made it possible to strike it rich, or at least improve your economic state, made the USA the destination of choice for the impoverished, like those fleeing the Irish potato famine or Scotland's Highland clearances.

Adding more incentives were America's vast physical resources that were unclaimed and often undiscovered up until the latter half of the 19th century. This allowed the possibility of coming across a fortune through a relatively small but lucky investment in land or industry. Many prospectors headed west to the Rocky Mountains or California to buy acres of cheap land in hopes of finding deposits of gold. The Gold Rush to Colorado and California was another tangible result of the American Dream.

Making Your Own Luck

The American Dream soon became the most powerful dream of all, so that even when Americans weren't actually pursuing it, many would dream of it. In the mid- to late-19th century the nation became addicted to dime novels, like those of the prolific Horatio Alger Jr, who idealised the American Dream. In his rags-to-riches novels, down-and-out bootblacks became powerful millionaires. But in this respect reality was even more captivating, and by the beginning of the 20th century major industrialist personalities became the new model for the American Dream. Many started life in the humblest of conditions but grew to control enormous corporations and fortunes. Among the most notable here were Andrew Carnegie and John D. Rockefeller. This acquisition of great wealth appeared to demonstrate that if you had talent, intelligence, and a willingness to work extremely hard you were likely to be a success in life.

Bourgeois Comfort

Not everyone could strike it rich, and, after the humbling Depression and the brutal Second World War, Americans began to redefine the American Dream in terms of something much more achievable. The dream became something that was theoretically within the grasp of most and became focused on securing your place in suburbia. Bourgeois comforts of every sort became the tangible results of a happy and successful life lived according to the American Dream, owning your own house the final stamp of approval.

The righteousness of this American Dream was seen as validated when the USA finally triumphed over communism at the end of the Cold War. However, today the American Dream is often seen as a somewhat discredited enigma; suburbia is no longer the draw it once was for those who grew up in it. Yet most of America's million or so annual immigrants still arrive in search of all those things that traditionally comprise the American Dream – freedom, opportunity and comforts – which are far harder to find in their home countries in Latin America or Asia.

Problems with the American Dream

A wholehearted belief in the American Dream implicitly damns those who fall by the wayside. For many reasons, including the way in which capitalism fundamentally works, it simply is not possible for everyone to become prosperous through determination and hard work. Yet those who don't succeed – that is, the conspicuously poor – are often considered to have failed through personal faults such as laziness or stupidity. Furthermore, the strong belief of many Americans that you basically get what you deserve helps explain why the parental role of the state is so minimal – even though this damns to even greater economic hardship those who struggle. This system is particularly unfair given that, as everywhere else in the world, many wealthy Americans are actually well off on the basis of what they have *inherited* – in the form of money, a supportive family and even biological traits such as intelligence, looks or physical fitness. Blind belief in the power of the American Dream also causes a misrepresentation of history since it suggests that the country's success was built on little more than hard work and determination. But this isn't entirely true, since another contributory factor to America's success is its over-abundance of natural wealth.

Getting to the USA

Travelling to the USA from the UK and Ireland is made painless and easy by the prevalence of flights over the pond and the rash of booking options that exist in the Internet age.

Hubs and Costs

The bulk of flights into the USA from Britain arrive in New York's airports or in Washington, DC, although direct flights to Atlanta, Chicago, Los Angeles and San Francisco are also easy to find and in total more than 20 US cities are served by non-stop flights from the UK. You can be in New York in seven or so hours, and Los Angeles in 12.

If you are heading beyond one of these major gateway cities, then you will likely first clear customs and immigration there before catching a domestic flight to one of the USA's countless regional airports. The two flights will almost certainly be issued on the same ticket and will be with the same or a partner airline.

Flight prices to the major cities start from around £200 from London in low season, but will more than double in high season. The cost can also easily go up by £200 if you need a connecting flight to London from a UK regional airport and if the ticket includes an onward flight to a smaller city in the USA.

Prices also vary depending on the season. In general, peak season lasts from July to September and includes periods around Easter, Christmas and New Year. Fares are at their cheapest in low season, which lasts from November to March. The months in between – April, June and October – are termed the 'shoulder season' and are a little more expensive – though not as expensive as peak season, and there should be less of a problem finding seats. The travel seasons are not universal throughout the USA, as destinations like Florida are less popular in their hot and sticky summers.

The more flexible you can be about your departure date, the more you will likely be able to save. Particularly try to avoid flying at weekends, when fares creep up.

Buying a Ticket

Buying a ticket through an agent has traditionally meant considerable savings for the consumer. Some agents – known as consolidators – buy blocks of tickets at low prices from airlines and then pass some of these savings on to their customers. Other agents may achieve low fares by specialising in discounted flights, student flights or the charter market. Charter flights can be good value, but since they are generally offered as inflexible tickets with only two or three weeks between departure dates they are not really a viable option for an extended stay – unless you can find a fare that's so low you can afford to throw the return portion away.

While travel agents of various kinds are still vital to the airline industry, buying direct from the airlines is becoming an increasingly popular way to secure your tickets. With the dawn of the Internet age the choice of vendors has become particularly bewildering, so it is highly advisable to look at some Internet price comparison sites to get an impression of typical fares and who seems to specialise in what. One extremely useful so-called 'travel portal', which lists the best fares from hundreds of providers, including both agents and airlines, is **www.cheapflights.co.uk**. This website allows you to quickly choose your destination and easily spot the agents or airlines offering the most competitive fares on the market. From here you can click through to their websites, which often include a booking engine that allows you to put in your travel details to arrive at a fare. Alternatively there is usually a booking centre you can call to find out the same information (which may result in a supplement). The fare you are offered will be based on availability, so it is worth moving the departure date around by a few days to see if this gives you a better price.

Before you finally decide on a ticket, carefully consider its restrictions, particularly the possibilities, costs and penalties of changing the dates and even the routing later on. Generally, most of the best fares are on advance purchase tickets – often called Apex – which enable the minimum of flexibility; but it is not unusual for conditions to vary between airlines and even within this ticket type.

Flights

The following non-stop flights head from UK and Irish airports to the USA:

From London

- **Atlanta**: British Airways, Delta, United
- **Baltimore**: British Airways
- **Boston**: American Airlines, British Airways, Delta, United, Virgin Atlantic
- **Chicago**: Air India, American Airlines, British Airways, Thai Airways, United, Virgin Atlantic
- **Cincinnati**: Delta
- **Dallas/Fort Worth**: American Airlines, British Airways
- **Detroit**: British Airways, Northwest
- **Houston**: British Airways, Continental
- **Las Vegas**: Virgin Atlantic
- **Los Angeles**: Air New Zealand, American Airlines, British Airways, Continental, United, Virgin Atlantic
- **Minneapolis**: Northwest
- **New York**: Air India, American Airlines, British Airways, Continental, Kuwait Airways, Thai Airways, United, Virgin Atlantic
- **Orlando**: British Airways, Continental, Virgin Atlantic
- **Philadelphia**: British Airways

- **Phoenix**: British Airways
- **Raleigh/Durham**: American Airlines
- **San Diego**: British Airways
- **San Francisco**: British Airways, Continental, United, Virgin Atlantic

From Birmingham

- **New York**: Continental

From Manchester

- **Atlanta**: Delta
- **Chicago**: American Airlines, BMI
- **New York**: British Airways, Continental, Delta, PIA
- **Orlando**: Virgin Atlantic
- **Philadelphia**: BMI, US Airways
- **Washington, DC**: BMI

From Glasgow

- **New York**: American Airlines, British Airways, Continental

From Edinburgh

- **New York**: Continental

From Dublin/Shannon

- **Altanta**: Aer Lingus, Delta
- **Boston**: Aer Lingus
- **Chicago**: Aer Lingus
- **Los Angeles**: Aer Lingus, American Airlines
- **New York**: Aer Lingus

Airlines

- **Aer Lingus UK, t** 0845 084 4444 or Republic of Ireland **t** 0818 365 000, **www.aerlingus.ie**.
- **Air India, t** (020) 7495 7950, **www.airindia.com**.
- **Air New Zealand, t** 0800 028 4149, **www.airnz.co.uk**.
- **American Airlines, t** 0845 7789 789 or Republic of Ireland **t** (01) 602 0550, **www.americanairlines.com**.
- **bmi, t** 0870 607 0555, **www.flybmi.com**.
- **British Airways, t** 0870 850 9850 or Republic of Ireland **t** 1800 626 747, **www.britishairways.com**.

- **Continental Airlines, t** 0845 607 6760 or Republic of Ireland **t** 1890 925 252, **www.continental.com.**
- **Delta, t** 0800 414 767 or Republic of Ireland **t** 1800 768 080 or (01) 407 3165, **www.delta.com.**
- **Kuwait Airways, t** (020) 7412 0006, **www.kuwait-airways.com.**
- **PIA** (Pakistan International Airlines) **t** (020) 7499 5500, **www.piac.com.pk.**
- **Thai Airways, t** 0870 606 0911, **www.thaiair.com.**
- **United Airlines, t** 0845 844 4777, **www.unitedairlines.co.uk.**
- **Virgin Atlantic, t** (01293) 450 150, **www.virgin-atlantic.com.**

Jet Lag

Jet lag – that fuzzy, out-of-sorts feeling that follows a long flight between different time zones – is a plight that affects all but a handful of travellers. It comes as the result of the disruption of the traveller's normal sleep/wake cycle and can present itself as indigestion, daytime drowsiness, headaches, irritability, fatigue, insomnia or poor concentration. Symptoms can range from mild to severe, but will often noticeably impair post-flight performance – as sometimes illustrated by the results of travelling sports competitors.

The physiological underpinnings of jet lag are in the hundred or so circadian rhythms that your brain generates for your body. These are the cogs of a complex internal clock that is driven by our environment and habits. This body clock is particularly designed for regular cycles of daylight and darkness. Jet travel, however, whisks us between time zones far too swiftly for it to adjust. As a rule of thumb, a day of recovery is needed for each time zone that you cross for your circadian rhythms to be completely restored.

Persuading Your Body

Rather than just waiting for your body to adjust, there's a lot you can do to help it overcome jet lag. A big part of this effort involves conscious meddling with the major time cues – diet, light, exercise, and social interactions – that your body normally receives.

Part of your efforts to crack jet lag has to involve adjusting these to the regime that your body will face at your destination as soon as you can. Often, though, few changes are really practical until you actually board the plane. Once you do, however, be sure to reset your watch to your destination time zone as soon as you can. Then think what you should be doing at this time of day and act accordingly. If you would be awake, then stay awake, if you would be sleeping then try to sleep. Getting to sleep can be hard, since aircraft are uncomfortable, noisy, busy and bright. So part of your tactic needs to be to create as quiet and dark an environment as possible. Eyeshades and ear plugs can be extra-ordinarily useful in this. Conversely you may need to force yourself to stay awake if the time at the destination demands it. This can be uncomfortable, but generally preferable to a sleepless night when you arrive. If you walk around and do isometric exercises (simply contract and relax as many muscle groups as possible while seated) while in flight this will improve your circulation and can help keep you awake. Additionally, try also to eat at times that suit the schedule of your destination – even if this means refusing your airline food.

Easing the Pain

While the disruption of the body clock is the true reason for jet lag, many other factors associated with jet travel contribute to the overall problem. Dealing with these as best you can will help significantly reduce the effects of jet lag. Generally speaking, air travel is hard on the body, so it pays to be in decent shape before you board a plane. If you are hungover, sleepy or run down before you start travelling, you're making yourself susceptible to severe jet lag.

One of the big physical stresses of flying is dehydration. The air aboard aircraft is generally stale and dry. The lack of humidity in particular can dry the nose and throat, encouraging coughs, sore throats, colds and viruses to take hold. The best way to help your body cope with this is to drink plenty of water. At the same time it's best to avoid alcohol and caffeine just before and during your flight; both will help dehydrate you. Additionally, alcohol causes drowsiness and can contribute to the sluggish feeling experienced by many travellers.

Low cabin pressure is another unavoidable stress of flying. At cruising altitudes of around 30,000 feet the aircraft is pressurised to about 8,000 feet. Unless you are accustomed to this altitude, you may well become lethargic and suffer from mild swelling of parts of your body – particularly your feet. While this won't contribute directly to jet lag, it is going to make you uncomfortable and perhaps keep you awake when you'd be best off sleeping. So be sure to wear comfortable, loose-fitting clothing and shoes.

Coping on Arrival

On arrival, try and build a little pampering into your schedule to allow your body to recover and adjust and defend you against jet lag. If possible, don't jump into a busy schedule straight away. And try to take a long bath as soon as you can to help return your body moisture level to normal.

If arriving in the morning you might be tempted to collapse and sleep, but actually you're generally better off finding diversions and some gentle exercise to do to keep you from falling asleep during the day – rather than napping and then finding yourself in the grip of night-time insomnia. If you are finding it difficult to adapt to the timing of your new sleep patterns you might try taking melatonin tablets in a fairly new but not uncontroversial treatment for jet lag.

This is the synthetic version of the human hormone that our bodies secrete into the bloodstream when it's time to sleep. Its release is normally governed by the absence of light as well as the timing of our meals. Light suppresses melatonin but at nightfall the body releases it, making you sleepy. Melatonin levels peak around midnight and then progressively drop off until morning. Several studies have shown that taking melatonin can help adjust your body clock and so alleviate jet lag, but the long-term side effects of taking these extra doses have yet to be established. The pills are available over-the-counter and in health food stores and pharmacies in the USA, but is not licensed for distribution in the UK.

   Less controversially, you can use your diet to help your adjust your body clock – and it this method that is often recommended to travelling athletes. This diet largely depends on eating starchy and sweet foods – high in carbohydrates – to cause sleepiness and then eating high protein foods, like meat, to make you more alert.

Red Tape

Give me your tired, your poor,
Your huddled masses yearning to breathe free,
The wretched refuse of your teeming shore.
Send these, the homeless tempest-tossed to me.
I lift my lamp beside the golden door.

Emma Lazarus, inscribed on the base of the Statue of Liberty

Apart from the relatively few Native Americans, all Americans are immigrants or the descendants of immigrants like those who first arrived on ships like the *Mayflower* or through the immigration channels on Ellis Island in New York. But the times when the USA actively encouraged the rebellious and impoverished to its shores are long gone, and recently it has done its best to shut the door on mass immigration. The land of opportunity has some of the strictest and complicated immigration laws in the world.

This regulation has become even stricter in the wake of the terrorist attacks in September 2001. These led to a complete rethink of security issues; attitudes have toughened up and new departments have been created. And there is a popular fear among many American people that foreigners (so called 'aliens') are 'overrunning the country' and more should be done to control their influx. Evidence of this includes the creation of vigilante civilian forces – calling themselves the Minutemen Project – patrolling the Mexican border in search of illegal immigrants.

Yet despite all this, one million legal and countless numbers of illegal immigrants still enter the USA every year. If you plan to be among either group, expect the bureaucracy to be difficult to deal with, unpredictable in its requirements and generally unsympathetic. You will need determination to deal with the system and a great deal of patience to cope with all the inevitable delays to your application.

You also need to be aware that, particularly in the present climate of heightened security, immigration policy and procedures are subject to modification, which may quickly render some of the information in this chapter invalid. Many regulations that were previously laxly policed are now being rigorously enforced. Changes in status between visa types are refused more often than in the pre 9/11 climate. Overall we can expect a further tightening of immigration controls and a greater emphasis being placed on the quality of skills that immigrants offer.

The best source of up-to-date information is your nearest embassy or **United States Citizenship and Immigration Service (USCIS)** office, though the monthly newspaper *Going USA* can also be a useful source. In complicated cases you may want to enlist the help of an immigration lawyer or consultant. The US embassy in London can supply a list of these, or you can browse a list of local options at **www.lawyers.com**. Alternative assistance is offered by the hundreds of immigration agencies within the USA. Many, like the **Irish Immigration Center** in Boston (**www.iicenter.org**), have useful websites and specialists on hand to offer free advice and support.

Administrative Departments

The first point of contact for Britons wishing to move to America is the **US Embassy** in London, 24 Grosvenor Square, London W1A 1AE, **t** (020) 7499 9000 or 24hr visa information line **t** 09068 200290 (60p per min); for further information call **t** 09055 444546 (at the prohibitive rate of £1.30 per minute); **www. usembassy.org.uk**. Its clear and well-organised website explains the difference between the different types of visa and should answer most, if not all, of your questions. It should give you a good idea of what category you are likely to fall into and the logistics involved in the application procedure itself. Fees and typical processing times are all explained on the website.

On its website the embassy crucially explains that, though they can recommend you for entry into the USA, its visas do not guarantee this; the ultimate decision will be made by a border official at your port of entry.

Officials at the port of entry work for the **Department of Homeland Security**. This state department divides into **USCIS** (**www.uscis.gov**), the **Bureau of Customs and Border Protection** and the **Bureau of Immigration and Customs Enforcement**. USCIS is the key department for those wishing to enter the country, since it deals with the immigration procedures of both foreign nationals entering the USA and those already within the USA who are seeking to alter their status. Their website is rather more detailed than that of the US embassy in London, but the layout is confusing – you may leave the website more bewildered than when you entered.

Entering the USA

The most straightforward way for British citizens to enter the USA is via the **visa-waiver scheme**, which generally boils down to filling out a simple form while on the aeroplane over. Essentially this method of entry is designed for tourists and business people, and is only available to those who do not intend on working or staying for more than 90 days. Should you break either of these conditions – and plenty of people do – you face deportation if you are caught and will not be allowed entry under this scheme again – making a full visa application necessary for future visits. The possession of a ticket out of the country and evidence of funds to support yourself during your stay are prerequisites to entering under the visa-waiver scheme. Incidentally, entry under the visa-waiver scheme is not available to those who have been arrested, even if this did not result in a criminal conviction, nor to those with criminal records or with serious communicable illnesses.

Britons wishing to enter the USA for longer than 90 days or to earn money require a visa. The range and number of these can be quite bewildering, but broadly they divide into permanent (immigrant) and temporary (non-immigrant) visas. An immigrant visa allows you to live and work in the USA indefinitely and is the necessary precursor to becoming a US citizen, while a non-immigrant visa allows you temporary admission to the country – in some cases for up to five years – for a reason specified in the visa.

Arrival and Customs

On arrival in the USA, everyone – no matter how long their intended stay – is **photographed and fingerprinted**. At this stage it is important to look as presentable as possible. Immigration officers have a lot of leeway to exercise their own discretion about whom they detain or refuse entry to, and it is not unknown for the bohemian or unkempt to be refused entry. You have no right of appeal should you be refused entry – unless you are seeking asylum.

On entering the country you will receive the **USCIS Arrival and Departure Record (form I-94)**, an extremely important document detailing how long you are allowed to stay in the country. Records of this will play a part in any subsequent dealings you may have with immigration officials.

You will also need to pass through customs, having filled out a **Customs Declaration** that will usually be given to you in advance on the flight over. Duty-free allowances are different for residents and non-residents. Non-residents cannot import gifts worth more than $100, and then only if you are staying for more than 72 hours and haven't imported anything for the last six months. Residents can import items to the value of $400 ($600 if returning from Caribbean countries, or $1,200 from Guam or the US Virgin Islands). You can also bring in 200 cigarettes, or 100 cigars or three pounds of smoking tobacco, and one litre of alcoholic beverages (provided you are over 21).

The list of import-restricted goods is long and often changes, but ultimately shouldn't affect most people. But fruits, seeds, plants and cheese will be viewed suspiciously and probably confiscated, as will meat in any form. The import-ation of the alcoholic drink absinthe is illegal, as is bringing in Cuban cigars. If you are thinking of bringing anything unusual into the country, check first on the US Customs and Border Prevention website at **www.cbp.gov**. There are no limits on the amount of money you can bring into the country but sums above $10,000 need to be mentioned on your customs declaration form.

Non-Immigrant Visas

If you don't intend to stay in the USA permanently, but just for a few months or years and for a specific purpose, then you will need a **non-immigrant (temporary) visa**, which can often be extended or adjusted. Even if you intend to settle in the USA long-term, you may be best off getting a non-immigrant visa first. These are easier to obtain than permanent residence status, and there is nothing to stop you petitioning for residency once you're within the USA.

However, since one of the qualifying terms of being granted a non-immigrant visa to the USA is your intention to return to your home country at the end, you will need to employ a certain amount of ingenuity to explain a change in circumstance. This will involve contacting and filing an application – usually via **Form I-539** – with the closest USCIS office to your place of residence. Should your application not be granted, you can request a review.

With over 30 types of visa available, the process of determining the appropriate visa can seem byzantine and overwhelming. Thankfully, though, most visas cater to small and specific groups like diplomats and the staff of international organisations like churches. These are applied for by the employer and the process is usually quick and straightforward. This leaves around half a dozen groups of visas that are commonly applicable to the needs of the vast majority of would-be temporary residents.

The first step to getting a visa is to get in touch with the nearest US consulate or USCIS office and find out which procedures apply. Should you be rejected once you have filled in and sent off the first round of the appropriate paperwork, you may appeal to the regional commissioner in control of the USCIS or the consulate to which you have applied. A prerequisite for all visas is that you have no drug or dependency problems, have no criminal record and are 'sound of body and mind'.

B Visas: Tourists and Business Travellers

The first step up from the visa-waiver scheme, and necessary if you if you are a British citizen staying for more than 90 days, are the B visas. You will need to prove that a stay of more than 90 days really is necessary to be granted this visa. The B-1 is the business visitor visa, B-2 the tourist visa.

J Visas: Exchange Visitors

If you'd like to have a working holiday – one involving a temporary holiday job, or working as an au pair or camp counsellor (*see* **Working in the USA**, pp.219–21) – you will probably need a J-1 visa. Gaining one is usually a quick and straightforward process and needs to be done via a sponsoring organisation, like Camp America or BUNAC, or a registered au pair agency.

Q Visas: Cultural Programme Participant

Q visas are designed for those on approved cultural exchange programmes. Generally you will be providing some training and sharing some of the cultural or historical traditions of your home country with the locals. The Q visa should normally be processed by your employer, but once you have it, it will enable you to take paid employment more widely.

H Visas: Working Visas

If you would like to work in the USA temporarily, and don't qualify for a J visa, you will need to file for an H-2 visa. This is a temporary worker visa and requires you to have a prospective employer who will approach the US Department of Labor for certification (*see* box 'Don't Steal Our Jobs!: Labour Certification'. p.124)

In the case of jobs that require graduates, you might be eligible for an H-1B visa. This is reserved for graduates with specialist knowledge, or a licence to practise in a specialist field, who are moving to a job that requires these skills. These visas enable you to stay up to six years (an initial three years with a possible extension for another three), but only 65,000 of them are available each financial year (October to October). However, certain applications are exempt from quota limitations, including: workers for non-profit research organisations, those working in higher education and those working for government research organisations. As with the H-2 visa, your employer needs to run the whole application via the authorities. The whole process can take some time, though in areas where America is experiencing a shortage of trained professionals – such as in nursing – some of the red tape may be waived or the process speeded up.

Should you be wanting to go to the USA as part of a traineeship, your employer will need to submit an application for an H-3 visa to the local USCIS office.

O Visas and P Visas: VIPs and Performers

If you are a leading light in your field, or a famous artist or entertainer, you might qualify for an O visa, for which the process of labour certification is not required. Similarly P visas are issued to performers and competitive athletes going to the USA in this capacity. In the case of either visa, your prospective employer or agent must first submit **Form I-129 (Petition for a Non-immigrant Worker)** to USCIS.

L Visas: Intra-Company Transfer

If your company is seconding you to the USA you should be eligible for an L-1 Intra-Company Transferee visa. You will need to have worked for the company for one year within the last three and the length of secondment is limited to five years, more for individuals with specialist knowledge – seven years for executives and managers, for example. Generally transfer visas are easy and relatively quick to obtain.

E Visas: Traders and Investors

E visas are designed for business people with either substantial financial investments within the USA, or those managing a large volume of trade between it and their home country.

Traders are eligible to apply for an E-1 Treaty Trader Visa, but to gain it you have to be an individual trader or executive who is essential to your company's presence in the USA. The company must also show evidence of a substantial and continuous trade with the USA.

Investors can more or less buy their way into the USA via an E-2 Treaty Investor visa. If you can demonstrate that you are seeking admission in order to invest in, or buy, a business in the USA then you should find the visa relatively easy to get. It will be largely based on how good an impression you create, since most of the criteria are not hard and fast. However, you will need to be investing a substantial amount (which is unspecified – though the benchmark of $100,000 is often used), be buying or investing in an enterprise that is already up and running, and demonstrate that your entry into the business will help unlock development potential or provide local employment. Employees of an E-2 visa holder may also be granted E-2 visas if they are executives, highly trained staff or essential to the running of operations. E-2 visas are initially available for one year, but can be extended almost indefinitely.

F Visas and M Visas: Students

Students accepted on academic courses in the USA should qualify for an F visa. Students on full-time vocational courses will gain entry to the USA under the M visa. The key difference between the two is that M visas do not enable you to transfer to an H-1B visa on the basis of your training. Neither visa grants you the right to take up paid employment, though you may find that there are positions legally available on campus. There is a means by which you can apply for permission to the USCIS to take up employment after the first year, but to be realistic, that is unlikely to be granted.

Immigrant Visas – Green Cards

Immigrant visas are known colloquially as 'green cards' after their original colour; they have since become blue then pink. These are officially called a Lawful Permanent Resident Card (LPR) and give the holder a quasi-citizen status. This includes many of the same rights and obligations of US citizens – with the notable exceptions of the right to vote and some welfare benefits.

Generally green cards are much harder to obtain than non-immigrant visas and most people from Britain who relocate to the USA do not arrive on an immigrant visa. Yet immigrant visas are worth pursuing if you intend to settle permanently in the USA, since they allow you to engage in any activity – not just the one specified on your non-immigrant visa. If you have family ties in the USA, or if your job falls into a special category that makes you a desirable immigrant, getting a green card may not be too difficult.

The first stage in acquiring a green card is a **petitioning process** that takes between three and six months depending on the complexity of the case and the workload of the regional processing centre. The next step is an **interview**, which, if it results in a successful application, is followed by the **wait** for the visa. The interview process will include checks for grounds for exclusion from the USA. These include checks of criminal records, extreme political affiliations, certain diseases and financial support. Interviews can take place either in the USA – if you are there on a non-immigrant visa – or in a consulate abroad. The latter is usually faster – four to six months compared to around a year. Note that if you are applying from the USA you cannot leave the country during the period of application without special permission – 'advance parole'.

A vital part of the process of getting a green card is having a guarantor in the USA. This can be an employer, but if your connection is through family ties it means finding a US citizen or green card holder who will guarantee that the applicant will not become a public charge for three years. In practical terms this means the individual needs to prove they have an annual income of around $25,000. If you can't find someone like this, you may be able to find an immigrant's aid organisation willing to serve as a guarantor.

Another important prerequisite to obtaining and keeping your green card is that you make the USA your place of permanent residence. If there is no clear evidence of this, your card can be confiscated at the port of entry. Unfortunately, there's no clear definition of what constitutes living in the USA, but spending

No Visas for an Easy Life: Retirement in the USA

Anyone can buy property, open a bank account, operate a business or own a house in the USA without a visa. But while some countries allow financially self-supporting people to retire or reside indefinitely, this is not the case in the USA. Proposals exist in Congress for a retirement visa, but for now all those who wish to work, live or retire in the USA require a visa. If you have a vacation or retirement home you are likely to find that the number of visits you make to it will eventually increase to the point where an immigration inspector will determine that you require a green card for your activities – at which point you have a home you can't use without a green card. Investing in a 'regional center' (*see* 'Employment-based Preferences', p.124) is a popular way around this, if you have $500,000 investment capital to spare.

most your time there, having a bank account, registered car, address and filing US tax returns will help build a convincing case.

Certainly if you leave the USA for more than a year and haven't filled out **form I-130** (Application for Issuance or Extension of Permit to Re-enter the United States) you will lose your green card.

Family Ties

If you have close relatives – such as a spouse, child or parents – who are US citizens and are living in the USA, then you should be able to get an immigrant visa fairly easily.

If you intend to marry a US citizen you can enter the country on a K visa for fiancé(e)s. This gives you much the same entitlements as you would under the visa waiver scheme. You need to get married within 90 days of entry and then lodge a petition with the USCIS for your adjustment of status to legal permanent resident.

In cases where the relative is more distant or simply a green card holder rather than a citizen, you have a chance of gaining a visa but must compete with other applicants for the half-million such visas issued every year. These are sub-divided into different quotas, including quotas for the immediate family of green card holders and the siblings of citizens.

In many cases applicants have been approved in principle but find themselves in an imaginary queue waiting for quota allocation for a visa to become available. These are subdivided by country – so that in countries with high demand, like Korea, India and Mexico, siblings may have to wait a decade before entering the USA. Foreign wives of green card holders may also have a significant wait – though this should not extend beyond three years, since a V visa exists to specifically prevent partners waiting for a quota to be reunited from being separated for more than three years. The V visa grants you residence and the right of employment until your permanent visa is ready.

Employment-based Preferences

The strength of your job skills or entrepreneurial success can also give you immigrant status. Applications are streamed into five categories based on the success and perceived usefulness of applicants as workers. All operate a quota system, although unused quotas can trickle downward through the system.

The kind of people that would qualify for O and P visas (see 'O visas and P visas', p.120) can often gain so-called **Employment-Based Preference Category One (E1)** status. If you have considerable international recognition in your field or are a well-published professor, multinational executive or manager, or are working in a religious occupation, you may find this door opening for you. You will be regarded as a priority worker and you will not need to provide labour

> ## Don't Steal Our Jobs!: Labour Certification
> All employee-based permanent residence applicants must first prove that no American citizens or resident foreigners meet the minimum job requirements. This is achieved by your prospective employer submitting an application to the US Department of Labor and then, certification in hand, applying to USCIS. Your employer has to prove that a US citizen or resident cannot be recruited for the post – a process that may require the employer to advertise locally first.

certification, though in most cases you will need to provide evidence of a job offer and apply to USCIS. An annual quota of 40,000 operates for this category.

Highly skilled and experienced professionals can also be considered for immigrant status and may fall into **Employment-Based Preference Category Two (E2)**, which also has an annual quota of 40,000. In this category you need to get labour certification (i.e. your employer needs to prove that they can't find a US citizen or permanent resident to do the job), or have a Schedule A designation (as nurses and other health workers have) or be qualified in an occupation considered to have labour shortages, as defined in the Labour Market Information Pilot Program.

The next rung down the ladder – **Employment-Based Preference Category Three (E3)** – is primarily designed for skilled workers with a minimum two years' training or experience, professionals with a bachelor's degree and some unskilled labour groups. All category three applicants must also get labour certification via a prospective employer.

The two remaining categories have much smaller quotas – 10,000 apiece – and deal with special cases. **Category Four** immigrants include professionals in religious organisations, overseas US government and armed forces employees and the retired employees of international organisations. **Category Five** is reserved for foreign investors, particularly those sinking capital into depressed areas, and needs at least $500,000 to be invested. If you don't have your own project in mind you could consider investing in a 'regional center' a group project financing an initiative in a depressed area. Effectively this raises the possibility of 'buying' a green card – though the business must succeed within the period of application – i.e. around two years. The immigrant investment category of visa is the fastest, safest and most expensive route to a green card. Opportunities in regional centres change quickly but up-to-date information is easily found via agents of immigration investment companies.

Diversity Immigrants

Since the mid-1990s this category of visa (sometimes called the 'Green Card Lottery') has involved selecting a defined number of applicants at random from certain countries. Applicants need to have completed secondary education or be trained for at least two years in a skilled job. This diversity immigrant lottery is of little concern to most people in the UK, since if you were born in Great Britain (but not Northern Ireland) you do not qualify for the scheme. However, if either you, your parents or your spouse were born in a qualifying country, you could be eligible to apply. Check with **www.travel.state.gov** for details.

Social Security Numbers

Your Social Security Number (SSN) exists to identify you for social insurance purposes, but has become the nationally recognised identification number. A social security number is usually required for many fundamental parts of US life including applying for a loan, credit card or driver's licence.

If you have a visa that allows you to work in the USA, or are a green card holder, you can bring this documentation into a social security office and apply on the spot. You will also need to provide proof of your identity and a letter from an organisation (such as a bank) that requires you to have a social security number – stating the reasons for their need.

Citizenship and Naturalisation

Unless you are born in the USA or of an American parent, the only way to become a citizen is by spending time as a green card holder, boning up on your knowledge of US history and government and being able to speak English. The US government happily allows you to hold dual citizenship, but the other country involved may rescind your citizenship if you become a US citizen.

If you are a US citizen you have the freedom to enter and leave the country as you please; the right to vote; and the possibility of bringing family members into the country relatively easily. Citizenship also makes you eligible for Medicare, the national health system for those over 65, which is not available for green card holders who have worked in the USA for less than 10 years.

After five years of being a green card holder (three if you're married to an American), you can become a US citizen by undergoing a naturalisation process. However, to qualify you need to have been in the USA for at least half the time you have had your green card. And if you have spent a significant amount of time away you will need to prove that the USA remained your primary place of residence in this time.

If you meet these residency requirements you can file for citizenship from three months before the five- (or three-) year time limit at a USCIS district office. They will schedule an interview, give you a fairly basic literacy test in the English language (unless you are over 65 or have lived in the USA for 20 years) and then test you on US history and government (about 20 questions). Most libraries and bookstores have study aids for this process. Questions cover your knowledge of the structure of government, the size of its various houses and

Case Study: Love Conquers Immigration

Ron, 32, first came over to the USA in the mid-1990s on the Visa Waiver Program to meet a woman he had met online. On arrival, he underwent close questioning in a private room, owing to the lack of money in his possession. 'There was one guy who didn't want to allow me entry but his supervisor was much more lenient and said I could enter and to have a nice trip.'

After almost 90 days the couple had fallen in love, and went back to the UK for a couple of weeks before returning to the USA together. Ron admits he was concerned. 'I was worried I hadn't been out of the country long enough, particularly due to the grilling on my previous visit. Again I had little money on me, but my girlfriend was working and had said she would be happy to support me for another visit.' Again Ron was sent into a private room for questioning, coincidentally by the same person who had wanted to refuse him entry the last time. 'The interrogation lasted almost two hours, and by the end of it he decided that, because I had done some gardening for a friend in the USA who had given me some money, I had broken the terms of my Visa Waiver and so my entry was refused. I was allowed 10 minutes with my girlfriend before being escorted to the next plane back to the UK.'

Ron was told he'd never be able to use the Visa Waiver system again and so had go through the full process of obtaining a fiancé visa (K1) before returning. He married the next day and has since become a green card holder, but recommends anyone coming to the USA to have more than enough money to cover your visit and not to do work and receive any money from anyone, since, in his experience, immigration officials show no leniency.

the names of crucial presidents in American history. The information in this guide will cover most of it, but you should check you are comfortable with the sample questions on the USCIS web page, **www.uscis.gov**.

See Appendix 1, pp.255–62, for a list of 99 typical questions taken from the US Naturalisation Test.

Living in the USA

Living in the USA, at least when starting out, is a complex endeavour. This is mainly because obtaining many of the things you need to set up your home and life in the States – mobile phone, bank account, driver's licence, a place to live, home utilities – are in many ways contingent on one another. For example, to get electricity hooked up in your home, you'll need a bank account, which you can only open by providing a piece of mail addressed to you at your home address. This means you need to have already rented or purchased a home, to which you'll need electricity flowing as soon as you move in – just one of the many Catch 22 situations you'll encounter when beginning to live in the USA.

That said, as a foreigner you'll find most people in the USA accommodating and helpful; the States still has a 'special relationship' with the UK, and many people across the country will act with politeness and hospitality to those with a British accent.

The single best piece of advice for the process of setting up home in the USA is to have ample funds available, as many letters of reference from banks, employers, and landlords as possible, and a patient attitude about the process. Soon enough you'll be comparing rents, complaining about price increases and lamenting the state of the economy with the best of them.

Finding a Home

Choosing a place to live will be your largest financial decision while in America. Before beginning your search you should try to learn as much as possible about the US housing market, which is huge, often confusing, and unforgiving to the uninitiated.

Unless you already know where in the USA you'll be living, your first decision will be where in the country you'd like to live. Different parts of the USA appeal to different people; for instance, do you want a warmer or colder climate? Are you looking for a kid-friendly small town or a brash big city? What are your politics? If you lean to the left, you might find California or New York City more welcoming than, say, Omaha, Nebraska – and vice versa. To help decide which part of the country appeals to you, read Chapter 02, **Profiles of the Regions**, which provides an overview of all US regions.

Having decided where you want to live, your next step is to determine what kind of housing you need. If you're a single person, an apartment or condominium might be best – though if you can afford it you might prefer to purchase a small house. If you have a large family, you'll probably want to either rent, lease, or buy a house. Most apartments are simply too small for couples with more than one child. Another factor to consider is which city neighbourhood you want to live in. Downtown areas of most cities are being rehabilitated and gentrified, and there is now ample apartment or loft-style accommodation available. Invariably this is near restaurants and nightlife – and commands higher prices as a result. If you don't have much interest in nightlife, or just want more space or a garden (yard), you might want to look in the shop- and grocery store-filled suburbs that surround all cities. You'll be able to get more square feet for your dollar the further away you move from the city centre, though these savings are often offset by increased time and money spent commuting. Suffice it to say, there will be pros and cons no matter where you choose to live; you just have to decide which mix is right for you.

Deciding your budget will be your final, and often most difficult, step before actually starting your home search. The US government recommends spending no more than 30 per cent of your income on housing, but in the centre of cities rents tend to be high and this figure unrealistic. However, if housing eats up more than 50 per cent of your income, you're likely to feel the squeeze. Try to underestimate what you can afford and then later, once you have a better feel for the city and your finances, you can always move to a more expensive place.

Renting

If you're moving to a large or medium-sized city, you should be able to find online rental information before you leave the UK. This doesn't necessarily mean that you'll be able to rent something before you get there – not that you'd really want to rent a place sight unseen, anyway – but this should give a good idea of prices, types of property available, and popular neighbourhoods. You might also want to get in touch with a rental agent or broker ahead of time, so that you can meet with them and get your search started on arrival in the United States.

Craigslist is an excellent resource for online apartment listings – in fact, listings of all types, from apartments and furniture to jobs and concert tickets – though only about 50 major US cities are currently served. Go online to **www.craigslist.org** (which takes you to the San Francisco Bay Area page, where Craigslist began) and look at the list of city links on the right-hand side of the page. Navigate to the apartment listings section. All of the listings on Craigslist are free (both to read and to post), though there may be fees levied for apartment rentals by those who post them, such as a broker's or application fee.

If Craigslist doesn't currently serve the city you're moving to, try typing in '[your town] apartment rentals' into an Internet search engine like Google. If you're moving to a smaller city or town, rental listings will be more difficult to find in advance. However, staying in a motel or bed-and-breakfast while you're looking for a place to live is unlikely to break the bank as it can in bigger cities. Unless you're moving into an absolute backwater, the place will have a website

Rental Adverts and Jargon

Rental properties are advertised in a sort of industry jargon that can, at first, be difficult to decipher. A one-bedroom apartment will commonly be listed as '1BD' or '1BDR', and so on for two-, three- and four-bedroom apartments. Apartments that comprise just one room, with a separate (or occasionally not) kitchen and bathroom, are listed as a 'studio' or 'efficiency'. These will invariably be the least expensive apartments. In more hip towns, lofts – large, open-space apartments often converted from warehouses or factories – might also be on offer; these are more expensive than a one-bedroom place, due to their cachet with artists, musicians and young professionals.

Other codes are used in apartment listings include 'EIK' or eat-in-kitchen (one that's large enough to accommodate a kitchen table); '1.5 bath', or one-and-a-half-bathrooms (meaning one full bathroom with shower or tub, and another, smaller bathroom with just a toilet and a sink); '4th-floor walk-up' (the apartment is located on the fourth floor and the building has no elevator); and 'cozy' – which means very small.

of some sort, and will probably have links to real estate information. While these small real estate outfits may not have a website, you will be able to phone and speak to someone directly about rental.

Should you be moving to the USA specifically for a job, you might want to ask your employer if they have a relationship with apartment buildings, landlords or rental management companies in the area. If so, this is a good way to find a reputable landlord or company, the rental process will be expedited, and you may even benefit from lower fees. For those moving to the USA to study at university, it's probably best to stay in on-campus housing where it's available. This is invariably cheaper and easier to find than off-campus accommodation.

The Cost of Renting

The size of your rent depends to a large degree on the city and the particular neighbourhood. A one-bedroom apartment in New York's SoHo neighbourhood, for example, can be as much as $5,000 per month, while the same in a small college town in Arkansas may be only $300.

To move into your apartment, you'll have to pay the first month's rent and a security deposit (usually one month's rent). Some landlords require the last month's rent up-front as well. In the largest cities (particularly in New York) many apartments are controlled by 'brokers'. These agents will show you available apartments in the city, with the understanding that if you rent one of these places you'll have to pay a 'broker's fee', which is anywhere from 10 to 18 per cent of a year's rent – quite a sizeable amount. To get around this fee, you can try to rent directly from a building's owner, from a 'no-fee broker', or from a property management company.

Signing a Lease

Once you find an apartment to your liking, you'll need the approval of the owner or management company before you can sign a lease. Commonly you are asked to provide a credit report and proof of employment, as well as an 'application fee' (usually around $50). Other items that can speed the approval process along are a letter from your current landlord (ideally with an official letterhead), personal references, bank statements and pay slips from your last job – basically just anything to help show responsibility and financial independence.

Once you're approved, you'll need to sign a lease in order to move in. Leases are typically drawn up for one year, though sometimes you can negotiate shorter or

Case Study: Renting Sight Unseen

Mark, now 30, moved to Austin, Texas, in the late 1990s to attend the University of Texas' renowned creative writing MFA programme. School for Mark was slated to start in mid-August, and unfortunately he didn't have much time in between backpacking around Europe that summer and the start of school. He knew that he didn't want to live in the dorms – living in college while getting his undergraduate degree in the UK had cured him of that desire – but he didn't have much time to look for an apartment, either. So, Mark turned to the world wide web.

'Because Austin's not a massive, ultra-expensive city like New York, I was able to find online quite a few places within my price range right off the bat. Eventually, I settled on a studio apartment not far from college, for $300 a month. I was able to view pictures – or so I thought – of the apartment online, and signed the lease for a mid-August move-in date before I ever left Aylesford to travel around Europe.'

However, when Mark eventually arrived in Austin, his apartment wasn't quite what he expected. 'First of all, the pictures I'd seen on the management company's website weren't even of my apartment, as I'd been led to believe. They were of another, much nicer unit in the building, one that had been recently renovated, with new carpet and new appliances. The carpet in my place, for instance, looked as though someone – or perhaps multiple someones – had been killed and left to die right there on the floor. And I hadn't seen appliances the likes of those since the late 1970s. All in all, the place was a wreck – but I didn't have any recourse, since I'd already signed a year's lease.'

Mark stuck it out in his flat for the full year, as he didn't want to lose his deposit by breaking the lease, but resolved he'd never again rent an apartment again without having seen it.

longer terms. Before you sign, be sure to look the lease over carefully and ask questions about any confusing bits; once entered into, the lease is legally binding and you don't want any surprises. Certain things to look out for are clauses about restrictions on pets, 'maintenance fees' and what sort of repairs the landlord is responsible for. After signing, you are given a copy of the lease, which you should keep somewhere safe. If you break your lease – move out of your apartment before completion of the term specified – you will forfeit your deposit, which ordinarily would be returned to you (minus any charges for damages and repairs) when your lease is up. That said, if you break your lease you will usually not be charged for remaining months of the lease.

Buying

Purchasing a house or an apartment is much more involved than renting. Not only is the amount of money changing hands far greater, but buying a home is also more permanent. Once the papers have been signed, there's no getting out of the deal – except, of course, by putting your house on the market and selling it on. Since buying a house in the USA is no small matter, if you're at all unsure or unfamiliar with the neighbourhood, city or region, you're probably better off renting a place first.

That said, there are many advantages to buying over renting: if you rent, you will never see any return on the money you pour into your place month after month. On the other hand, if you buy, your monthly mortgage payment does not disappear, but rather accumulates, so that if you decide to sell your house, you'll have money invested in the place that you'll be able to put towards your next home. There are also many tax breaks given to home-owners in the USA.

Tax Breaks for Home-owners

The tax breaks for home-owners in the USA mean that even though you'll be locked into paying off a 15- or 30-year mortgage, you might actually end up spending less per year on housing than you would if you were renting an apartment. Tax breaks for home-owners work out as follows: whatever you pay as interest on your mortgage (which makes up most of a mortgage payment, at least during the first years of paying the loan off), as well as whatever you pay in property taxes, can be deducted from your federal tax return.

What this means is that your federal taxable income – and thus the taxes you'll be required to pay – will be lowered, often significantly. Depending on the state you live in, you may be able to deduct interest paid on a mortgage from your state tax return as well. In order to deduct mortgage interest paid on a home (and thus reduce your tax liability), you must be the person responsible for repayment of the loan – you can't just be living in a house to get this credit; you also have to be the one paying for it.

Lawyers

Lawyers do a variety of things in the process, including checking to see if the home you intend to purchase is legally the seller's (carrying out a 'title search'); making sure that there are no outstanding legal claims ('liens') or property taxes due on the home; drawing up the necessary documents to transfer ownership; and so on. Fees vary depending on where you are in the USA and the complexity and extent of the legal services required, but generally these amount to a few thousand dollars.

Realtors

If you decide to buy a home, you will want to work with one or more estate agents or 'realtors', members of the **National Association of Realtors** (**NAR**). These realtors have completed a course in selling homes and are bound by a strict code of ethics. To find realtors in your area, look in your phone book's Yellow Pages under 'realtors' or 'estate agents' (for directory enquiries dial 'o' – the operator – on any phone). There are no fees payable to a realtor when buying property; these are paid by the person selling, not the person buying.

These agents have lists of new and old properties that they will be able to show you, and will broker the deal in the event that you decide to purchase one of them. Some realtors operate independently; others are associated with large realty companies. The latter invariably have more listings than private realtors. If you go with a private realtor you'll probably get more personal attention, while fees (for those selling) are lower and options wider with a realty company. Either way you should ensure that the realtor or company in question has a good reputation around town.

Houses are advertised on the Internet, but usually this is just a preliminary to actually meeting whichever realtor has that home's listing.

Looking at Property

Once you've decided on a realtor, it's time to start looking at homes. Much of the same information applies when deciding on what kind of place you want to buy as with renting, though you'll want to look that much longer and harder, since buying a home is a big investment and not one to be taken lightly.

If you have a family, or plan on starting one, you'll want to make sure that your home is in a suitable neighbourhood. Does the neighbourhood have other children for your kids to play with? Does it have a park or a swimming pool? What's the crime rate like? What are local schools like? What are the neighbourhood membership fees, if any (the latter are often used to pay for upkeep to any community property, such as walking trails or playgrounds)?

Surveys

It is not obligatory to have a home inspection, or survey, of a property carried out before getting a mortgage. Whatever financial body you get your mortgage from isn't concerned with the condition of whatever house you plan to buy (you can, in fact, get a mortgage before ever viewing a home). A survey (or inspection) is important, however, because it identifies any major problems that might not be readily apparent to the buyer – and thus might affect how much the buyer is willing to pay, or even if the buyer still wants to purchase the house. Visit the **American Society of Home Inspectors** at **www.ashi.org** to learn more or find a home inspector in your area. You could also just look in your local Yellow Pages under 'Building Inspection Service' or 'Home Inspection Service'. The cost of a home inspection varies depending on the area and how large the property is.

Getting a Mortgage

For most people a mortgage (or home loan) is necessary to afford the considerable cost of buying a house or apartment. Mortgages are available from a wide variety of lenders, such as banks, savings and loans organisations, homebuilders. The basic idea of a mortgage is that you borrow somewhere between 70 and 95 per cent of a home's purchase price (allowing you to actually buy the place), and pay this amount back, with interest, over a long period of time – 30-year mortgages are the most common in the USA. The amount you are allowed to borrow depends on your earnings (usually no more than three times your annual salary), your credit history, and the size of your initial deposit ('down-payment'). The greater your mortgage, the more you'll have to pay back each month. Similarly, the higher your down-payment is, the less you'll have to pay back from month to month. Interest rates on mortgages vary in the USA according to a variety of factors, the biggest of which being the current state of the economy.

Currently, the average home loan interest rate is around 5 per cent. So if you buy a $100,000 home on a 30-year mortgage, your monthly payment will be $536 a month, and you'll eventually end up spending around $193,000. This figure will vary depending on the length of your mortgage, fluctuations in the interest rate, and the amount of your down payment. To determine exactly how much you'll pay per month on a particular mortgage, simply search online for 'mortgage calculator'. Most lenders offer this free service, which allows you to input the amount of your mortgage, an interest rate, and the length of your loan to calculate your monthly payment. Bear in mind that this figure is unlikely to include initial 'closing fees' of around 5 per cent of the purchase price (which will need to be paid up front), nor property taxes or home-owner's insurance, which must be paid yearly. These latter two fees vary widely, depending on the state in which you reside and how much your residence is worth; they can run from hundreds to thousands of dollars per year.

Finally, there are two primary types of mortgages in the USA: the first is what's known as a fixed-rate mortgage, where the interest rate will not vary over the life of your loan; these are generally recommended for buyers whose incomes are not expected to rise rapidly. The second type is the adjustable-rate mortgage, where the interest rate will fluctuate depending on a number of factors, most notably the state of the US economy; these are best for buyers whose income is likely to rise significantly during the term of the mortgage, thereby allowing for higher payments. All the above is just a primer; there are countless books devoted to getting a mortgage, available from most bookshops or local libraries.

Moving

Only the very wealthy are able to afford moving the entire contents of a home from the UK to the USA, as everything must go by ship and there will be lots of labour involved on both ends to move your belongings. Fees can range from a few thousand to ten thousand dollars or more, depending on how much you want to move and where in the country you're moving. Generally, moving to US coastal areas is less expensive than moving to the interior. To find a removals firm, just search online for 'removals UK'; quite a number of good options will turn up. Also make sure, if you go this route, that your belongings are insured while in transit. If you decide not to move the contents of your home, moving into a place in the USA will be a much simpler affair.

If you've been renting a place and then you buy a home, you can contact a local moving company to take whatever you have across town – the fees for this are of course much less than international removals, though depending on how much you possess they can still be significant, from several hundreds of dollars to a few thousand. For those without much to move, you might want to consider renting a truck or van and taking care of it on your own. This will always be the cheapest option, especially if you have a few friends who can lend a hand. **U-Haul** (**www.uhaul.com**) and **Ryder** (**www.ryder.com**) are among the largest moving truck companies, with branches nationwide. Rates vary depending on what size of vehicle you need, how long you'll need it, and whether you'll be returning the vehicle to the same store at which you rented it or to another office somewhere else (as in the case of moving to a different town or cross-country). Rates start from around 30 dollars per day for a small van.

Home Utilities

Part of moving into your new place will be to set up and pay for some or all of the electricity, water and gas utilities. In addition to these essential services, you may also choose to install a phone, though nowadays many eschew a landline in favour of an all-purpose mobile (or 'cell') phone.

Two good places to start when looking to set up your utilities are the phone book or Yellow Pages and the Internet. In medium-sized to larger cities the phone book will be a heavy, inches-thick tome, while in smaller towns it may look like nothing more than a small yellow paperback. In both cases, the phone book will be made up of a 'White Pages' section – for alphabetical listings of individuals and businesses – and a 'Yellow Pages', for business listings grouped by pursuit, such as 'chiropractors' or 'electric companies'. To begin your search online, simply visit your favourite search engine and type in your soon-to-be town's name: the city's official website, which will invariably have links to or contact information for the local utility companies, should be listed within the first few entries.

In most cases, you won't have to worry about which electricity, water or gas company to choose: owing to the high costs of running a utility company, along with limited infrastructure for utility delivery, there will usually be just one game in town for each service. And don't worry about price gouging or abuse by a utility monopoly: in each state a regulatory body known variously as the Public Service Commission (PSC) or Public Utilities Commission (PUC) serves to keep the utilities in check.

Electricity

Every residence in the USA, whether house, apartment or somewhere in between, will have its own electricity meter, which records actual electricity use. Usually, this meter will be 'read' monthly by the electric utility, and you are billed accordingly. Energy costs vary from state to state, though prices are generally highest in the summer, when constant use of air-conditioning (AC) units puts an extra strain on the energy infrastructure. In the interest of saving yourself from killer summer electricity rates, you'd be wise to invest in a couple of ceiling fans (you may want to look for a place that already has these installed) or box fans and learn to live with the heat – except, of course, if you live in the south or the southwest, when regular summer temperatures all but necessitate central AC or at least a window unit.

Once you've found the electricity provider in your area, you should call the company at least two weeks in advance of your moving-in date and ask for service to be turned on one day prior to your moving in. You will need to provide the address of your residence, a deposit (usually between $50 and $200) and some form of official ID. For most Americans, this will be either a state-issued driver's licence or ID card or a social security card. Most foreigners, however, won't have either of these items – at least not for some time. In place of these items you can use your passport number, though don't be surprised if the utility company asks you to come down to their office in person to open your account; there are often a few extra bureaucratic hoops for non-citizens to jump through.

Your electricity bill, which will arrive monthly by mail, may well look like a bewildering mess of numbers, KWHRs (kilowatt hours, the unit by which usage is measured) and bar graphs, but don't fret: the important bits for you to pick out will be your account number, the amount due, and the payment due date – usually 21 days from the bill (or 'statement') issue date. On your first bill there will also likely be a connection fee (from $10 to $50), which will be folded into the total amount due. (In all likelihood this connection fee does not mean you will have been visited by an actual electric company employee; rather it's just what they charge to flick the 'on' switch – but such is the utility business.) Besides telephone, cable TV, and Internet fees, your electricity bill will be your largest monthly utility expense.

Gas

Natural gas and electricity may be supplied by the same utility company, though each is itemised separately on your bill. If not, simply follow the same procedure (phone book or Internet) to obtain contact details for the gas company. Natural gas is used primarily to heat your home, and as such, your gas bill will likely be higher during the cooler months. That said, natural gas is relatively cheap and your bill should be a good bit less than your electricity bill – though costs are rising, owing to the increased use of natural gas to produce electricity.

To begin service, ring the gas company about two weeks ahead of your move-in date and, as with electricity, request that service commence the day before you take up residence. A deposit is required, and a connection fee, again folded into your first bill, is charged; these are likely to be lower than the deposit and connection fee levied by the electricity company. As with electricity, you will need to provide some form of official ID along with the address of your new residence.

Water

In most cases water should already be on and running the day you move in. Water is usually paid for as part of your property taxes (paid for by yourself in a house, or by the landlord in an apartment), and usually you shouldn't have to worry too much about usage. An exception to this is in the south and (especially) the southwest and California, where water usage is often restricted by the state after a particularly dry winter or during a particularly dry summer – which is common in these areas.

As for cleanliness, you have nothing to worry about: US water is some of the cleanest in the world, and is safe to drink directly from the tap. That said, the taste of water varies in different parts of the country; if you find that you don't like the taste of your town's water, you can either wait and get used to it, which you most certainly will after a time, or purchase a water filter for your tap or a water jug with a filtration system. Both are inexpensive. Brita is the largest manufacturer of these devices, and their products are widely available. Failing that, you can purchase bottled water cheaply in bulk from the grocery store.

Paying Utility Bills

Utility bills, paid in arrears for the previous month's usage, can be paid by mail with a personal cheque, drawn from your current ('checking') account. When paying your bill by mail, be sure to include the payment stub from the bill, and also to write your account number in the 'memo' portion of the cheque. Some larger utility companies allow you to pay your bill online or over the phone with a credit or debit card. In addition, many banks now offer online bill payment options; this saves the bank the cost of processing your cheque, saves you postage and ensures your payment will never be lost in the mail.

Resolving Disputes

If you get the feeling you are being charged too much, or are dissatisfied with your service, first call the customer service phone number for the company in question. This number will usually be found on your monthly bill or, failing that, somewhere on the company's website or in the phone book. Don't be afraid to ask for the name of the person you speak to, and to call back if your query isn't handled in a reasonable amount of time. If, after talking to the customer service department, you still aren't satisfied, you can get in touch with your state's **Public Utilities** or **Service Commission**. You can find contact information for these bodies in the 'Blue Pages' of the phone book (these contain phone numbers for various government offices) or by searching online for '[your state] Public Utilities (or Service) Commission. If the company you're having trouble with isn't regulated by the PUC or PSC (as is the case with mobile phone companies), you can contact the **Better Business Bureau** (**www.bbb.org**), a consumer advocacy group that assists in resolving disputes between individuals and businesses.

Terminating Service

With the exception of mobile phones, all utilities can be terminated by calling at least two weeks in advance of when you'd like service to end. Simply let the utility know when you'd like service to stop and a final bill is issued. If you'd like your final bill to be sent to a different address, you should inform the utility company of this at this time. Be sure, too, to enquire about when and how your deposit is refunded.

Communications and Entertainment

Home Phones

Once on a time, AT&T (or 'Ma Bell') was the only phone company in the USA. Then, in 1984, the government broke up this vast monopoly into seven smaller, though still large, service providers, dubbed the 'Baby Bells'. Today, after many mergers, start-ups and acquisitions, only four major providers remain. Depending on what part of the country you live in, one of these companies – **Verizon**, **Qwest**, **SBC Communications**, **Bell South** – will be your home phone service provider. To get contact information for these companies (or to request the very handy phone book), just dial 'o' on any phone.

Unlike with your electricity, gas and water supply, you have a vast set of options for your home phone service. These include local, regional or nationwide coverage, various long-distance providers, and extras like caller ID, three-way calling, and Internet access. The options and prices vary a great deal, so you'd do well to look around the relevant company's website and examine all the different packages closely before making a decision. A few key questions to consider might be: do you have relatives or friends in another part of the country that you'll want to call often, or will most of your phone use be local (in town)? Will you also be purchasing a cell phone, or will this be your only phone? Do you require Internet access at home? (Bear in mind that cable Internet access through the TV company is now fairly commonplace, so that you may not even need a phone line to connect to the Internet).

Except for the most bargain-basement plans, $20 a month should get you a phone line and unlimited local calls. Depending on where you live, a local call may be defined differently, from every number that shares your area code (the first three digits of your phone number) to all numbers in a region, no matter what the area code. Any phone number dialled beyond this area is subject to a per-minute long-distance surcharge – unless, of course, you choose a plan that includes in-state, regional, or nationwide long-distance. These premium packages usually cost around $50 per month. Add-on options such as dial-up or DSL Internet access can add between $20 and $50 to your monthly bill.

Mobile Phones

The selection of plans and companies offering mobile (or 'cell') phone services is even more bewildering than the choice of home phone services. A multitude of companies offer a vast array of plans: including pre-paid, contract, local, and nationwide long-distance. It really helps to do some research before settling on any particular provider. A few of the larger companies are **Verizon** (**www.verizon.com**), **SprintPCS** (**www.sprintpcs.com**), **Cingular** (**www. cingular.com**) and **T-Mobile** (**www.t-mobile.com**). There are also local options, but most people who often travel are best off with one of the big companies, as their coverage is more comprehensive and their prices more competitive.

The aforementioned companies all offer 'contract' cell phone plans. What this means is that when you begin service with the company, you sign a contract that says you will stay with the company for a certain amount of time – usually one to two years. If you change your plan during your contract period, the contract usually starts from scratch. So even if you've been with a cell phone company for 11 months of a year-long contract, and you change your plan during that 11th month, you're now signed up for yet another full year. If you break your contract before the term has expired, you'll be subject to a hefty fee – usually $100–200. As such, be sure to read the fine print of your contract before you sign on the dotted line; you'll save yourself a lot of headaches and frustration if you enter into the agreement well informed.

Of the myriad available mobile phone contracts, most involve a certain number of 'anytime' minutes (also called daytime minutes, usually between the weekday hours of 6am to 9pm) combined with a certain number of 'night and weekend' minutes. Most companies now offer unlimited night and weekend minutes along with free 'nationwide long distance' – meaning that those lengthy evening calls to that friend across the country in California will be, effectively, free. **Keep in mind that, unlike in the UK, 'minutes' are used up both when receiving and making a call.**

With regards to pricing, most contract plans that offer around 300–400 anytime minutes, unlimited night and weekend minutes, and nationwide long distance (i.e. calling across the country will use up minutes at the same rate as if you were to call across the street) will run you around $40 a month. Taxes and fees will add about $10 per month onto that total. From there, each extra $5 per month should correlate to an additional 100 to 150 anytime minutes, and so on. You should be careful to choose a plan that provides just a bit more than the amount of anytime minutes you'll be needing each month; if you go over your allotted minutes, the charges add up quickly, while purchasing a plan that leaves you with a good chunk of excess minutes every month is a waste of money. There are dozens of add-ons to such plans, including web access, text messaging (which is nowhere near as popular in the USA as in the UK), and picture and multimedia capabilities. These extras will typically cost you between $5 and $25 more per month. Free voicemail is standard with almost all providers and plans.

Depending on what part of the country in which you begin your contract, you may or may not need to pay for your first phone: in the south, for example, a free phone when you start your contract is fairly easy to negotiate, while in New York City you'll be forced to pay for even the most low-end model. Prices for phones start at around $50 and really have no upper limit. Mobiles brought over from the UK (unless they are one of the 'tri-band' phones) will not work in the USA, as the two countries operate on different bands.

Finally, 'pay-as-you-go' or 'top-up' plans are nowhere near as common in the USA as they are in the UK. That said, a few major phone companies do offer these plans, notably Cingular and T-Mobile. For around $50, you'll be able to get a phone with around 100 minutes 'pre-loaded'. After that, you'll need to purchase additional minutes directly from the company, usually with a credit or debit card over the phone or using top-up cards from convenience stores. T-Mobile, for example, charges $50 for 400 anytime minutes, while Cingular has a sliding rate depending on how many minutes you buy: from a high of $0.15 a minute up to 400 minutes to a low of $0.11 a minute up to 650 minutes. These pay-as-you-go schemes can be good if you won't be using your phone that often or if you're not sure how long you'll be needing a US cell phone; if you decide to quit one of these plans, you won't be charged a hefty penalty as you will if you break a traditional cell phone contract.

Another option if you're not going to be in the USA for very long is to rent a phone: look in your Yellow Pages under 'cellular' for companies offering this service, which is generally only available in the larger cities.

Calling Home

Making international calls from the USA is not cheap. It can be reasonable, however, if you shop around and exercise caution. When you set up your home or cell phone, enquire as to how much international calling plans cost per month, and how much the 'per-minute' charges (during the daytime, night time, and at weekends) are after that. (They will usually be fairly pricey.) If you don't mind using a **calling card** to call home, this is often the best option. Look around online for a calling card that suits your needs: there are literally hundreds of companies out there offering prepaid international cards. If you choose wisely, you ought to be able to manage calling home for as little as a couple of cents a minute. Be sure to read your calling card's fine print, though; sometimes cards with very cheap per-minute rates turn out to have hefty connection fees, which can deplete your balance quickly. Also look at which areas these cards cover. Some only have certain local access numbers and even the 'free' 1-800 numbers (which invariably attract a surcharge) may only serve small regions of the country.

Fax

The ever-increasing ease of sending documents electronically over the Internet means that fax machines may soon go the way of the dodo. For the time being, though, a fax machine is a good investment for the home office. You can purchase a second phone line to use as your dedicated fax line, but this isn't absolutely necessary: as long as whoever's sending you a fax lets you know ahead of time, you can just not answer your phone and let the fax machine pick up; many newer machines can, as well, distinguish between when it's a another fax machine or a person calling. If you do decide to get a second phone line (useful if you'll be sending or receiving lots of faxes) it will probably cost you around an additional $35 a month. If you need only to send a couple of faxes every now and again, you're better off to just forgo a home fax machine and simply run down to the nearest copy centre, where you'll be able to fax documents for around $1 to $2 a page – not cheap, but it won't break your bank if you fax infrequently. Kinko's is the largest copy centre chain in America; check **www.kinkos.com** for locations.

Post and Private Couriers

Unlike in Britain, the post office in America serves pretty much just one purpose: sending and receiving mail and packages. Visit **www.usps.com** for all you ever wanted to know (and probably much more) about the United States Postal Service (USPS), or look up 'post offices' in the phone book's Yellow Pages. Opening hours vary from office to office, but are generally 8 or 9am to 5 or 6pm on weekdays, 9am to 12 noon or 1pm on Saturdays and closed on Sundays.

Mail is delivered to your home or apartment from Monday through Saturday and, depending on what sort of residence you live in (usually stand-alone houses or apartments), it may also be picked up directly from your home as well. Rates vary depending on the size and weight of your letter or package, beginning at $0.37 for a standard letter. If you're not sure of the postage rate, you should visit the post office to mail your letter or package – there they'll weigh whatever you're mailing and tell you exactly how much it will cost to send. Standard delivery time for a letter mailed first class (with a $0.37 stamp) is around three to five days nationwide. At the post office you'll also be able to choose from various special-delivery options, such as Priority Mail (two days nationwide), Express Mail (overnight nationwide), insurance and so on. These options all cost extra.

Though the post office is fairly reliable, you may want to use a private **courier company** for more valuable or time-sensitive packages or documents. **FedEx** (**www.fedex.com**) and **UPS** (**www.ups.com**) are the two largest courier companies in America, and will be happy to ship whatever you've got to any corner of the globe; their rates are, surprisingly, not that much more than the post office's, and their reliability and service are top-notch.

Internet

The US is the most wired country in the world: according to the most recent census data, over half of all Americans are connected to the Internet in their home. Increasingly, broadband service (DSL, cable and so on) is replacing dial-up access, even in rural areas. What this means for the expat is that you should find it very easy to get online – at a high connection speed, and most likely at lower cost than back home – no matter what part of the USA you're in. All you need to connect for dial-up access is a phone socket or 'jack', which your home will doubtless already have. For digital subscriber line (DSL) or cable Internet, you'll need some extra hardware, which is usually supplied by the company.

Pricing varies for unlimited dial-up access (usually at a baud rate of 56 Kbps) ranges from around $10 a month to around $50 or $60, for the highest connection speeds. High-speed cable access is usually offered by whatever company offers cable TV service in your area, and often comes as part of a cable TV package. One advantage of cable access (besides the speed) is that you don't need a home phone line to use it – which, if you've decided to use a cell phone for all calls, will save you a good $20 to $50 per month on a land line. With dial-up and DSL service, you will need a home phone line. When using dial-up, you will tie up your phone line while surfing, while with DSL you can browse the Internet and take calls simultaneously. Unless you're on a tight budget or don't use the Internet often, you should pay the extra money for a high-speed connection. Also, unlike in Britain, local calls – including to Internet service providers (ISPs,) with local access numbers – are not charged by the minute, meaning that, beyond the cost of a monthly service, surfing the Internet is effectively free.

There are countless ISPs in the USA. **America Online** (**AOL**; **www.aol.com**) is ubiquitous, while **NetZero** (**www.netzero.com**) and **EarthLink** (**www.earthlink.com**) are newer, upstart ISPs, with lower rates than AOL's standard $24 a month for unlimited dial-up access. You could also choose a local ISP – check the phone book for contact information, or search online for '[your town] local ISP'. However, if you plan on travelling around the country and want to be able to get online while on the road, you should choose a national ISP. Rates for local and national ISPs are pretty much the same – around $10–$25 a month for dial-up access. Keep in mind, too, that many hotels and coffee shops around the country now offer free wireless (WiFi) Internet access; to take advantage of these hotspots, your laptop computer will need to be wireless-enabled.

You may well be able to use your British e-mail account in America. If your e-mail is a web-based account such as those provided by Hotmail or Yahoo!, you'll certainly have no trouble accessing it across the pond. If, however, your e-mail is provided by a local British company that also provides your home Internet service, you may need to get a new, American e-mail account. Check with your current ISP to see if your email will be accessible in the States. If you do require a new address, simply visit **www.hotmail.com** or **www.yahoo.com** and sign up for their free e-mail service; you'll be able to access either of these accounts from anywhere in the world. There are many other free web-based e-mail services; just search online for 'free e-mail'. Soon, too, Google will be offering their snazzy 'Gmail' service to all comers; right now it's in the beta stage and available by invitation only; check **www.gmail.com** for current status.

Television

Television in America is set up very differently from in the UK. Unlike the partially state-funded and regulated system in the UK, TV in the USA is all about free enterprise (though with some government oversight, in the form of the **Federal Communications Commission**, or **FCC**). There are no **licence fees** for or taxes on owning a television, and basic network service is free: all you need to watch the basic channels is a TV, an electrical outlet and possibly an antenna (often called 'rabbit ears'). With this set-up you'll be able to watch at least NBC, CBS, ABC, Fox and PBS (the Public Broadcasting System, a non-profit network featuring news and shows of cultural or educational merit).

Beyond that, things get much more complicated. **Cable TV**, depending on the package, will cost you anything from $20 to more than $100 a month. 'Basic' cable will include 20 or so stations in addition to the major free networks: these are channels like CNN, ESPN, MTV and so on. From there the sky's the limit, with literally hundreds of additional cable channels, 'premiums' such as HBO and Showtime, movie channels, digital cable, digital video recording (DVR) services, and even high-speed Internet.

Many of the higher-end packages also include some form of the BBC; enquire directly with your local cable company about availability – again, just look in the phone book under 'cable companies' or search online for '[your town] cable TV' (or see **www.bbcamerica.com**).

Many homes and apartments have existing cable 'jacks', meaning you should only have to initiate service with the cable company and plug in. If your home does not have cable jacks, someone from the cable company will have to come by and install them – for a fee, of course.

There are other options besides cable TV, such as **satellite** or **DirecTV**; these may be a good choice if you live in a rural area not served by cable, though the gear and set-up costs associated with these services, not to mention the monthly fees, can be high. For DirecTV, look online at **www.directv.com**; for satellite service, check the listings for 'cable television & satellite companies' in your phone book's Yellow Pages.

See also **The USA Today**, pp.88–9.

Money, Banking and Taxes

For a foreign national, opening a bank account in the USA can be a frustrating process, involving many application forms, and requirements for certified documents and proofs of ID. But, with patience and plenty of time to overcome all the hurdles, you will eventually be able to open a US bank account. In the States, the two primary bank accounts are checking (current) and savings (deposit). Checking is used for day-to-day transactions, such as paying rent and utility bills, and can be accessed via personal cheques ('checks') and an ATM or debit card. A savings account is used for storing money that you don't need right at the moment, and will earn a low level of interest while in the bank. Depending on the bank and the checking plan you choose, your checking account may also earn interest.

Opening a Bank Account

The first thing you must decide is whether you want to open a bank account while still in the UK, or wait to do this until you arrive in the USA. There are pros and cons to both options: there aren't many banks in the UK that offer international banking, though arriving in the country with a US bank account will help a lot in terms of getting a house or apartment and setting up your utilities. On the other hand, once you reach the USA there will be countless banks with which to open an account, though you may have to perform some financial acrobatics to fund initial payments on your apartment or home.

If you choose to open an account while in the UK, your main options are large, multinational banks, like **Citibank** (**www.citibank.com**) or **HSBC** (**www.hsbc.com**). Before you begin this process, check to see if whichever bank you decide to go with has a branch in your stateside town – if they don't, then your account will be fairly useless for necessities such as setting up home utilities, writing rent or mortgage payment cheques, etc. With Citibank or HSBC, your best bet is simply to visit a branch in the UK and ask to open an inter-national account. You will need to provide two forms of picture ID (usually a passport and driving licence), proof of residence (a utility or phone bill sent to your UK address should suffice), and, if you aren't already a customer of that bank, a letter of reference from your current bank. You will also need to provide an initial deposit into the account – the amount required varies.

If you decide to wait until you get to the USA to open an account, you'll need to be a resident – have a home or apartment in the States – before you can open one. As such, your initial housing and utilities transactions will have to be funded from your UK account. What this means is that, since most companies won't accept international cheques, you'll need to use cash or your British debit or credit card until you get a bank account. It won't be difficult to obtain cash:

Case Study: Establishing Credit

When Sally, 36, moved to New York City to be a freelance writer in the autumn of 1999, she'd only been out of college for a couple of years, and had never owned a credit card. She'd never had to use one back home since her father allowed her to use the family's credit card when she needed to. When she arrived in New York, however, she encountered quite a different situation. 'Everywhere I went, all I heard was 'credit report' this and 'credit history' that. I had no idea what these things were, much less how to get them. And, it turned out, they were almost a necessity for renting a flat.'

After throwing a good bit of cash at the situation – paying several months' rent up-front, rather than the usual first-month's and security deposit – Sally was able to move into her own place. She didn't want to go through the difficulties again, though, so she set about finding out how to establish her credit history.

'I went to the bookstore and looked through a book on obtaining credit. They advised that, if you have no prior credit history, you should first apply for a low-limit, easy-to-obtain credit card – something from a department store, perhaps – and promptly spend some money. Then, as you pay this back monthly, always on time, you'll begin to establish a credit history, which will enable you to have a good credit report.'

Sally followed the book's instruction, got a credit card, purchased a load of clothes – 'a brilliant side-effect'– and began to receive regular bills on the balance; no more than $20 a month as a minimum payment. She also went on to get another credit card and use it for as many purchases as possible – though always clearing the credit every month. When she moved into a new apartment two years later, she had a fine credit rating and was treated as a valuable customer by the apartment management company.

the USA is blanketed with ATMs (automatic teller machines or cash machines), and almost all will accept your ATM card. A safer option than cash is dollar traveller's cheques, which can be replaced if lost or stolen, and are accepted by almost all companies as equivalent to cash (though you may have to visit their office directly to pay, rather than being able to pay by mail as you normally would). Visit **www.americanexpress.com** for more information on traveller's cheques. Another option is a TravelMoney or Cash Passport Card, available through Travelex (**www.cashpassportcard.com**); this card can be loaded up with money before you leave home, and then used at any ATM just like a debit or credit card – and, like traveller's cheques, if lost or stolen these cards can be replaced.

To open a US bank account, simply walk into the nearest branch of the bank you wish to join, and let them know you'd like to open an account. Depending on the bank, their requirements for opening an account may vary, but you'd do well to have with you proof of residence (in the form of a utility or phone bill sent to your US address, with your name on it), your passport, a letter from your bank back home, and travellers' cheques, cash, or wire transfer information for your initial deposit. You will also be asked to provide your social security number (SSN, see **Red Tape**, p.125), which, unless you have already been hired by a US company and applied for an SSN, you won't have. You can get around this by providing additional forms of ID, such as a driver's licence or credit card from another bank.

Most banks will have several different 'checking' schemes. Some charge a monthly fee (usually from $10 to $15) if a minimum balance is not maintained from month to month, while some are advertised as 'totally free checking' (or some such), with no fee being charged no matter what your balance. All banks will provide you with an ATM card, used to access your cash in both checking and savings accounts, and many will offer a dual ATM/debit card, which acts like a credit card (and will have a MasterCard or Visa symbol on it) but which, when used, directly 'debits' money from your checking account. Unlike in the UK, not all banks currently offer overdraft protection, though this convention is being steadily adopted. Cheques can be purchased directly from your bank, usually for a fee of around $20 to $25 for a goodly amount. These are most often used to pay rent, utilities and other such bills. In smaller towns many companies will accept a personal cheque (with ID) for goods and services. Out-of-town cheques are usually not accepted, and many companies in larger cities simply don't take personal cheques at all; instead they'll accept cash or a debit or credit card.

If your banking plan does not offer overdraft protection, be sure to know your account balance before writing a cheque; if you don't have enough money in your account to cover a cheque, the cheque will be returned, and you'll be charged a punitive fee – usually in the neighbourhood of $20 to $30.

Money Transfers

Wiring money from the UK to the USA is fairly easy, and there are two ways to go about this. The fastest is to use a company like **Western Union** (**www. westernunion.com**) or **MoneyGram** (**www.moneygram.com**), both of which allow you to send money online with a credit or debit card. You can also send money via phone (call **t** 0800 833 833) or by visiting a Western Union or MoneyGram office. The fee for sending money varies depending on the amount sent: for example, sending £100 via Western Union will cost you £14, while sending £500 will cost you £37. The recipient will be able to pick up the money at any of the company's offices within a few minutes of sending. Office locations (in the UK and the USA) can be found online at each company's website, or in your phone book's black business pages.

The other way to wire money is between two banks. Both people involved in the transfer must have bank accounts, in this case one in the UK and one in the

USA. If you don't yet have a US bank account, having money wired to you via Western Union or MoneyGram will be your only option. To wire money through a bank, you'll need the recipient's account and routing number (listed at the bottom of all personal checks) and bank address and phone number. The person sending the money should visit their bank in person or online and initiate the transfer. This way of sending money takes a few days to go through, but the fees are lower and the maximum amount you can send is higher. A good rule of thumb is that Western Union and MoneyGram are good for quick, small- to medium-sized cash infusions, while bank transfers are best for more significant amounts. Attempting to transfer money via a personal cheque is the worst way to go (though the fees as low), as the cheque in question will have to be sent off for 'collection', and it can take up to two weeks before the money will appear in your US account.

Income Tax

Everyone who works in the USA is required to pay **federal income taxes**. Depending on what state and city you live in, you may also have to pay **state and local taxes**. The percentage of your income that will be taken up by taxes varies with how much you earn, but a general range is from 20 to 30 per cent of your wages. Social security contributions may also be deducted from your wages, though you might be exempt from this – check with your employer to see if you are.

If you make any money at all in the USA over the course of a year, you will be required to file a 'tax return' before 15 April of the following year. The **Internal Revenue Service (IRS)** is responsible for tax collection, and the necessary forms to file taxes – the '1040' form is the most-used – are online at **www.irs.gov**.

As for paying British income taxes while working and tax resident in the USA, you will not be required to do so as long as none of your income derives from the UK, and as long as you were not officially tax resident in Britain for that tax year; a person will generally be treated as resident in the UK if he or she spends 183 or more days per year in the UK.

For tax planning, and if you need assistance in filing your taxes, you can contact **H&R Block**, the largest tax preparation and financial services company in the USA, or perhaps a local firm – just look in your Yellow Pages under 'tax return preparation'. H&R Block can be found online at **www.hrblock.com**, where you can ask questions, file a return or find office locations.

Tax Residence

Income tax is paid by **US citizens and resident foreigners** (and by some types of non-resident foreigners) on their **worldwide income** – all interest, dividends, wages, or other compensation for services, income from rental property or royalties, and other types of income. Those earning any income in America usually have to file a US income tax return even if they are only in the country temporarily.

Some tax laws that apply to **non-residents** are different from those that apply to resident foreigners. Generally speaking, non-resident foreigners are exempt from paying tax on monies earned outside the USA. If you are an alien (not a US citizen), you are only considered a non-resident 'alien' if you do not you meet either the **green card test** or the **substantial presence test** for the calendar year (1 January –31 December). Even if you do not meet either of these tests, you may be able to choose to be treated as a US resident for part of the year if this results in more favourable treatment for you.

The Green Card Test

You are a resident for tax purposes if, pursuant to the immigration laws, you are a lawful permanent resident of the USA at any time during the calendar year. This is known as the green card test. You are a lawful permanent resident of the USA at any time if you have been given the privilege, according to the immigration laws, of residing permanently in the USA as an immigrant.

The Substantial Presence Test

To meet this test, you must be physically present in the USA for at least:

- **31 days during the current year,** *and*
- **183 days during the three-year period that includes the current year and the two years immediately before that, counting:**
  - **all the days you were present in the current year,** *and*
  - **one-third of the days you were present in the first year before the current year,** *and*
  - **one-sixth of the days you were present in the second year before the current year.**

Example. You were physically present in the USA on 120 days in each of the years 2003, 2004 and 2005. To determine whether you meet the substantial presence test for 2005, count the full 120 days of presence in 2005, 40 days in 2004 (one-third of 120) and 20 days in 2003 (one-sixth of 120). Since the total for the three-year period is 180 days, you are not considered a resident under the substantial presence test for 2005.

Do not count days for which you are an 'exempt individual'. The term 'exempt individual' does not refer to someone exempt from US tax, but to anyone in the following categories:

- **An individual temporarily present in the USA as a foreign government-related individual (i.e. diplomats).**
- **A teacher or trainee temporarily present in the USA under a J or Q visa, who substantially complies with the requirements of the visa.**

• A student temporarily present in the USA under an F, J, M or Q visa, who substantially complies with the requirements of the visa.

• A professional athlete temporarily visiting the USA to compete in a charitable sports event.

Tax Residence in More than One Country

Remember that you can be tax resident in more than one country under the respective rules of those countries. For example, in the year you move to the USA you might spend 230 days in the year in the USA and 135 days in the UK. In this case you could end up, under the rules of each country, being responsible for paying the same tax in two or more countries. This would be unfair, so many countries have signed reciprocal '**Double Taxation Treaties**'. The UK and the USA have such a treaty. It contains 'tie breakers' and other provisions to decide, where there is the possibility of being required to pay tax twice, in which country any particular category of tax should be paid. The US tax residency rules do not override tax treaty definitions of residency. If you are treated as a resident of a foreign country under a tax treaty, you are treated as a non-resident alien in assessing your US income tax.

Local Taxes

Both residents and non-residents pay **local real estate (property) taxes**. These taxes are paid if you own a residential property. They are paid by the person who owns the property on the tax due date, often towards the end of the calendar year. If the property changes hands in one particular year, the tax liability is pro-rated by the closing agent. The tax is raised and spent by the town hall of the area where you live. It is calculated on the basis of the assessed value of your property. You can appeal against the valuation decision, but the sums involved are usually lower than the actual value. The amount you will be charged will generally range from 1 to 2 per cent of the value. A demand for payment is sent each year. The sum claimed must be paid by the specified date (which varies from place to place). Failure to do so incurs a penalty. It is probably simplest to arrange for payment from your bank by direct debit. If your property is subject to a mortgage, your mortgage payment will include a partial pre-payment for this tax. In such cases, your mortgage lender will pay the taxes directly.

Other Taxes

Other taxes include:

• **Capital gains tax** – levied on the profits made from the sale of an asset – usually land, buildings, equipment and the like; usually from 8 to 20 per cent of the profit made.

• **Estate tax** (or 'death tax') – levied on assets (money, property and so on) passed from a person to his or her heirs; the rate varies from 35 to 49 per cent on estates worth $1.5 million or more, though this boundary will be raised to $3.5 million in 2009; estate tax is set to be repealed in 2010, though this could change with the American political climate.

Health and Emergencies

While the USA is unsurpassed in terms of healthcare technology and scientific advancements, the country's public health options are woefully inadequate. President Clinton attempted to create a national healthcare programme, though his efforts ultimately came to nought, and remain so to this day (*see* **The USA Today**, pp.82–3). This means that, but for a couple of exceptions, unless you have health insurance through your employer or have purchased private health insurance for yourself, you are liable for all costs stemming from a visit to the doctor, a trip to the emergency room, or – most costly of all – surgery or a lengthy stay in the hospital. What this does not mean, contrary to horror stories you might have heard, is that in the event of an emergency you will not be picked up by an ambulance or treated at a hospital without proof of insurance or a credit card: you certainly will be – though you may also be hounded by those seeking payment until the end of your days.

Health Insurance

Most Americans who have health insurance have it through their employer. Except for the lowliest wage-earning jobs (those paid by the hour, usually in the food service industry), most employers offer some sort of health insurance, though you may not instantly be eligible; some companies require you to have worked with them for a certain period of time (a few months to a year) before you can become eligible for insurance. If you are eligible, you must choose which 'plan' you want to be covered by, and a fee will automatically be deducted from your wages along with your taxes. Your employer will normally cover most of each month's insurance premium, though the amount an employee is liable for can vary widely: the cheapest option is for 'single' coverage (just for yourself) and the most expensive a 'family' plan, which covers your spouse and your children. Even if an employer offers single-person health insurance, they might not offer 'family' or spouse-coverage plans. If you come to the USA on a company-sponsored visa (meaning you may work only for that company), you probably will not have many options when it comes to employer-provided health insurance. Still, given that the cost of healthcare in America is so steep, it's worth getting information on what sort of health plan a company offers before you accept a position.

Dental and Vision Plans

Many employers also offer dental and vision plans, which cover some of the costs of dental work and contact lenses or eyeglasses, again either for just yourself, you and your spouse, or your entire family. These plans are generally cheaper than health insurance, and are excellent – especially in the case of dental – as preventative care; since most dental plans offer a couple of free 'cleanings' per year, this means you're less likely to get cavities and have to pay for a costly filling or other, more extensive dental work.

Private Insurance

If your employer does not offer health insurance, or if you are unemployed, you'll have to go it alone and purchase private insurance for yourself and your family. This can be a very expensive undertaking, costing hundreds of dollars a month or more, depending on the number of people the plan covers, you and your family's health, and whether or not you want a smaller or larger excess (or 'deductible'). The 'deductible' is the amount that, in the event of a major health emergency, you will have to pay 'out-of-pocket' before health insurance benefits kick in. Generally speaking, the higher the deductible, the lower your monthly premiums are. To find companies that offer health insurance, look in your phone book's Yellow Pages under 'insurance'. You could also visit the BlueCross BlueShield Association online at **www.bcbs.com**; this is an association of a great many BlueCross BlueShield health insurance providers across the nation, and is an invaluable resource.

Doctors, Hospitals and Emergencies

Most health insurance plans require you to pick a '**primary care provider**', or PCP. This person will be, for all intents and purposes, your doctor, whom you'll visit for check-ups, general illnesses and so on. This doctor will be associated either with a hospital or a private practice, and will be able to refer you to other, more specialised doctors should the need arise. If you need to make an appointment, simply call your doctor's office and speak with the receptionist, who will tell you when the doctor can see you. Don't be surprised, especially in larger cities, for there to be a significant waiting period – though if you need to see someone immediately, the doctor's office will be able to accommodate you. With health insurance, you will need to pay what's known as a 'co-pay' for your visit, which will usually be somewhere in the neighbourhood of $10 to $25. With no insurance, you will have to pay for the entirety of your visit's cost, which can be very expensive.

If you need immediate medical attention and the doctor's office is not open (as at night or at weekends), you should visit the nearest hospital emergency room. Get there on your own or have a friend take you if at all possible, as ambulance visits and 911 calls should be used only for major, life-threatening injuries or illnesses. To find a hospital close by, check your phone book's Yellow Pages. Some hospitals specialise in fields such as children or mental health, so be sure to pick a hospital with a primary focus on general medicine, as it really wouldn't do to show up at the psych ward with a kidney infection.

Prescriptions and Pharmacies

A prescription written by your doctor will need to be taken to a pharmacy to pick up your medicine – though sometimes the doctor's office can phone it in, after which you must either go in person to pick it up or, with some pharmacies, the prescription can be delivered to your home. You can visit any pharmacy to have prescriptions filled, though it's best to find one you like and stick with it, as the staff will come to know who you are and what medications you take. Prescriptions, like healthcare, can be very expensive without health insurance – a simple dose of antibiotics can cost upwards of a hundred dollars without insurance. If you have insurance, prescriptions – as with doctor's office visits – are subject to a co-pay, which will vary depending on what the medicine is and whether or not it is a generic or brand-name medicine. Generally, though, the prescription co-pay will range from $10 to $50 per refill. For more on pharmacies *see* 'Shopping', p.163.

Women's Health

The first and last word on the reproductive side of women's health in America is **Planned Parenthood**, a nationwide organisation that is dedicated to providing affordable, accurate reproductive and sexual health information and assistance to all comers, female or male. Planned Parenthood provides STD and HIV testing, birth control, pregnancy testing, gynaecological examinations and, among a whole host of other services, abortions or abortion referrals. The organisation has offices in all 50 states except Arkansas; addresses and contact information for these can be found online at **www.plannedparenthood.org**.

Many women, in addition to having a general practitioner (GP) doctor, who treats them for illnesses and broken arms and such, also have an obstetrician-gynaecologist, or OB-GYN, who focuses on reproductive health and administer gynaecological exams, pap tests (smear tests) and breast cancer checks. During your first visit to your primary care provider, you should ask him or her to refer you to an OB-GYN. Should you need it, your OB-GYN will also be able to write you a prescription for birth control. This will have to be filled at the pharmacy like any other prescription, but will usually have more refills.

Pharmacies are also a good place to pick up women's hygiene products, as well as home pregnancy tests and condoms.

Children's Health

In addition to your family's primary care provider, your health insurance plan will allow you to choose a paediatrician for your children. Many doctors specialise in this sort of medicine, so don't hesitate to be choosy when looking for a doctor that makes both you and your child comfortable. Children in the USA are required to have a slate of shots (jabs), so check before leaving the UK as to just what inoculations your child has already had, and bring proof of this to America – after all, there's no sense in subjecting the child to extra shots.

Children's aspirin and other medications are available in all pharmacies.

Social Services and Welfare Benefits

Social services and welfare benefits don't refer to quite the same thing in the USA as they do in the UK, and, on the whole, the American system is much less comprehensive. That said, in the USA each state's **Department of Social Services** is generally responsible for the protection of children (including reports of child abuse, child support payment oversight, and adoption and foster care); assisting the blind, hearing-impaired and disabled; and financially helping out poor adults or families, usually in the form of welfare payments or food stamps.

Unless you decide while living in the USA that you want to adopt a child, probably your only contact with your state's Department of Social Services (DSS) will be if you are somehow injured while at work or if you lose your job, in which case you may be eligible for **disability or unemployment benefits**. Keep in mind that qualifying for unemployment assistance (which is calculated as a certain percentage of what you earned at your last job, and will only pay out for a limited amount of time) is more difficult than it is in the UK. You can only get unemployment benefits if you were fired or made redundant from your last job, not just if you don't happen to be currently employed.

Another way in which you might use social services is if you or your family has a low income or you are above the retirement age of 65. **Medicaid** and **Medicare** are government programmes that pay for medical care for these two groups, and can be a good safety net if you are unable to afford health insurance.

To find your state's Department of Social Services, either search online or check your phone book's 'Blue Pages', which lists local government offices.

Maternity leave is something that varies depending on your employer. Only employers with more than 50 employees are required by law to offer maternity leave, so make sure before you decide to have a child just what sort of plan your company offers (if any). Maternity leave is usually unpaid, and an employee will be allowed 12 weeks of leave within any 12-month period – providing the employee has worked for the company for at least a year. **Disability leave**, for oneself or to care for an immediate family member, is also available under similar guidelines. Both of these leaves are mandated by the Family and Medical Leave Act of 1993, which can be read online; it's a good idea to know your rights in this arena.

See also **Working in the USA**, pp.208–210.

Retirement and Pensions

Retirement

The benefits of retiring in the USA are many: warm, sunny regions that suit the elderly (Florida and the southwest are the most popular regions), the fact that money you've saved (or your pension) will go a lot further in the USA than at home, and that on the whole retired persons in the USA are treated exceptionally well, not sidelined as they often are in the UK. The **American Association of Retired Persons (AARP)** is a good source to look at when thinking of retiring in America. The group publishes a magazine and maintains an informative website, **www.aarp.org**. AARP is also one of the most powerful lobbying groups in Washington.

The public retirement scheme in America is run by the **Social Security Administration (SSA)**, which was signed into law by President Franklin D. Roosevelt in 1935 as a key component of his historic 'New Deal' social reform programme. Originally, Social Security (as the entire programme is commonly known) only dealt in retirement pensions for the 'primary worker', though later additions extended benefits to the worker's spouse and children, as well as the disabled. To pay for these benefits, every worker in the USA is required to contribute social security taxes from his or her wages; this amount is deducted in the same way as federal, state and local taxes. The money raised by this process is collected by the SSA, invested, and then, when a worker reaches retirement age, he or she will begin to receive monthly social security cheques. Currently, social security is in flux, as the Bush administration attempts to partially 'privatise' the programme – divert some of the money collected by social security to Wall Street. The reason that reform is needed is that, as more and more baby-boomers (the immediate post-war generation) retire, the amount that will need to be paid out will begin to overshadow how much is paid in. If something is not done about this situation, the programme will be forced to reduce benefits in order to avoid bankruptcy.

Retirement Benefits

To qualify for retirement benefits in America, you must have worked and paid social security taxes for at least 10 years. If you were born in 1937 or earlier, the current 'full retirement age' (FRA) in the USA is 65; for those born after 1937 but

Case Study: Retiring in the Sun

Jan, from London, is 67 and has been living in the USA for over 10 years, and has finally retired with her husband in Florida. For a long time the couple lived in New York State but when it came to retirement it just had to be Florida: 'There are kilometres of sandy beaches and no winter – what more could you ask for?' However, Jan warns that retiring in the USA is not to be taken lightly.

'For a start, there is no visa that specifically allows you to retire in the country. You may get in if your children are already here or if you have the spare cash to invest in a business, otherwise you'll have to just come in for six months at a time. This means a lot of travelling and you have to finance two residences. My husband originally came into the country as a civil engineer on an intra-company transfer visa. We were able to stay on after he finished working for the company by successfully changing our visa status by buying a business (a bar), and have since both become green card holders.'

The next big problem, explains Jan, is medical insurance. 'If you could even get any as a pensioner it would probably run to thousands of dollars every month. You could go without but if anything happened, you would be in real trouble. Prescriptions and a doctor's appointment will cost hundreds each and a major illness and will run into tens of thousands of dollars. My husband's job included a good medical insurance package, which we have since stayed with, and it's essential that you check this out before accepting any job here.'

Jan's advice to pensioners thinking of moving to the USA is simply don't. She suggests you're much better off living somewhere on the Mediterranean where there's at least some free medical care and you can easily get back to the UK if you need serious healthcare.

before 1960, the FRA is between 65 and 67; and if you were born in 1960 or later, your FRA is 67. You can retire early when you turn 62, though your monthly benefits will be reduced permanently by a percentage that's based on how far away you are from your full retirement age. Similarly, if you retire after your full retirement age, your monthly benefits will be increased. Exactly how much you will be paid by the SSA after you retire depends on a number of factors: your birth date, how much you used to earn, how much you currently earn (if anything), and so on. You may also be eligible for a private pension, depending on the company you work for; ask your employer if they offer one. Keep in mind, though, that one must work at a company for a long period of time – usually most of one's working life – in order to be eligible.

The 401k Account

Another option that many Americans choose to exercise is a 401k account. This is a tax-deferred personal retirement savings programme, usually offered through your employer, but also available privately. Over the course of a working year, you can contribute a fixed amount of dollars before taxes from your wages to a 401k account (the maximum amount is set by the federal government). This money will be invested in a mutual fund of your choosing and managed by an independent financial services company. Often, employers will in some way 'match' employee contributions: for example, say you contribute $100 per pay cheque (usually paid bi-weekly or semi-monthly in the States) to your 401k; depending on their policy, your company may match 50 per cent of your contribution, putting in $50 of their own money.

The idea is to contribute steadily throughout your working life, and to leave the money alone and let it grow with the market. If you access this money before you reach retirement age, you will be subject to financial penalties and taxes (though it always remains 'your' money); however, if you wait until you retire to draw on your 401k, you will avoid much of the tax burden that you would otherwise have to pay. All in all, the 401k plan is excellent, and if you contribute often and invest wisely you should have no trouble funding your retirement.

Other investments, such as stocks and bonds, are not tied in any way to retirement.

The Reciprocal Social Security Agreement

The UK and the USA have a reciprocal social security agreement, so if you retire in the USA and you qualify for a UK pension, whether state, occupational or personal, you will be able to receive it while abroad. However, most pension funds will insist on paying your allotment directly into your UK bank account – leaving you responsible for transferring the funds to your US account.

Unlike in some countries, such as Canada, Australia and New Zealand, if you retire to the USA your UK pension will not be 'frozen', but rather will increase over time, as it would if you were still living in Britain. If, in addition to qualifying for UK pension, you have also worked in the USA long enough to be eligible for social security, you will be able to collect from both of these accounts on your retirement.

Death Certificates and Wills

Death certificates are filed automatically for anyone who dies in the USA, but it may be necessary to request a personal copy of one. If the deceased originally came from England or Wales, you must forward the death certificate to the UK **General Register Office** (**GRO**; **www.gro.gov.uk**) in order for the death to be registered; Scotland and Northern Ireland have separate general offices.

While living in the States, you might also want to prepare a will, to ensure that your belongings and assets are dealt with properly after you die. In many states, Americans cannot do just as they please with their property when they die;

inheritance rules often apply to protect the surviving spouse. These rules generally set out a minimum portion of the estate which must go to the spouse. Wills are therefore complicated documents, and should be drawn up by a lawyer. To find a lawyer who specialises in wills, simply look in your Yellow Pages under 'attorneys' and scan for the 'wills & trusts' sub-head.

Shopping

If one thing is certain, you won't be at loss for shops in the States: from food and drink to clothing, electronics, furniture, and more, the USA is awash in consumer choices – sometimes unrelentingly so. Shopping takes place pretty much everywhere in the USA, from small-town main streets to Rodeo Drive in Beverly Hills and New York's Fifth Avenue. There are malls aplenty in the USA, the country that developed this all-in-one-building consumer carnival of shops, food courts, movie theatres and video arcades. Increasingly, though, malls are falling by the wayside in favour of strip malls – long outdoor collections of stores in one complex, served by a stadium-sized parking lot, and big 'box stores' – Home Depot, Best Buy, Target and Wal-Mart. These are usually located in the suburbs, and will be mixed in with fast-food restaurants, 'family dining' establishments like Chili's and Applebee's, video rental shops, clothing stores, pharmacies (chemists) and countless other consumer ephemera. The question becomes, then, not how to find things to buy, but rather how to shop without breaking the bank.

Whatever you buy, you are almost certain to have to pay a **state sales tax** – though in some states items such as food and clothing are exempt. This tax will almost never be included on the price tag, and varies depending on the state, from around 4 to 7 per cent. There is no federal sales tax. If shopping online or by mail order, it is worth bearing in mind that you don't pay sales tax on items ordered from outside the state in which you are receiving them. This often more than offsets the price of next-day delivery, no matter where it is in the USA that you are ordering from.

Food and Drink

For most of America, the supermarket is the one-stop shop (if such a word can be used to describe a building that's often bigger than a football field) for all groceries, as well as home products like cleaning supplies, laundry detergent, light bulbs, batteries and so on. Most regions have a few large supermarket chains, such as Kroger, Harvest Foods or Safeway, and an outpost of one or more of these will likely be within a short drive from your home. If you're in a larger city, such as New York, there will usually be at least a couple of (smaller) supermarkets within walking distance of your apartment.

The supermarket combines all aspects of the food-and-drink experience: here you'll be able to buy bread, meats, grocery produce, desserts, dairy products, all manner of snack and junk foods, and, in some cases, alcohol (though usually not spirits – 'liquor' or wine). While the food at most supermarkets is of fairly good quality, you'll have to search out speciality stores for items like organic or free-range chickens, imported cheeses, organic vegetables and other delicacies. These speciality shops are often difficult to locate in the suburbs (dwarfed as they are, if in evidence at all, by the big box stores), and will more often be clustered in the more quaint or hip parts of town. A good way to find these stores in a city not readily associated with gourmet cooking (anywhere other than the major cities like Boston, Seattle, Los Angeles, San Francisco and Chicago) is to find a fellow foodie, and ask them where they shop for particular items. Part of the fun, of course, is finally locating that one treasure-trove store.

Many towns and cities also hold regular farmers' markets, where low-yield farmers (often organic) from kilometres around will bring their wares to market. Here you'll be able to find lovely eggs, chemical-free produce, cuts of meat from humanely treated animals, fruit straight from the orchard, and often fresh flowers, plants and herbs. Look in the local papers for announcements of these farmers' markets; they're often held on Saturdays and maybe once during the week as well, usually from early morning until around noon.

As regards drink, what you've likely heard about America is true: the country that once outlawed all alcohol still has a strong Puritan streak and, depending on the state, you may not be able to buy hard alcohol anywhere other than a specially licensed liquor store. In some states and towns you can buy beer in the supermarket or convenience (corner) store, though the selection will always be better in a stand-alone liquor store. These aren't hard to find: just look for the neon signs of various brewers in the store window (or, if you're especially lucky, a 'guns & liquor' sign along the highway). Most liquor stores also sell wine, though there are shops bent more towards the wine-lover; you'll have to search these out in much the same way as you would speciality food shops. Keep in mind, too, that the drinking age in America – whether to purchase alcohol at a store or buy a drink in a bar – is a strictly enforced 21; if you look young, you'll be asked for ID to prove your age. In most states, liquor stores are closed on Sundays, and in some you may not be able to buy beer from the supermarket or convenience store, either.

Clothing

Though not as fashionable as Europe, the USA still has plenty of places to find stylish, 'now' clothing, especially in the larger cities. For staples such as underwear, shoes, jeans, trousers ('slacks'), shirts, blouses, skirts and what-not, you can visit a local department store, such as Macy's, Dillard's or J. C. Penney's. Prices are usually reasonable, and the selection sizeable, often with multiple floors of offerings for men, women and children. There are stand-alone clothing stores such as Gap, Old Navy and Banana Republic in suburban malls or strip malls, or in cities along shopping district streets, such as Broadway in New York's SoHo neighbourhood or North Michigan Avenue (also called the 'Magnificent Mile') in Chicago. For cutting-edge clothing, your best bet is to check out the small boutiques in hip neighbourhoods of medium-sized to larger cities – but beware the prices. Depending on the size of your town, thrift-store (charity shop) shopping (Salvation Army is a big chain) can yield some great, cheap finds, though the larger and trendier the city, the more thrift-stores tend to morph into vintage clothing boutiques, with inflated prices to match. Some New York vintage shops actually send vans down to thrift stores in Florida, scouring them for cheap stock and bringing it back to sell at huge profit. Children's and maternity clothing can be found in small, often locally owned businesses; check the Yellow Pages listings for 'children's clothing' or 'maternity clothes'.

Appliances

On the whole, home appliances in the USA are much larger than their counterparts in Britain: it's not uncommon for a family of four to have a six-foot-tall stainless steel refrigerator in their kitchen, stocked full with food (as shopping is usually done in bulk, weekly or fortnightly). Most apartments are furnished with at least a refrigerator and stove, while in houses you may well have to purchase these items for yourself. There aren't many national chains that sell home appliances – Sears (**www.sears.com**), Home Depot (**www.homedepot.com**) and Best Buy (**www.bestbuy.com**) are notable exceptions – so when beginning your search, the best place to start may be your phone book's Yellow Pages.

If you don't want to purchase a major appliance outright, there are many companies who will rent or lease them to you. Most US homes are outfitted with a dishwasher and clothes washer and dryer. With an apartment, these may or may not be present, depending on the building's age and how much the apartment costs; generally speaking, the more modern appliances an apartment has, the higher the monthly rent. If an apartment doesn't have a washing machine and the complex doesn't have a communal laundry, check before renting if there's a laundromat relatively nearby; it's a hassle to schlep your laundry for blocks on end.

Home Furnishings

Now that you've rented an apartment or purchased a home, the question arises: what do you fill it with? Unless a rental property is specifically advertised as 'furnished', all you'll have in your new place is a refrigerator and a stove – and

Online Trading

In recent years, online trading has become wildly popular in the USA, originally for such specialities and collectibles like vintage lunch boxes and concert posters, and now for everything from kitchen appliances, clothes, and books to cars and even houses. The name that springs to most people's mind when the subject of online trading comes up is invariably **eBay** (**www. ebay.com**), an auction site where individuals can list items for sale that are in turn bid on by whoever's interested, with the prize in question going to the highest bidder. Some devotees take a perverse pride in 'winning' these auctions – surely the zenith of the American consumer condition – though you really can get things on the site you couldn't elsewhere, and all from the comfort of your computer chair. If you're the winner of an auction on eBay, you'll usually pay for your purchase via **PayPal** (**www.paypal.com**), a symbiotic company that allows consumers to securely send or receive money (via a credit or debit card or a checking account) to or from a third party – all for a small fee. This fee depends on the amount of money changing hands; similarly, eBay charges a fee to the seller depending on how much an item is sold for.

Though surely the most popular site, eBay isn't the only game in town for online shopping: **Amazon** (**www.amazon.com**) sells virtually everything under the sun, usually for prices less than you'd be able to find elsewhere; **FreshDirect** (**www.freshdirect.com**) peddles high-quality groceries, delivered directly to your house; and **Toys in Babeland** (**www.babeland.com**) offers, ahem, adult toys that some might be too embarrassed to purchase in person.

possibly not even these. Obviously you'll need a bed, some living room furniture, and perhaps a desk and dining room table. The list can go on and on, depending on the size of your residence and what you want, but these are the basics.

For a bed, 1-800-Mattress (**www.mattress.com**) is a fine company with competitive prices that will deliver a mattress and box springs right to your door, usually the next day. They have warehouses nationwide, so pretty much wherever you're at in the States they should be able to get you a bed. However, 1-800-Mattress does not have showrooms in all states – so if you'd like to try out your bed before purchasing, you might want to look more locally, in your phone book's Yellow Pages under 'mattresses'. For a full-size mattress and box spring set, prices range from a low of around $400 to highs of around $2,000.

Even fewer national chains sell home furnishings than sell appliances, so again you'll want to check your Yellow Pages under 'furniture' for local store listings. Most places will sell individual pieces (sofas, dining room tables and so on) as well as room 'sets', which, for a hefty price, will provide you with everything you need to set up, say, your dining room or living room. Prices for home furnishings are not cheap – a relatively low-end sofa can go for $500 or more – so be careful not to over-extend yourself when purchasing. A cheaper and often more rewarding way to buy furniture is from a flea market or antique fair. These affairs are much like farmers' markets, in that small dealers from around the area will come in and set up their wares, usually in a big warehouse-type building or occasionally outdoors. Here you'll invariably find more interesting pieces and, unlike at a regular furniture store, you can bargain with the sellers – especially when purchasing multiple items. As with farmers' markets, check the local papers for news of when and where these flea markets or antique fairs will be held.

Books and Music

Despite what you might have heard, reading in America is not dead. In fact, more books are being read in the USA now than ever before – but just what exactly is being read, well, that's a different story. Best-selling authors such as John Grisham and Dan Brown, along with whatever Oprah's latest book club choice happens to be, can be found almost anywhere, from airports to Wal-Marts. For something more literary, though, you'll need to do a little more searching. In places like San Francisco and New York, small, interesting bookstores abound, and you're sure to stumble across a few just by walking around the city. In towns not known for their literary tendencies, you'll probably have to look a bit harder for that special bookstore. When you do find it, ask the staff about other good, independent bookstores in the area; they're likely to be able to point you in the direction of shops you might never have found on your own.

If you aren't able to locate an independent bookstore to suit you, Borders (**www.borders.com**) and Barnes & Noble (**www.bn.com**) are both good, very large chain bookstores. They'll never have in stock that tiny journal of poetry from the University of Illinois Press (though they will be happy to order it for you), but both have vast amounts of books, and it's easy to get lost in them for hours while browsing. Check each chain's website for store locations.

As for music, the USA has plenty of small, independent record stores, though these are only slightly less hard to find than their bookstore brethren. Looking through the music section of your town's independent newspaper(s) is a good place to start, as is asking around at local music venues and bars. Compact discs (CDs) are sold at many different stores, from Best Buy to Target, but to find a really excellent selection you'll need to seek out a locally owned shop. Both Borders and Barnes & Noble sell music (Borders has the better selection), though prices at these two stores are often high – as much as $19 for a single CD, in some cases. In larger cities there might be a massive Tower Records (**www.tower.com**) or Virgin Megastore (**www.virgin.com**), both of which offer virtually every CD ever pressed, most at reasonable prices.

Other Stores

Hardware stores in the USA are either massive, warehouse-sized chains (Home Depot, Lowe's and so on) or small, friendly, neighbourhood shops. If you're embarking on a large project such as building a deck or putting in a bathtub, a large chain store is your best bet, since they'll have every single thing you'll need – and likely a few things you didn't know you needed – to get the job done. Also, the employees at these large hardware stores are generally very helpful and knowledgeable. The 'mom-and-pop' neighbourhood shops won't have lumber or large items, though for a hammer, a power drill or some nails, they're perfect.

You'll never come across a 'chemist' in the USA, but instead **pharmacies** or, more colloquially, drugstores. At these places you'll be able to get prescriptions from your doctor filled, as well as purchase a large variety of cosmetics, personal hygiene products, over-the-counter medications (available without a prescription, like headache, cold and flu remedies), home cleaning supplies, and other assorted odds-and-ends such as cameras, batteries, videotapes and so on. There are three types of pharmacies: independently owned shops, major chains such as Walgreen's (**www.walgreens.com**) and pharmacies inside supermarkets or stores like Wal-Mart. Prescriptions in the USA are expensive, so you'll want to have health insurance to help you pay for these (*see* pp.151–4).

Video rental stores are ubiquitous in America. The largest chain is the antiseptic, often frustrating Blockbuster (**www.blockbuster.com**). You'll often find the best selection at a smaller, independently owned video store, though these are fast falling by the wayside as the chains increasingly take over the market. Usually you'll have to sign up for a free membership before renting a movie; the cost is around $3 to $5 for a few nights' rental. Another good way to rent movies is via Netflix (**www.netflix.com**), which, for a monthly fee, allows you a certain number of DVD rentals, which are mailed directly to your home. Blockbuster has also recently begun offering this service.

Foreign newspapers and magazines are difficult to find except in the larger cities; Barnes & Noble and Borders usually have a decent number of titles, though stand-alone magazine stores like Hudson News in New York City have the widest selection. Tobacconists, at least as they exist in Europe, aren't really to be found in the USA. Instead cigarettes are sold at all convenience stores, though for a finer smoke you'll want to seek out a cigar store, which will usually also sell top-quality cigarettes and pipe tobacco.

For **stationery** or **office supplies**, your best bet is a large office-supply store such as Staples (**www.staples.com**) or Office Depot (**www.officedepot.com**); visit each chain's website for locations in your area. **Dry-cleaners** are found all over the place in most cities, though these are most often locally owned businesses. For **greeting cards**, Hallmark (**www.hallmark.com**) has cornered the market, though pharmacies and grocery stores usually peddle these as well.

Transport

The USA is truly the land of the car: in most of the country, having a car or truck is a virtual necessity for getting to work, shopping, and going out for entertainment. Only in the larger, older cities such as New York and Boston is it really feasible to do without a car entirely; newer cities are just too spread-out and generally have only a skeletal public transport service. This is changing, as cities begin to adopt environmentally friendly public transport like light-rail trains and downtown trolleys and buses. But, even if you live in a city that's adopted such measures, a car will likely still be a necessity; light-rail systems are used more for ferrying commuters from the suburbs to downtown, and the stations will often be kilometres from your home.

Getting around the country itself is a different story: while there's nothing more American than tearing down the interstate on a long road trip, you don't need a car to see much of the States. Internal flights are reasonable – New York to Los Angeles can cost as little as $250, for instance – and the Greyhound bus company goes to most places you'd want to visit (and quite a few places you wouldn't). Travelling by train is a unique, romantic experience, and can still be done easily on long-distance trips, but the prices are almost as much as a flight – so, unless you want to take your time in getting to your destination, you're better off just buying a plane ticket.

Public Transport

Travelling by Bus

The **Greyhound** (**www.greyhound.com**) bus company has a very extensive network of bus routes crisscrossing the USA, with stops in 3,330 cities and towns across the country. Fares are reasonable, and usually (though not always) less than a plane fare for the same trip. Tickets can be purchased online or by phone (**t** 1-800-231-2222) for either one-way (single) or round-trip (return) journeys, or at any bus terminal (or 'station'). For a longer trip, you should purchase your ticket well in advance, as popular routes could be sold out if you just turn up at the bus station on the day you want to leave. Fare and schedule information can found had online or by calling the toll-free number above. You should check online, too, for regular fare specials, usually to or from a specific city for a reduced rate. Students and seniors are also eligible for reduced fares; to qualify as a student, you must have a **Student Advantage Card** (which costs $20, and can be purchased online at **www.studentadvantage.com**), while seniors must be aged 62 or above. The discount is 15 per cent off regular fares for students, and 5 per cent off for seniors.

Bus travel is, needless to say, not glamorous. In many towns the bus station is in a seedy part of town, and frequented by shady characters – many of whom

The Green Tortoise

If you'd like to see a good chunk of the USA, but don't much relish the idea of travelling in an anonymous Greyhound bus with mildly deranged travelling companions, you might want to look into the anything-but-anonymous Green Tortoise (GT). Since its inception more than 30 years ago, the Green Tortoise has taken half a million travellers on 'adventure trips' across America in their bright green converted sleeper coaches, complete with dinette tables, beds, bunks, and a jury-rigged stereo system.

The most popular trip the Green Tortoise takes is the cross-country tour, with northern and southern routes across the States. Trips begin from either Boston for westbound journeys, or San Francisco (GT's headquarters) for eastbound, with stops in famous cities like New Orleans or Chicago, state and national parks, monuments such as Mount Rushmore, natural wonders including Niagara Falls and South Dakota's Badlands, and a few out-of-the-way places known only to the drivers. Along the way you'll either sleep nights aboard the bus while driving, or occasionally camp out. With regards to food, you'll cook breakfast, lunch and dinner – hopefully always delicious – with your travelling companions, invariably a fun, young, mixed lot hailing from all over the world; friends are made easily on the Green Tortoise.

Prices are very reasonable: for a two-week cross-country trip, expect to pay between $550 and $650, plus $150 to $170 for food and park admission costs. If you'd like to give the Tortoise a try but don't have time for a two-week jaunt, check out their website, **www.greentortoise.com**, which has details on all sorts of other trips, from a few days in California's Death Valley to a week touring the stunning national parks of Utah and Wyoming, including Zion and Yellowstone – not to mention a night out in Las Vegas.

may well be getting on the bus with you when the time comes to leave. Avoid being at the bus station at night or, if you have to be, stay awake and alert, in a well-lit area, keep an eye on your belongings at all times and be wary of offers of help or companionship from strangers. That said, riding cross-country on a Greyhound bus can be an unforgettable experience: you'll meet a whole host of eccentrics, drifters, dreamers and archetypal American characters. Greyhound buses are fairly well maintained, though in no way luxurious. Seats usually recline and are fitted overhead with reading lights; you may want to bring a pillow and a blanket for an especially long journey. There is a toilet in the back of the bus, though the driver will also make stops for food and bathroom breaks every few hours. Smoking and drinking are not allowed on the bus.

A great option for anyone wanting to see a large chunk of the USA by bus is the **Discovery Pass**, which allows for unlimited travel via Greyhound during a certain number of days. Currently, for international visitors, passes are available for 4, 7, 10, 15, 21, 30, 45 or 60 days. Prices begin at $149 for a four-day pass and top out at $539 for a 60-day pass. If purchasing from abroad (you can buy a pass while in the USA, though prices are higher), you'll need to buy your ticket at least 21 days in advance, so that there will be enough time before you leave to have your ticket mailed to your UK address.

Travelling by Plane

Internal flights within the USA are a great way to get between cities – though if you plan to hop around the country via aeroplanes, the price can quickly become astronomical. So it's best to fly when you're just going to one place and back for a short period of time; otherwise you probably will want to drive or take a bus (fares for the train can add up just as they can for flights). Good websites to use when looking for plane tickets are **www.travelocity.com**, **www.expedia.com** and **www.orbitz.com**. Each of these offers pretty much the same service, comparing prices from many different airlines for whatever itinerary you desire. Keep in mind, though, that these websites sometimes don't include prices for budget or regional carriers, such as **JetBlue** (**www.jetblue.com**) or **Frontier Airlines** (**www.frontierairlines.com**), which operates out of Denver. If you know what regional carrier operates in a certain area, you'd do well to check with them as well as with the major national carriers.

Plane fares are usually reasonable, as long as you purchase your ticket 21 days in advance of your flight date; after that, the rates go up sharply. Fares are also affected by the size and volume of whatever airport you're flying out of and into, more so than the distance between the two. For example, a ticket clear across the country from New York to Los Angeles is much cheaper than, say, a ticket from Jackson, Tennessee, to Wichita, Kansas.

If you have a good deal of flexibility in your travel plans, you might want to try an online flight 'auction' site such as **Priceline** (**http://tickets.priceline.com**). Here you can either purchase a flight as you would at Travelocity, or you can 'name your own price' – meaning you tell Priceline how much you're willing to pay for trip X, and they offer this price to airlines that fly that route and may have planes that haven't yet been filled. The catch is this: you won't be able to see flight times until after your bid is accepted, so you may well get stuck with a 5am departure time or 1am arrival time. As long as the uncertainty doesn't bother you, you can save some money this way. Whatever your strategy for finding a well-priced ticket, **www.cheapflights.com** makes an ideal first stop in the search for inexpensive and reliable agents and options.

Travelling by Train

Trains are the least popular way to travel long distances in the USA: prices are often comparable to flights, routes are limited, and the trains are often slower than buses. **Amtrak** is the national carrier and, like most train companies the world over, survives only by commercial railroad and state subsidies. With the exception of southern California and the Northeast Corridor (from Washington, DC to Boston), pretty much the only people who still travel by train are those who want to get off the beaten path and take their time in getting around the country. You also need to be extremely flexible as many smaller destinations are only served by one daily train, which often only passes through in the middle of the night. On the positive side, trains are cleaner and far more comfortable than buses, and often travel through some beautiful scenery.

To book a ticket, go online at **www.amtrak.com**, or call **t** 1-800-USA-RAIL. One option available only for non-US or non-Canadian citizens is the **USA Rail Pass**, which allows for unlimited travel over a 15- or 30-day period in one of three regions (west, east and northeast, which also features a five-day pass) or nationwide. Prices for the rail pass vary depending on whether you travel during 'peak' or 'off-peak' times, which are generally defined as around Christmas and during the summer (peak) and during the spring and autumn (off-peak). To give some idea of the fares, a 15-day off-peak pass in the west will cost you $210, while a 30-day peak nationwide pass will cost $550. Keep in mind that the pass can only be purchased before leaving for the USA, through one of Amtrak's international agency representatives; in the UK, **Trailfinders** (**www. trailfinders.co.uk**) is the largest of these. Full fare and schedule information is available on Amtrak's website.

City Buses and Subways

Only the most major cities in the USA (New York, Boston, Chicago, Los Angeles, Miami, San Francisco, Seattle and Washington) have any sort of comprehensive public transport system. Most medium-sized cities have some type of city bus service, though these usually make infrequent stops and generally are just not very handy. Even in the major cities, the scope, make-up and quality of the system varies widely, though with each you should be able to get around town effectively (occasionally being able to do without a car at all) for little money. Fares range from $2 to $5 for a single ride, and multiple-ride cards (such as New York's MetroCard) can be purchased at a discount. Most cities also offer a discount for senior citizens and the disabled. Transport systems vary tremendously, and the best place to orientate and inform yourself is at the central bus station in medium-sized towns or at any subway or train station in the major cities.

Private Transport

Getting a Driver's Licence

If you already have a British driver's permit, you can drive on it in the USA for up to one year after entering the country as a tourist; if you enter on a study or work visa you must obtain a US licence within 30–90 days depending on the state. This will involve taking a US driving test.

For extra peace of mind you may also want to get an **International Driving Permit (IDP)**, which should be used in conjunction with, not in place of, your UK permit (in the USA, having extra forms of ID and proof you're allowed to drive is always a good thing, especially as a foreigner). An IDP can be obtained in person at many post offices around Britain; the **Automobile Association (AA) has** a list of these offices on its website at **www.theaa.com**.

If you don't have a British driver's licence, but plan on driving while in the USA, you are strongly advised to go ahead and get a licence in the UK; if you try to apply for licence in the USA, you'll have to go through all sorts of legal and immigration issues.

Each state's own **Department of Motor Vehicles (DMV)** administers driver licensing for that state; a list of web links for these offices can be found online at **www.anydmv.com**. Generally speaking, to get a US driver's licence you'll first need to have a learner's permit, which is granted after passing a written test (study guides are available at each state's DMV). Then, after practising for a bit with an experienced driver, you'll need to return to the DMV to take an actual driving test. If you pass this final test, you'll be given a US driver's licence.

Renting a Car

If you want to hire a car, contact any rental car agency in your area. There are quite a few national chains, such as **Alamo** (**www.alamo.com**), **Hertz** (**www.hertz.com**) and **Budget Rent-a-Car** (**www.budget.com**); the websites for each will be able to give you contact information for an office in your area. Prices vary widely depending on what kind of car you rent (sub-compact, economy, compact, sedan or luxury), how long you want to rent the car, and whether or not you'll be returning the vehicle to the place you rented it or to some other branch of the car rental chain. You can find car rental agencies in your area by looking in the phone book under 'car rental'. Also, if you're flying into a city, there will invariably be several car rental companies stationed at the airport, often with a free shuttle to their (usually nearby) offices. Most rental car companies in the USA require you to be at least 25 years old to hire a car.

Be sure when you rent a car to examine it all around for dents, scratches and other damage before you drive off; if there is damage to the car that you fail to point out before you leave the lot, you'll likely be liable for these damages when you return the car. Vehicles are usually rented at a per-day rate (beginning at around $15 or so, at the least expensive end of the scale), with a certain number of kilometres allowed (sometimes unlimited). Rental prices will invariably be cheaper from a local agency (look in your phone book) than from one of the big, nationwide companies; you may also be able to get a discount if you are an **Automobile Association of America** member (**AAA**; **www.aaa.com**). Keep in mind that US car rental rates are quoted without insurance, as renting a car with a US credit card usually will allow for built-in Collision Damage Waiver (CDW) coverage. This will not be true, however, if you rent a car with a credit card issued from outside the States – so be sure to enquire about insurance (rates can vary from $10 to $20 a day). Lastly, before you return the car to the rental office, be sure to fill up the gas tank; otherwise, they'll fill it up and charge you at a much higher per-gallon rate than if you were to fill it up at an independent gas station.

Buying a Car

Buying a car in the USA might as well be considered a national pastime, such is the fervour with which people of all ages, backgrounds and finances devote themselves to the process. It's not uncommon for someone to buy a new car every year, trading last year's model in towards the new set of wheels – which means that there is a healthy used car market in whatever town you happen you live. While buying a new car does have its advantages, as soon as you drive the car off the lot it loses a good chunk of its value, so buying a used car just makes more sense financially. That said, you must be careful you don't get, as the all-too-appropriate saying goes, 'taken for a ride'.

The best first step to take when buying a car, new or used, is to do some research: check the latest magazines, trade reports, safety ratings and so on. A great resource is Consumer Reports (*see* box, below). A second excellent resource is the Kelley Blue Book, which can be found online at **www.kbb.com**. The 'Blue Book', as it's more commonly known, lists average prices for new and used cars, depending on condition, accessories, mileage and your location within the country. All of this information can be found on their easy-to-use website, or in print from major bookstores. You should use the Blue Book price as a benchmark when negotiating any deal for a new or used car; if what a seller is quoting as his price is way off the Blue Book value, you might want to consider taking your business elsewhere.

Now that you've decided on the car or truck you want to purchase, you'll need – unless you're swimming in cash – to get an auto loan. These can be obtained

America's Which?

The equivalent to Britain's *Which?* magazine, **Consumer Reports** is a non-profit consumer advocacy group, which publishes a monthly magazine and also maintains a significant presence online at **www.consumerreports.org**. For $26 a year, or $5 monthly, you'll have access to Consumer Reports' extensive tests and ratings on almost all car makes and models. In addition, Consumer Reports has just as much information on home appliances, electronics and other consumer goods, all of which can help a great deal when deciding what to buy for your home.

directly from the car dealership, though if you can get a loan from a bank beforehand you'll have more negotiating power when it's time to make the purchase. Generally, auto loan terms are from three to five years, paid back monthly, with an interest rate (APR) that varies depending on your credit history. As such, you'll want to obtain a copy of your credit report from the UK; you should bring this with you when applying for your loan, along with anything else that can attest to your financial well-being, such as bank statements or pay stubs.

Auto Insurance

Before you take your new or used car for a spin, you'll need to have purchased insurance. There are three different types of auto insurance – collision, liability and comprehensive – but the only one you're required by law to have is liability. Liability insurance covers costs should you cause an accident. For this, a hefty insurance premium is charged, often several hundred dollars every six months; exactly how much this fee will be depends on your age, accident history and the type of car you buy – a red sports car will command a higher insurance premium than a beige mini-van. To find companies that offer auto insurance, look in your Yellow Pages under 'insurance' – or go online, if you subscribed to Consumer Reports and check out its information on various insurance companies.

Vehicle Registration

Within a month of purchasing your new or used vehicle, you must visit your local DMV and have it registered. To accomplish this, most states require documents proving ownership, odometer and damage disclosure statements, proof of auto insurance, proof of identity and date of birth (your passport will do), and proof that you paid the sales tax for the vehicle.

You will need to fill out an application form and make a payment (usually by personal cheque) of around $35 to $50. On completion, you'll receive licence plates for your vehicle as well as registration documents, the latter of which are required by law, along with proof of insurance and your driver's licence, to be kept inside the car with you at all times; if you're ever pulled over by a police officer, the standard opening line is 'licence and registration, please'.

Motorcycles, Mopeds and Bicycles

Motorcycles, mopeds, and bicycles are seen quite often in the USA, though they're generally used for recreation rather than transport. You must hold a driver's licence to drive a motorcycle or moped legally (enquire what you need to do to get this at your local DMV; see 'Getting a Driver's Licence'), while cycling requires no permit. Keep in mind that two-wheeled vehicles are much less common on major roads in the USA than they are in Britain and, as a result, other drivers might not know how to behave around such vehicles. As such, you

Winter Driving

While driving in the USA during the temperate months is not much different from driving in the UK, driving in America during the winter is another beast entirely. Except for those living in southern Florida, southern California or Hawaii, there really isn't any place that's exempt from the dangers of winter driving – it can snow or be icy in the South just as it can in Chicago. In fact, whenever it does get treacherous in a place that doesn't usually receive much winter weather, it's often more dangerous than in areas where snow and ice are the norm: people up north are more used to driving in harsh winter conditions, while the inexperience of those elsewhere can be deadly. That said, given a few precautions and some common sense, you should be able to get through driving during a harsh winter just fine.

Your first lines of defence will be an ice-scraper, which you should keep in your car's glove box or trunk – after all, it's hard to drive safely during the winter if you can't see through your windscreen – and, for those living in high-precipitation areas, a snow shovel for digging your car out of the inevitable drifts. Chains for your tyres are also a good idea (though only necessary in the snowiest areas); these help your tyres grip the road more effectively in icy conditions, and you can have these put on at most full-service gas stations. Finally, when it's snowing or icy out, always drive very carefully and keep away from other drivers (who will often be the most dangerous factor in bad conditions). If you start to slide while driving (and don't have anti-lock brakes or 'ABS'), don't slam on the brakes; instead, pump them repeatedly until you regain traction. If your car begins to spin, turn gently, not sharply, in the direction of the spin in order to right yourself. Above all, though, the best way to avoid an accident is to drive slowly.

should exercise caution when piloting these bikes on heavily trafficked roads frequented by standard cars and trucks.

Traffic Violations and Parking Tickets

When driving around town or on the highway, be sure to adhere to all rules of the road, especially the speed limit and stop lights and signs. **Speed limits** vary from state to state and also depend on what type of road you are driving on. Interstate speed limits, for example, can be as high as 75mph, while roads through neighbourhoods can be as low as 15mph. Generally, though, on highways and interstates the speed limit varies from 55 to 75mph. Some states have different speed limits for trucks and cars, and also for day and night. It's best to just pay attention to the signs along the road; speed limits are posted.

If you don't observe the limits, besides being a danger to yourself and others, you run the risk of getting pulled over by a police officer and charged a sizeable fine. If you receive too many of these traffic tickets, you can have your driver's licence suspended or even revoked – and, as traffic tickets mount up, your insurance premium will also increase.

Parking tickets – issued when you park illegally or stay over your time limit in a metered parking space – are less serious than traffic violations, though the costs can still add up. If you do get a parking ticket or traffic violation, it's best to pay the fine straight away.

Gasoline

Gasoline (petrol) is inexpensive in the USA compared to Europe. It's sold by the gallon, and prices vary depending on what part of the country you're in (urban areas are higher than rural areas), what 'octane' you choose (usually 87, 89 and 91; these correlate to the purity of the gasoline), and the state of the global crude oil market – prices often rise sharply after crises affecting supply.

Gas stations are found all over in the States, especially along interstates and highways. Most stations are pretty interchangeable; a few of the big US brands are Shell, Exxon, Citgo and BP. Currently, fuel prices are hovering just over the $2 per gallon mark.

Crime and the Police

Though crime is certainly a problem in the USA and the country has over two million citizens in jail, it's not nearly as bad as TV, movies and the news would have you believe. Local news programmes in the States, for example, seem to operate on a policy of 'if it bleeds, it leads', which creates an overly violent impression of the USA in the minds of viewers.

The parts of the country that suffer most from crime are the inner cities, particularly in the industrial north, certain cities up and down the east coast (Baltimore, Maryland has a particularly bad reputation), southern California, and the poverty-stricken south – though this is changing as the process of gentrification is rehabilitating previously off-limits downtown areas.

Another positive factor is President Clinton's Crime Bill, signed into law in 1994, which provided money for 100,000 additional police officers across the nation, crime-prevention social-services programmes, a ban on many types of semi-automatic weapons and, among other provisions, the 'three strikes and you're out' law, which mandated that any criminal convicted of three violent crimes would be put in jail for life. Violent crime has declined markedly in the USA since the passage of the bill.

For the political backgound on crime, *see* also **The USA Today**, pp.84–5.

Drugs

One type of crime that has increased in the last decade is drug offences. Drug-related arrests have mounted steadily over the years, and nothing seems to be able to stop this trend – least of all continuing to incarcerate for lengthy periods those arrested on relatively minor offences (such as simple possession). Currently, 55 per cent of those held in federal prisons and 20 per cent of those in state prisons are there because of drugs – and the vast majority of both these populations are non-white. There have been some inroads made by those seeking change, such as in the case of New York's draconian 'Rockefeller Drug Laws', which recently were reformed to provide for lower mandatory sentences and more treatment programmes. Nevertheless, much still remains to be accomplished.

Petty Crime

In all likelihood, the worst crime you might have the misfortune to encounter while in the USA will be pick-pocketing or mugging. Being a victim of the former is best avoided by being aware of your wallet or purse when in the midst of large crowds or on public transport, while the latter can largely be avoided by staying away from deserted or high-crime areas during the night. Keep your wits about you, stay alert – talking obliviously on a cell phone while walking home is a big no-no – and, if you must be in a dicey part of town at night, take a friend with you. If you are mugged, immediately give up your belongings – it's simply not worth trying the patience of a criminal who may be armed and dangerous. Afterwards, call the police immediately – the emergency number for police, fire and ambulance is t 911, a toll-free call from any phone – and file a report. You probably won't get your belongings back, but you may well help police prevent the person who mugged you from striking again. If you should happen to be the victim of a more violent crime, such as rape, make your way to a safe public place and notify the police immediately.

The Police and Other Authorities

Police officers in different states have varying uniforms and cars, though all are recognisable by their dark blue or black outfits, tool belts with handcuffs, nightsticks and guns, and police cars (usually white and black) with red and blue lights on top. Though you may feel uneasy about American police as a result of high-profile police brutality cases such as the beating of Rodney King in Los Angeles, most officers are helpful and understanding; you shouldn't hesitate to approach one if you feel unsafe or are in need of assistance (even just for directions).

On the outside chance that you do have an unpleasant run-in with the police, be sure to report it to your town's police headquarters. In this day and age, allegations of misconduct are taken very seriously. Otherwise, it is likely that the only contact you'll have with the cops is if you're pulled over for speeding. If you don't have any prior traffic violations on your record, most officers will simply give you a warning – which will be recorded – and send you on your way. They can, however, write you a ticket, even for a first offence. Be sure, if you are pulled over, to stay in your vehicle and as the officer approaches to keep your hands on the steering wheel. Anything else could be interpreted as suspicious behaviour that might mean you are armed.

Other uniformed authorities in the USA include members of the fire department, emergency medical technicians (commonly referred to as EMTs) and state troopers. You probably won't see the fire department unless they're en route to the scene of a blaze; if you happen to be on the road while they're coming towards you with lights flashing and sirens blaring, it's required that you quickly and safely make way for the fire truck, usually by slowing down or shifting lanes. The same is true for ambulances (which are driven and staffed by the EMTs) and police cars that are obviously responding to a call.

State troopers will not be encountered within city limits, but rather patrolling the nation's highways and interstates, looking for speeders, drunk drivers and drug smugglers. Their uniforms are different from police officers, but they still should be easily recognisable as cops.

If you are pulled over late at night by a state trooper or police officer, you are well within your rights to ask for ID before opening your door or rolling down the window; though infrequent, there have been cases of women being abducted and raped by men posing as officers of the law. If you feel especially unsafe, you may proceed slowly, with your right-hand 'turn signal' switched on, to the next well-lit public space or highway exit before pulling over.

Education

The education system in the USA is not markedly different from that in Britain: there are pre-schools, various 'grades' for students between the ages of 4 and 18 (1st through 12th grade – different from the letter grades given out to indicate the quality of a child's academic performance in school), and a vast assortment of universities, colleges, and vocational and technical schools. The largest divide in the USA education system is between public and private elementary and secondary schools.

Public (state) schools are run by each city's Board of Education, whose members are elected by the general public. These public schools are funded by state and local taxes, which every working person – no matter whether or not they have a child – must pay. The federal government contributes to the schools in various ways, such as President Bush's 2001 'No Child Left Behind' Act, which requires states to set student achievement standards that schools must meet. Private schools, on the other hand, are often associated with a religious group, though many private schools have no religious affiliation, and are simply dedicated to quality education.

Public schools are free for all children to attend (in fact, depending on the state, most children are required to attend until the age of 16 or so), while private school tuition can run the gamut from reasonably affordable (as with many Catholic schools) to incredibly expensive. Attendance at private schools is voluntary (and they are often hard to get into), while a public school will be assigned to your child based on where you live in your town or city. Before buying or renting a home, make sure that whatever school your child will be placed in is acceptable; school standards can vary widely within a city.

Pre-school

Depending on the state in which you live, public pre-school programmes (often referred to as 'K3' or 'K4', according to the age of child they will admit) may or may not be offered. Traditionally, pre-schools have been primarily private and fairly pricey, though this is changing as more and more parents (both of them) go back to work soon after their child is born.

Pre-school programmes, like private schools, may be associated with a certain religious faith, but more often they will be non-sectarian and instead focus on simple games, stories, sharing and other creative activities. Essentially they are a sort of day-care plus, where children are introduced to the school setting in a gentle, fun way.

That said, not all pre-schools are this laid-back: certain pre-schools in Manhattan, for instance, have long waiting lists, with parents jockeying viciously to get their child into that all-important first step that will eventually lead, they hope, to Harvard and a Nobel Prize.

Elementary School

Elementary (or 'grade') school is where education proper in the USA begins. Typically, elementary schools encompass the grades of 'K5' (for kindergarten, which children are admitted to at age 5) through 5th or 6th. In most of the nation, a school year runs from late August or early September through to late May or early June, with a two-week (or so) break at Christmas, a week-long 'spring break', and various other holidays and 'teacher conference' days off during the year. The period between when school lets out in the early summer and resumes in the early autumn is commonly known as 'summer vacation', and

Case Study: School District Screw-ups

In the summer of 2002, Valentina, now age 45, moved with her husband and daughter from London to Connecticut, where her husband had recently been transferred by his financial services company:

'We didn't really know much about buying a home or renting in the USA, so we basically let Tim's company lead us to a neighbourhood not far from his office. The house seemed suitable, not too small, and our neighbours were friendly, if somewhat older than we were. There didn't seem to be many other children in the neighbourhood, but we assumed Izzy would be making friends at school.'

Valentina and Tim wanted their child to really experience America – they didn't want to insulate her at a posh private school – so when the school year rolled around, Isabelle was enrolled in the 7th grade at the public school to which she had been assigned based on her parents' home address.

As it turned out, there was a reason there weren't many other children in Valentina and Tim's neighbourhood: the school to which Isabelle had been assigned was widely known as one of the worst in the area, with gang violence problems and generally run-down facilities. 'We didn't expect that at all,' Valentina says. 'We assumed that most public schools were of similar quality – and when we asked for Isabelle to be transferred to a better school, we were told that, because of where we lived, this was where Izzy had to attend.'

Thankfully, Valentina and Tim were only renting and had not purchased their home, so when the lease was up they moved across town to a better school district, and the next year Isabelle began her second year of junior high at a much better school – and in a neighbourhood where there was a swimming pool and lots of other kids about.

school will not be held (except for remedial students, who may be required to take summer school) during this time.

School hours generally run (from elementary on up through high school) from 7 or 8 in the morning until 2 or 3 in the afternoon.

Elementary school is where students will begin to learn how to read, do mathematics, study American and world history (commonly referred to as 'social studies'), and often learn how to play music, paint or sing. There will invariably be a number of recitals or plays put on throughout the year by your child's elementary school; these are taken very seriously by parents, who show up dutifully to every event, camcorder in hand. Elementary school is also where the Parent Teacher Association (PTA, or sometimes, in the more politically correct school districts, the PTSA, Parent Teacher Student Association) will begin. Essentially this is a forum for parents to discuss their child's progress with his or her teachers, and to address any problems (with the child or the teacher) that may have arisen. PTA meetings are held several times a year.

The school year is typically divided into four 'nine weeks' – two sets before Christmas, and two after the new year. At the end of each nine weeks your child will receive a 'report card', which will indicate the grade your child has received in each subject (reading, maths and so on). Grades of 'A' and 'B' are the highest and 'D' and 'F' the lowest. A 'C' grade is considered average. A grade of 'F' indicates that your child has failed the subject in question – though grades this low don't really start to be given out until junior high school. It's possible – though not likely in elementary school – that if your child fails too many subjects he or she will be 'held back' (have to repeat the same school grade) or be required to attend remedial classes. However, schools have all but ceased the practice of holding back young children, as this is thought to do too much damage to their fragile self-esteem to be really effective as a learning aid. At the end of the year, provided your child has 'passed' all classes (attained a grade of D or better), he or she will graduate and be allowed to move up in school next year.

Junior High

Depending on the school, junior high may encompass 6th, 7th, and 8th grades; 7th, 8th, and 9th grades; or just 7th and 8th grade. If your child attends a private school, it's possible that he or she will not have to switch schools in the transition from elementary to junior high; many private schools incorporate grades K through 12. If your child is attending public school, however, he or she will most likely have to switch schools. Unlike elementary, junior high is where school becomes a bit more serious, and the prospect of being held back for failing grades becomes very real. Unlike in elementary, where students usually stay in one classroom all day with one teacher who teaches all subjects (except for specialities like art or music), junior high students shuttle from one classroom to the next during the day. Each teacher in junior high typically handles one or two subjects, and students come to them (rather than the other way around) for instruction. Your child may well have a locker (secured by a combination lock) in junior high, in which he or she will keep all books, personal belongings, lunch and so on. Junior high is also where worries about school safety begin to manifest themselves, and it's not uncommon for schools in high-risk areas or with a history of gangs or violence to have metal detectors and employ a small security staff.

The structure of the junior high school year is essentially the same as in elementary school: report cards are issued every nine weeks, PTA meetings are held regularly, and the same holidays and school breaks are observed. Two major differences between elementary and junior high, though, are sports and clubs. 'Junior varsity', or JV sports, begin in junior high, and your child (girl or boy) will have the opportunity to try out for a number of different teams, depending on the school; basketball and football are the two biggest school sports in

America, though others may also be offered, such as baseball, volleyball, tennis and even golf. Cricket will most likely not be on the menu. Clubs and organisations are also big in junior high, including such pursuits as the yearbook, foreign languages, Model UN and the chess club, among countless others. If you plan on your child going to college, encourage him or her to get involved early with any number of these activities; colleges eat this stuff up.

High School

High school, for which your teenager will again have to transfer schools, continues the trend of specialisation that began in junior high. During the 10th, 11th and 12th grades (9th is sometimes included in high school), students will have much more control over what classes they take. There will be certain required courses, but if your student shows a desire to learn more about art than, say, physics, the opportunity will likely be there. Many high schools (some junior highs, too) offer 'advanced placement', or AP, classes. These are for especially gifted students, and sometimes can count towards college credit. Sports are very important in high schools across America, and often the most 'popular' students will be those on the basketball or football teams or their cheerleaders. It's worth going to a high school game or two, as the energy and school spirit on autumn football-game nights really is something to experience.

Sports aside, high school is the grooming ground for college, and many students as they near their 12th grade or 'senior', year (9th-graders are 'freshmen', 10th-graders 'sophomores', 11th-graders 'juniors') will begin to obsess over which college they would like to attend. All this is tied up with grades and grade point averages, or GPAs, which assign a number value to each letter grade. For example, an 'A' is worth 4 points, a 'B' 3, a 'C' 2, and so on. Over the course of high school, all of a student's grades will be averaged together to determine his or her GPA. Thus, a student with two As and 2 Bs would have a GPA of 3.5. Graduating with a perfect 4 GPA is highly desired by motivated students – and relatively rare. Another big factor that determines what colleges will accept your student is the scholastic assessment test – or, as it's universally known and feared, the SAT. The SAT is a voluntary test that measures a student's learning in three areas: critical reading, maths and writing. It is scored on a 200- to 800-point scale for both critical reading and maths, with additional scores for the writing section. Many different companies offer study guides and courses to prepare for the SAT, and most actually can help your student improve his or her score; a good one to start with is Kaplan, which can be found online at **www.kaplan.com**. Depending on your state, your student might also want to take the ACT, a similar, competitor test to the SAT.

Colleges and Universities

It's become almost de rigueur for students in the USA to attend some sort of college after they graduate from high school. The reason for this is that people applying for all but the most low-paying jobs (with the exception of factory or construction work) now require a college degree in order to be hired. As with elementary, junior high and high school, there are public and private colleges and universities (these two terms are used somewhat interchangeably, though technically a university is an institution that contains several colleges).

However, unlike in grade school, one must pay to attend public universities (or 'state schools') in the USA – though the cost of tuition is usually much lower than that of a private university such as Yale or Harvard. That said, college tuition in America is very expensive – sometimes as much as $30,000 per year – and, as in the UK, students often take on substantial student loans to pay for their education.

Scholarships and financial aid are also available, and these are applied for during the same period that students apply to college itself. Scholarships are given either for academic merit or financial need, while financial aid is given only to those whose families don't otherwise have the money to pay for college. Sports scholarships are also awarded, though these usually only go to the most talented athletes. Details of scholarships and how to obtain financial aid will be available from your student's high school guidance counsellor.

Choosing Where To Go

Choosing just what college to attend is often a fraught experience for high-schoolers, such is the emphasis placed on how important selecting the 'right' school is to the rest of one's life. This is partially true, as those students lucky enough to attend an Ivy League school (Harvard, Yale, Brown, and so on) will be set up for life with connections (*viz* both candidates for the 2004 presidential election). However, the quality of education at most schools is solid, and should prepare your student very well for a career in whatever field they choose. Universities contain many different colleges, such as a liberal arts school (encompassing everything from art and literature to biology and physics), a business school, and a fine arts school (dance, drama and so on). While it's easy to change one's 'major' (primary course of study) within any particular college, it's often difficult to switch, say, from liberal arts to business, even within the same university. The reason for this is that each college has its own set of course requirements – meaning that if you spend two years in the liberal arts college and then decide to switch, those two years' worth of courses might not add up to much in your new college.

In choosing which college to attend, keep in mind that state schools (the University of Southern California, the University of Michigan, and so on) will offer reduced tuition only if you are resident of that state – the idea being that if a student spends four years at an in-state college, he or she is more likely to remain in-state after school, thereby contributing tax dollars from their (ideally high-paying) university-fuelled career. Private schools, whether in your state or not, will charge the same amount to everyone. Prices for tuition vary, but most state schools will charge around $10,000 to $15,000 per year. The time required to complete a degree is around four years, though many students nowadays – owing to switching majors, study abroad, or general slacking off – are taking much longer.

Some, in lieu of attending a 'regular' four-year college, instead choose to enrol in a **vocational or technical school**. Programmes like this abound in America, and, though not as desirable as a four-year degree, can still lead to high-paying jobs, especially in the trades (such as plumbers, electricians and carpenters), computer programming, and truck-driving. The time required to complete a 'vo-tech' (as they are known) degree varies, but in general is less than a university. Classes are usually also offered at night, so you can work during the day and get your education at night. (The same goes for most universities.)

Recreational Courses

No matter what your area of interest, countless recreational courses in the USA offer pretty much any type of class you can imagine. If you'd like to learn how to do something **artistic**, such as paint or throw pots, you're probably best off contacting your local community, recreation or arts centre or a local art museum. In addition to such pursuits as putting on plays and exhibitions, these centres often double as classrooms, usually with night or weekend classes. The local theatre in your town might offer drama or acting classes. To find out contact information for these groups, look in your phone book's Yellow Pages under 'recreation centres', 'museums' or 'arts centres'.

Cooking classes are popular in the States, especially in 'foodie' cities like New York and San Francisco. In New York, the Institute of Culinary Education (**www.iceculinary.com**) offers a wide-ranging slate of courses, for skill levels from novice to advanced. Costs range from a high of $535 for its five-session 'Techniques of Cooking 1' class, to a low of $95 for their one-day 'Essentials' classes (Essentials of Cantonese Cooking, Greek Cooking, and so on). Often these classes will end with a several-course meal served with wine; they're a great place to meet people. To find a school that offers culinary courses in your area, search online for '[your town] recreational cooking classes'.

Scuba-diving is another big area of recreational courses in the USA, particularly in warm coastal areas such as Florida and California. The Professional Association of Dive Instructors (PADI) is associated with dive centres all over the country where you can learn how to dive; to find the location nearest you, visit

www.padi.com. Scuba-diving courses are fairly pricey, often a few hundred dollars for just a couple of sessions (though this includes gear, which you probably won't have). After completing the required courses, you'll be given a PADI dive certification card, which will allow you to dive on your own anywhere in the world. Most centres also offer more-advanced diving classes.

For something even more adventurous, you might want to consider an **Outward Bound** course. These are something of a mini-vacation – though don't think you'll be sipping cocktails and having your gear lugged around for you – and usually range from five days to two weeks. Outward Bound (**www. outwardbound.com**) offers courses in a wide variety of outdoor pursuits, from canyoneering and rock-climbing to skiing and sea kayaking, and encourages a philosophy of problem-solving, pushing past difficulty, and teamwork. Most courses involve a period of training by instructors, a practice period, a solo outing, and a final trek, where your class – without the instructors' help – will put to use the skills you all have learned. The quality courses are expensive: depending on the activity, a five-day trip will cost around $900, a seven-day trip $1300, and a two-week trip $2600.

If you'd rather have your nose buried in a book than your body hanging from a cliff face, an **adult education class** at a community college or university may be appealing to you. Many colleges offer reduced-rate night classes in all manner of subjects for non-degree-seeking students. You can study world literature, art history, or even take a poetry- or fiction-writing workshop; check the course catalogues of local colleges to see what they have on offer. Community colleges, meanwhile, offer similar, traditional classroom fare, though they also often have classes on such practical pursuits as car maintenance, home improvement and personal computing. Classes at community colleges will be much cheaper than those offered by a university, though the quality can vary widely.

Taking Your Pet

Bringing your pet cat or dog (or six turtles, the maximum allowed for 'non-commercial purposes', according to the Centres for Disease Control, or CDC) to the US is a fairly simple affair. Since the UK is listed as a 'rabies-free country', dogs who are from the UK or have been there for the previous six months are not required to be vaccinated for rabies prior to arrival in the USA. Cats are not required to have ever had a rabies vaccination.

On arrival in the USA, your dog or cat (or turtles, as the case may be) will be inspected for evidence of infectious diseases to which humans are susceptible. If it seems that your pet may be sick, a veterinarian may have to have a look at the animal in greater detail. Otherwise, if your pet is healthy, he or she will be admitted to the USA with no problem. The USA does not require a health certificate for your animal. However, certain airlines may require one, so you should check with your airline before departure.

If you are moving to Hawaii, or plan to visit and bring your pet there, be aware that Hawaii has much more stringent requirements than the rest of the States; for more information, visit **www.hawaiiag.org** and click on the 'Animal Quarantine in Hawaii' link. For more information on guidelines for the rest of the USA, visit the CDC's 'Importation of Pets' webpage at **www.cdc.gov/ncidod/dq/animal.htm**.

Working in the USA

Being employed in the USA differs in certain fundamental ways from having a job in the UK, though increasingly, as the UK adopts more American work practices, the gap is narrowing. What tends to differentiate the USA most is its more casual business manner. Deals are struck less formally – not least between employer and employee. The labour market in the USA is far more cut-and-thrust than in the UK. The notion of a job for life has disappeared and most workers have virtually no company loyalty – they are often travelling between jobs, sectors and parts of the country. Conditions of work, too, are less secure. When you have a job, financial stability is easy to maintain – albeit through working much longer hours – but there are relatively few government safety nets in place when things go wrong. Long- and short-term sick leave, redundancy and pensions are all issues you need to think about and provide for well in advance – and in most cases private insurance is the only viable means to ensure peace of mind.

On a more positive note, the USA amply and easily rewards the self-motivated and dynamic entrepreneur. Small businesses are easy to set up and run and the country has an exceptional business-to-business commerce, so that it is always easy to outsource and get professional advice for every business, big or small.

Without the legal right to work on arrival in the USA, the chances of finding a good job are slim. In some circumstances, casual employment is possible though not recommended. If you do find work illegally, be aware that should you be caught you will immediately be repatriated and refused entry to the USA in the future.

Business Etiquette

Most business in the USA is conducted with limited formality, though certain unwritten rules certainly exist. During interviews and in meetings, personality is as important as credentials and success may hinge on how well you are liked. There is some decorum to learn, but caution, respect and common sense should make up for a lack of cultural knowledge. Face-to-face encounters are also a chance to market things about yourself that are not in your résumé or sales brochure – don't miss this opportunity.

Dress Codes

The casual veneer of doing business in the USA is mirrored in dress codes. With the exception of jobs in finance and sales, the classic suit and tie for a man have given way to casual business attire – typically involving less formal trousers and shirt. Generally, the smaller and warmer a city, the more casual the attire will be.

Increasingly popular are 'dress down Fridays' when employees of companies with a more formal dress code can wear more casual attire that would not be acceptable during the rest of the week. But no matter how casual an environment, it doesn't hurt to dress smart for a job interview or an initial meeting; it is always better to be over-dressed than under-dressed. Men can wear any sort of shirt and tie; with a white shirt and a red or blue tie considered the most conservative choice. The women's business suit is less popular than in the past, and smart trousers and a blouse are acceptable in most circumstances. Often women dress more smartly than men to help project extra professionalism, and it would be highly unusual for a woman to wear the same outfit more than once in a week. Most women will have at least enough outfits to ensure daily variety for 10 days' work. Men can get away with a smaller wardrobe by varying their shirt and tie combinations.

Greetings and Business Meetings

Initial encounters should always be approached conservatively. The appropriate greeting for men and women is a firm handshake with eye contact. Titles such as 'Dr', 'Mr' or 'Ms' should be used, though most Americans will immediately insist that their first name or a nickname be used. This cultural norm reflects the casual American style and should not be confused for anything else. To fit in, it is useful to reciprocate immediately, by offering your first name. Most interviews and business meetings will begin with some light-hearted banter and your accent may be the source. Play along and avoid any controversial topics. Don't bring up business until your acquaintance does (presuming they are the more senior, or have the balance of power in the meeting on their side), and let them determine how long the conversation stays there. While business is being conducted, Americans tend to be direct and to the point and will appreciate the same from you.

Business meetings may be held 'over lunch' in restaurants or bars. Business will usually be conducted before or after the meal, which should be used as a time to establish trust via light conversation. It is not customary to drink alcohol and it would be unwise to order any unless your host does so first. If they do, don't feel obliged to join them; they won't be offended. On the other hand the after-work cocktail can be a time to foster casual relationships that could improve your standing in the office. Smoking is permissible in fewer and fewer places and increasingly frowned on. If smoking is permitted, ask permission before lighting up and don't be surprised if someone objects.

When eating out, Americans tend to be big tippers. The size of a tip often has little to do with the level of service received and is usually given out of custom. If hosting a lunch, tip at least 15 per cent; if you don't, your company may well be embarrassed and feel the need to make up the difference.

Immediately following an interview or meeting, a 'thank you note' is a wonderful opportunity to remind the person about you and let them know how much you valued their time. A hand-written note will be most effective, but an e-mail can also serve as a quick and easy reminder. It's a competitive market, and anything you can do to set yourself above the competition is a good idea.

Language

Most Americans speak only one language and may be impatient towards those with a thick accent or whose English is not entirely fluent, but British accents are typically considered rather charming and refined regardless of type. Most Americans cannot differentiate between an English or Australian accent so any stereotypes associated with various English accents will certainly not apply in the USA. With occasional exceptions, Britons and Americans will be able to converse with few problems. Americans do tend to use a lot of idioms and acronyms, though, so if language is ever a barrier, don't be afraid to ask for clarification.

Bonuses

Holiday bonuses are becoming less popular though are still sometimes awarded by companies large and small. In the absence of a bonus most bosses will provide a small token of gratitude like a food basket or a gift certificate for a department store. The boss will not expect something in return, although some employees pool together for a nominal gift. Doormen, maintenance men, and cleaning staff are usually given a monetary gift at holiday time as well.

Many big companies own season tickets for a local sports team. These are usually handed out to clients, but are sometimes also given to employees and should only be accepted if they are going to be used.

Equal Opportunities and Sexual Harassment

Though America prides itself as the land of equal opportunity, white males still fill the chairs at most board meetings. But further down the hierarchy you can expect to see people of different sex, religion and ethnicity in all positions. The United States has very strict anti-discrimination and sexual harassment laws. Jokes about race, religion, or sex are not tolerated in the workplace and in the last few years there have been a number of cases involving employees being reprimanded or even dismissed for viewing and sending offensive material over company e-mail. Many companies have policies on the use of e-mails and the Internet for purposes other than work, which can extend to the monitoring of web traffic for the purposes of enforcement. Sexual harassment is also taken

Play Meets Work

The use of idioms from the sporting world in the workplace is common and, inevitably, most come from American sports such as baseball and American football. In some cases these sayings are so common that the reference to sport has all but been lost. Here are some common expressions.

7th inning stretch	A pause near the end to refresh
Armchair quarterback	Someone who makes suggestions from a position where their input will not matter
Ballpark figure	An estimate
Batting 1000	Doing perfectly, 100 per cent
Below the belt	Unfair, unjust, uncalled for
Big leagues or Major leagues	The highest level
Bush league	Unethical, unacceptable behaviour
Call the shots	Give orders
Double play	To achieve two things at once
Field questions	To handle questions well
Fumble	To make a mistake
Game plan	An approach, a business plan
Getting to first base	Getting started
Home run or Homer	A great job
Monday morning quarterback	Someone who suggests what should have been done after the fact
Out of left field	A comment or action that comes out of nowhere
Playing hard ball	Cut-throat, no holds barred
Saved by the bell	Getting out of a bad situation just in the nick of time
Second string	Not top quality, usually a person
Slam dunk	A great job
Strike out	To fail
Take a rain check	Postpone an event
Taking a dive	Losing on purpose
Team player	A co-operator, someone who works well with everyone
Throw a curve	To trick, deceive
Time out	A rest, a breather
Touch base	Keep in touch, update
Touchdown	A great job
Two strikes	Only one more mistake is allowed

very seriously. Employees at larger companies are informed about what constitutes sexual harassment and are expected to sign a compliance statement. Men in power should never ask subordinate women on a date unless the woman in question's interest is unambiguous. Violations can result in immediate dismissal and possibly further legal action.

The Labour Market

Employment opportunities in the United States have worsened since the recession that began in early 2001, and despite occasional signs of recovery the situation at the time of writing remains comparatively bleak. The booming economy of the late 1990s was fuelled by a rapidly growing technology sector, which has since been particularly weakened. Once a new technological infra-structure was in place and new markets were cornered, Wall Street caught up with reality. Then, with the market already ebbing, the September 11 terrorist attacks later that year caused a downturn in consumer confidence that hurt all parts of the economy. Since then, employers have largely stopped enticing skilled workers from around the world with generous compensation and ownership packages.

Unemployment in 2005 lies at just over 5 per cent, though this figure hides the real scope of the problem. The statistic is the product of the United States **Bureau of Labor Statistics** (**BLS**; **www.bls.gov**) which conducts monthly surveys of sample households across the USA. The BLS readily admits their procedure makes their figures inexact, but it's those factors that are hard to register in statistical terms that make an even larger difference. Unable to obtain a position similar to one they have been made redundant from, many Americans have chosen to retire early, return to school for more training or have a crack at starting their own business. Moreover, the statistics also fail to account for the vast number of people who are currently under-employed – those who have taken on work below their training and experience when they find themselves left with little alternative.

Yet despite its current economic woes, the United States still maintains the lowest unemployment rate in the industrialised world, and opportunities exist for those with the right skills, a good work ethic and a flexible and opportunistic approach to employment.

Background

The USA is the land where capitalism famously runs wild – offering the minimum amount of protection and support for those at the bottom of the ladder, but at the same time ensuring premium conditions and rewards for talented individuals who successfully operate within the system. Out of this comes one of the world's most energetic economies, though perhaps partly, critics would say, at the expense of the weak.

Job security and company loyalty are almost non-existent in the USA and labour unions have little real power. Most states operate under 'employment at will' law, allowing an employer or employee to terminate a work agreement at any time with little or no reason. Unionised labour, at its strongest just decades ago when heavy industry still flourished, is also on the wane and has little political influence today. Currently, less than 10 per cent of private sector – and only around a third of government – workers are unionised. Most private sector unions are stronger in the east and in the north, while western states have little organised labour; teachers and grocery store workers are significant exceptions.

Big business in the USA has also been helped by other political trends of the last few decades, including the stagnation of the federal minimum wage. This hasn't been raised since its 1997 increase to $5.15 an hour and so marks one of the lowest values – when adjusted for inflation – since its inception in 1938. While the relative freedom from unions and the minimal number of restrictions on the labour market crushes many individuals underfoot, these factors are also considered to generate a flexible and vibrant economy: the USA has few strikes that slow down the economy or bring cities to a halt.

Current Policies and Issues

As in many developed countries, the immigration of workers from poor countries is an emotive issue and one that certainly has a profound effect on the American economy in several different ways.

The massive influx of migrant labour from Latin America, annually involving millions of people, consititutes the largest group of economic migrants, and causes no end of consternation among most Americans. Most immigrants do jobs that most Americans are unwilling to do, moving around the country performing backbreaking work. In this sense they don't directly compete with most Americans, though their presence, and the fact that many of them work illegally for quite a bit less than the minimum wage, tends to drive down wages generally.

Another powerful foreign component of the US labour market is made up of highly skilled foreign workers who enter the country under the H-1B visa programme (*see* p.120). Annually 65,000 H-1B visas are offered, with many going to those with considerable experience in computers or engineering. With so many highly skilled Americans seeking jobs, there is increasing pressure to lower the number of H-1Bs offered. The quota of 65,000 was established during significantly different times when skilled guest workers were in demand. However, big business often benefits from hiring H-1B workers and fights to maintain the programme. One reason is that, although the law requires H-1B workers be paid the median wage for each job, these workers are less likely to ask for – or receive – pay rises and are much less prone to leave the company in search of a better job.

Finally, Americans are not just competing with foreigners within the country but also internationally. With no real encouragement in place for doing otherwise, as in other countries companies are increasingly 'outsourcing', where they can, using cheaper overseas labour wherever viable. With a highly educated workforce that speaks acceptable or even fluent English in Latin American countries or India, US companies can pay foreign workers a fraction of what American workers receive. This principle has been a major cause of recent job losses in the USA ,with the technology sector hit the hardest.

Prospects

Over the last 100 years, Americans have watched as jobs in textiles, manufacturing and now technology have moved overseas. With each transition they have feared the worst, yet over time the USA has proved itself economically buoyant and adaptable, and the country has repeatedly helped itself – and the world economy – out of difficult circumstances. So, despite the current lag in economic growth, given its historical record, the USA will almost certainly bounce back and is also the most likely candidate to spearhead the next global economic boom.

What appears to sustain the long-term success of the American economy, apart from relaxed US labour laws, seems to be the flexibility and pro-activeness of the American workforce. Americans have historically been willing to change careers or move thousands of miles as circumstances have demanded it, and this continues to be a characteristic of the labour force today.

This workforce get-up-and-go will likely be a root cause of a future American economic revival, and will probably make or break your own long-term economic success in the country, too. Historically US population patterns have always shifted with employment opportunities. From textiles in the South, to manufacturing in the Midwest and technology on the West Coast, Americans have always literally moved with the times. The region most likely to see the next increase in job opportunities is thought by many to be the 'Sun Belt', made up of the southern states of Arizona, California, Florida, Georgia, Nevada, New Mexico and Texas. As the US population ages and more Americans retire, increasing numbers are moving south to enjoy year-round warm weather. With a growing proportion of non-working residents in the region, job opportunities there are likely to increase.

Job Ideas

In countries where English is not the primary language, British expats tend to gravitate towards certain jobs. This is less so in English-speaking countries like the USA, where a proficiency in English is normal and will not open any doors. Scope for teaching English as a foreign language is understandably minimal –

and it's the knowledge of a second language that is more likely to strengthen your application.

The natural advantages that Brits bring to the USA are more subtle, but notably include your accent, which will immediately distinguish you at the interview stage and in business. All British accents are widely considered intelligent and professional, which may well give you a small advantage over American competition. Generally, the British are also more knowledgeable about other countries than most Americans, who only have very limited foreign experience and education about the rest of the world. This will be accentuated if you have already worked abroad in other countries or done business with them. Either way, in positions with obvious international trading or other links, you are likely to have some natural advantages over US applicants.

Yet in general the special characteristics that British expatriates can offer to the American labour market are relatively minimal. Ultimately the job you find will, as in the UK, depends on your skills and experience – and your ability to sell yourself. Competition is keen, since Americans tend to be very adept at promoting themselves, and they have the advantage of a more opportunistic and flexible attitude to finding work than most Britons. You will probably also have to adopt this, since the rewards for those with energy and initiative are particularly great in the USA. Keeping up to date on current trends in the USA labour market is a vital part of this process. Some areas considered to have bright prospects are discussed below.

Teaching

Many places in the United States are desperate for teachers, so if you have experience in teaching children – or would like to give it a try – this is a good opportunity, and one that sometimes requires no more than a general degree to get started. The requirements for certification are often far lower than in the UK, but vary in all 50 states, as well as between school boards in each state. Some school boards require a degree in education while some states experiencing severe teacher shortages, such as New York and California, offer an accelerated certification programme for anyone possessing a bachelor's degree. Around 15 states require US citizenship to teach in publicly funded schools, but private schools in every state typically have lower standards, albeit with lower pay. Supply teaching (known in the USA as substitute teaching) has even more relaxed requirements and pay for this varies from around $60 to $140 a day, depending on the school board. Without a long-term assignment, it can be a difficult way to make a living, but is a great way to network with schools in your area.

Before being certified in any state you will need to have your education credentials evaluated and compared with those in the USA. This is done at the applicant's expense through a third party such as the **Educational Credential**

Evaluators (www.ece.org), or **International Education Research Foundation** (www.ierf.org). Contact a state's **Department of Education** to find out more about certification requirements: these are listed at **www.americanteachers. com/certifications.cfm.**

If you have experience teaching in Britain you might consider working for **British Schools of America** (www.britishschool.org), which regularly requires top-notch teachers to teach the UK national curriculum to the children of British expats. Currently there are British schools in Boston, Charlotte, Chicago, Houston and Washington, DC, but there are plans to expand into other major cities across the country.

Teachers looking to spend a year or less in the USA should look into opportunities offered by the Fulbright US–UK Commission. They organise the transfer of around 50 UK teachers each year. The **British Council** and the United States **Department of State** administer the exchange, placing teachers across the country in schools with children ranging from age five all the way up to adults in community colleges. Participants are matched in a school befitting their experience and desired location and placement can be for the whole or just half an academic year. All qualified teachers with three years' teaching experience in the UK are eligible. Interested teachers should visit the British Council website at **www.britishcouncil.org/learning-fulbright-teacher-how-to-apply.htm.**

For university faculty and professionals, the **United States Fulbright Commission** offers about 800 research or lecture grants to non-United States residents each year. A host institution must provide a letter of invitation to fulfil application requirements. Application details can be found at **www.cies. org/vs_scholars/vsfulb.htm.**

Healthcare

Healthcare workers are currently in high demand in the USA and will certainly remain so in the long term, so that healthcare forms perhaps the country's most reliable source of future employment. As the 'baby boomers' – the generation born in the immediate post-Second World War years – begin to reach retirement age, the demand for qualified healthcare workers has begun to skyrocket.

Experienced doctors, nurses, home healthcare specialists and biotechnology researchers are always in high demand. Much of the high cost of US healthcare goes towards paying these healthcare professionals. Such positions command high respect and salaries are among the highest in the world. British nurses in particular are frequently recruited, and in the USA can expect salaries of up to $50,000, or more for specialists. Requirements for certification vary by state and information on this is obtainable from the **National Council of State Boards of Nursing**, 111 East Wacker Drive, Suite 2900, Chicago, Illinois 60601, **t** 312-525-

3600, **www.ncsbn.org**. Recruitment agencies that sponsor green cards for nurses can also be found in the UK and include **Adevia Health Ltd**, 6 Dukes Gate, Acton Lane, London W4 5DX, **t** (0870) 033 0500, **www.adevia.com**; and **O'Grady Peyton International**, 1–3 Norton Folgate, London EC1 6DB, **t** (0870) 700 0140, **www.ogpinc.com**.

Trends and Opportunities

The US famously deems itself as the land of the self-made, and rewards entre-preneurial initiative as much as any country in the world. But be warned: this opportunistic business culture is a cut-throat one, and in this land of entre-preneurs you may find it hard to come up with anything original. No matter whether you are looking for employment, wish to be self-employed or intend to start your own business, it's always worth keeping a close eye on trends. One excellent source of information with projections of job opportunities – organised by region and state – is the annual *Occupational Outlook Handbook* (**www.bls.gov/oco**), published by the Bureau of Labor Statistics.

Possible Growth Areas

Sustained long-term growth is anticipated in several key areas of the economy. However, if you're starting your own business, research the market well and try to find an innovative twist that sets you apart from the competition. The USA is the land of hype, so if you can make it sound innovative and good, then more often than not it will work.

• *Technology*: According to the latest projections, and despite the current outsourcing trend, job opportunities in information technology are projected to grow. The sector is becoming increasingly specialised, so niche skills increasingly lead to lucrative jobs. By fusing experience in promising growth areas like management, security, technical consulting or sales areas, you are likely to find new and interesting lines of work.

• *Counter-terrorism*: Combating terrorism is of paramount concern in the USA today. Individuals with experience in defence, law enforcement, secu-rity or intelligence are actively sought.

• *Financial planners*: Expertise in international markets is in demand. Knowledge of international market potentials and nuances may lead to a well-paid career. Investing in overseas markets is increasingly popular, even among relatively small-scale investors.

• *International consultants*: US businesses are always looking to expand their market and increasingly look overseas. With the right experience and overseas contacts, foreigners may command premium consulting fees from mid- to large-scale organisations.

• *Business brokers*: These international experts match businesses around the world that need each other's goods and services. You will be ideal for this sector if you have a network of useful contacts on both sides of the Atlantic.

• *Home caregivers*: Many older Americans aren't ready for a nursing home but may need some help around the home. Home helps ('caregivers') deal with anything from the shopping and cleaning to helping someone climb in and out of bed.

• *Internet trading*: The popularity of eBay and other auction sites has many Americans selling things they no longer need. The opportunity is here for small-time traders to earn their keep, buying and selling in this way. If you have a good knowledge of an area through a hobby, this may give you a good eye and so a keen advantage in the market.

• *Spas*: Health and beauty spas are increasing in popularity and the trend is unlikely to slow. The trick for a new spa is to cater to a specific crowd like young people – or even dogs. Training in massage can be rewarding and lucrative, with a variety of short and longer, more medically informed courses available.

• *Translation services*: The emerging global economy means many businesses are expanding their market overseas. Translators are needed for everything from business documents to sales brochures. There may even be a need for translation, or at least professional proofreading, between American and British English.

• *Tagging and tracking*: People are beginning to protect their valuables by attaching immovable or hidden tracking devices. Global positioning system technology is exploding and this market is sure to expand.

Part-time Work

Part-time work can be a great way to earn a few extra dollars while you search for full-time employment, or can provide a sociable activity for those with some time to spare. You may find part-time work is an easy, or even the only, way to get your foot in the right door. Some employers hire part-time employees on informal probation when new additional staff are needed but they are reluctant to take on full-time employees.

Part-time work – usually defined as less than 35 hours a week – is governed by many of the same regulations that apply to full-time employment. Since employers are not required to provide any benefits to full-time employees, most will not offer any to their part-time employees. Part-time employees can also expect to receive 10–20 per cent less pay than full-time employees doing the same job.

Generally finding part-time work is far easier than finding full-time positions. However, currently large numbers of Americans are employed only part-time in the absence of being able to find full-time work, so finding part-time work in some fields may prove difficult.

Bars and Restaurants

One area where positions regularly come up is in bars and restaurants. Waiting on tables and bartending are among the most lucrative forms of part-time work in the USA. Some well-educated Americans have even made a career out of it in preference to their less well-paid specialist fields. Particularly those who staff the best restaurants and bars, and work the busiest shifts, can earn more than $30,000–$40,000 a year, which is as much as the starting salary for a teacher, policeman or certified accountant; no other country tips the way America does, with 15–20 per cent of the total bill generally being the minimum.

Telemarketing

Perhaps the most ubiquitous form of part-time work available is in the field of telemarketing. The work can be very challenging and the turnover rate is very

Case Study: The Accidental Salesman

Tony, age 50, wasn't too concerned about finding work when he moved from south London to Virginia in 1998. An American bank paid his wife, Lisa, well and needed her expertise in their US office so set up a transfer. Tony had worked hard all his life and planned to retire early in the States. But once they'd settled in their home, he soon became restless and decided he needed at least a part-time job. Tony had been a successful accountant for over 20 years back in the UK but wasn't at all qualified to practise in the States.

With no work for Tony anywhere near their home, Lisa suggested they get a second car so Tony could explore other options. The following Sunday they stopped by a local car dealer. Lisa hasn't forgotten that visit, since it lasted all afternoon. 'Tony always fancied himself a Formula 1 driver. Once he starts talking about cars, he can't stop.' Since the model that caught Tony's eye wasn't available in the UK, he persisted with questions until the sales manager had to assist the salesmen. The sales manager was impressed with Tony's knowledge of cars and they chatted for quite a bit. The moment Tony mentioned he was looking for work, he was offered a job on the spot. 'He told me that with my knowledge of cars and my accent, customers would have no choice but to trust me,' Tony recalls. 'He also said my accent would make me irresistible to the ladies, but I haven't told Lisa that part.'

Five years later Tony is one of the top salesmen in the state and happier than he ever was in front of a spreadsheet.

Case Study: Barman's Paradise

Simon, 26, didn't plan on going to university for three years just to work behind a bar. After growing up in northwest England, he met his bride-to-be during his final year at Newcastle University. Not sure what to do after graduation, he passed up the opportunity to backpack across Asia with his mates. Instead he followed his heart and his girlfriend to New York. 'Honestly, I knew we had a chance of spending our lives together as soon as I met her,' Simon declares, while mixing a martini behind a bar on Manhattan's Upper West Side, 'but we certainly wouldn't have married so soon if it hadn't been our only option.' Karen, originally from New Jersey, still had another year before she completed her masters degree at Columbia University.

When the money and the clock were running out on Simon's stay, they decided to take a chance. They married at New York's City Hall, and Simon began to look for work. His first instinct was to put his new degree to some use and he began to search Manhattan for a job. During the hunt he was offered $75 to help clean out the basement of their local watering hole, but in accepting it he had no clue it would lead to a well-paid job.

A week later the boss needed a shift filled for one night. 'The next thing I know I'm working four nights a week and making more money than any of my mates back home.' When Simon first started behind the bar the boss didn't even have him on the books – 'I just worked for tips' – but that didn't matter. 'I pocket between $200 and $300 in cash on a Friday night. I still can't get used to it.' Simon shakes his head...'And people are giving me their hard earned dollars, for what? Filling a pint glass?! I might as well have skipped uni and just spent more time in the pub!'

high. However, top telemarketers can make full-time pay working only part-time. Persistent salespeople with the gift of the gab can earn substantial commission selling anything from satellite dishes to aluminium siding (cladding). For a less demanding position, some newspapers and non-profit companies pay an hourly wage for calling enough homes to reach a quota without necessarily making any sales.

Changes in legislation may reduce the number of telemarketers needed in the near future. A federal 'do not call' list has been established and anyone not wanting unsolicited calls may join the list. However, big business is finding ways around the new law and some opportunities for new telemarketers are likely to be available for the foreseeable future.

Working Freelance

Certain skills such as writing, photography or computer programming may prove ideal for finding freelance work. With the right talent and contacts, freelancing can be very rewarding and may even lead to you starting a small business in the field.

For some, the thought of working on their own is very attractive. Freelancers are free from any boss, decide their own hours and are able to accept only the work they choose. Your success as a freelancer will hinge on your ability to be organised, self-motivated, disciplined in your work patterns and able to find assignments. While some freelancers receive what sounds like a fairly high hourly rate for their services, it is important to bear in mind the amount of unpaid hours invested in finding work and the time spent between commissions. Freelancers also need to maintain their own office space and buy the latest technology and software.

If you think you have what it takes, the USA is one the most welcoming places in the world to work for yourself, and regulations regarding freelance work in the USA are few.

Once you have accepted any freelance work for payment, you have technically opened a sole proprietorship (*see* p.212).

Looking for Work

As long as you are legally entitled to work, finding a job in the USA isn't much different from in the UK. Having a well-crafted résumé (CV), knowing where to look, and performing well at an interview, are the keys to finding the right job.

The Résumé (Curriculum Vitae)

Preparing an American style résumé is the first important step in any job search. A well-prepared résumé available on quality 8½ by 11 inch (approximately A4) paper and in digital format is essential. A British-style CV is only appropriate for academic or clinical positions or if your application is being processed in a UK office and should not be submitted otherwise.

Below are some guidelines for preparing a US-style résumé, but should you lack access to a computer or have any doubts about being able to prepare an immaculate résumé, you are strongly advised to use a résumé service, which will convert your CV to a résumé for less than $100. Just search the Yellow Pages or the Internet for 'résumé services'.

Should you decide to build your own résumé, be sure to have the spell check set to American English and have a qualified American review it. Résumés often land in a pile of hundreds; one imperfection and yours will likely be discarded. All résumés need to be concise; for those with extensive experience relevant to the position, two pages are acceptable, otherwise stick to one. In either case, try to create one that is exactly one or two pages long without much clutter or empty space. Presentation is vital.

Sample Résumé

Daniel M. Barrow
1811 Grove Road • Arlington, VA 22246
(703)-627-1392
dmbarrow@yahoo.com

Objective:

Management position in network operations where 11 years of experience in Network Administration will add value to operations

Summary of qualifications:

Cisco IOS 12.3	Red Hat Linux	Network Security
HTML Programming	Windows XP Professional	Checkpoint Firewall
Voice Over IP	C++ Programming	Disaster Recovery
Team Management	TCP/IP	McAfee Virus Protection

Experience:

Oct 2002 to present – Network Security Manager, Intellitech Corp, Manassas, VA
  – Promoted to manage the information security program to protect enterprise-wide critical information on company systems
  – Led the implementation of Checkpoint Firewall system
  – Managed a project to adopt company policy on network security and user rights throughout the nationwide network
  – Responsible for managing network administration team of 12

Jan 1998 to Oct 2002 – Senior Network Administrator, Intellitech Corp, Manassas, VA
  – Designed and implemented the migration of an office-wide LAN system
  – Responsible for installation of Frame-Relay connections between home office and satellite sites
  – Configured and maintained Cisco 7200 and 2500 series routers

Aug 1994 to Jan 1998 – Network Administrator, E Commerce Group, South Gate, MD
  – Installed RedHat Linux for firewalling, DNS, HTTP and file sharing
  – Maintained availability of company computer systems including servers, workstations, laptops and printers
  – Supported and administered mobile computing environment, RADIUS and VPN services

Education:

1994   Bachelor of Science (Honors) Information Systems
1997   University of Salford, Manchester, England

Certifications:

1999   Cisco Certified Network Professional
1997   Cisco Certified Network Administrator
1995   A+ Hardware Technician

No tried-and-true formula exists for the perfect résumé, and each person needs to follow a format that will best highlight skills and achievements. A key choice is between the two acceptable formats that exist: the traditional chronological résumé and the increasingly popular functional résumé.

An 'objective' should be placed on every résumé directly below your contact information. Your objective should clearly state what an employer would gain from hiring you. Ideally the objective should be tailored specifically for the desired position. If you only have one objective, be sure it clearly states your short-term employment goals and highlights what you bring to an employer.

Cover Letter

A cover letter should be included with any résumé. If sending a résumé by e-mail, the cover letter can serve as the text of your message with the résumé included as an attachment.

Sample Cover Letter

23 Vickers St
Oneonta, NY 13820
(607)-555-6384
ericmathers@gmail.com
November 12, 2005

Ms Rachael Watson
Elite Telecomm
34 Fairview St
Binghamton, NY 13790

Dear Ms. Watson,
One of your associates, Irene Hannity, suggested I contact you regarding the customer service position that you are seeking to fill. As you will see from my enclosed résumé, I have four years of customer service experience in the communications industry.

During my time with Express Data Communications my role extended well beyond the usual one of a customer service representative. Working in an environment providing 24-hour service proved especially demanding and I often led the night shift when management needed additional help. I was also responsible for training several new employees and evaluating their progress. Most importantly, I learned that satisfying customers really does take precedence over everything else.

I am sure that my experience closely matches the skills you seek. I have heard a lot about your company's plans for future growth, and I would love to be a part of your team. Please feel free to contact me at any time by phone or e-mail.

Thank you for your time and consideration.

Sincerely,

Eric Mathers

Job Application Dos and Don'ts

Do:

- place your most recent experience at the top of the résumé.
- place recently received degrees or technical training above your work history if you have no experience in the field.
- be sure to emphasise your strongest points.
- be certain that your referees (called references in the USA) know that they may be contacted and that they will only paint you in a good light.
- try to address cover letters personally, otherwise use 'dear sir or madam'.
- be sure your cover letter is prepared with as much attention to detail as your résumé – and on the same high-quality paper if sent by mail.
- if e-mailing your résumé as an attachment, be sure to mention the file format and use rtf (rich text) files in preference to anything other than a Microsoft Word document.

Do not:

- include any work experience more than five years old that is irrelevant to the position for which you are applying.
- include personal information such as age, sex or marital status or a photo.
- include personal interests and travel experience unless they are highly relevant to the position.

Cover letters should be at least three paragraphs but should never exceed one page. The opening paragraph should discuss the position you are applying for and where you heard about it. If someone referred you to the employer, put that person's name in the first paragraph of the letter. Use the second paragraph to emphasise any information not in your résumé that may help land you the job. Finally, the closing paragraph should be used to stress how excited you are about the position, what a great match you will be and mention any further action. If salary requirements are requested, they should be included in the final paragraph.

How to Get Started

Finding a job can be a daunting and time-consuming endeavour anywhere and the USA is no exception. If your employer has arranged for you to work at a US office then the hardest part of your move is over, but for many, finding a job will be the most difficult step in their journey to a new life abroad.

The more prepared you are, the easier it will be, but, that said, unless you are applying for a position in the USA through a UK office, it will be difficult to actually receive an offer before you arrive in the country. Except for those who possess highly specialised skills, the chances of being hired to work in the United States from abroad are slim.

However, there are certain things you can do to give you a head start when you arrive. A look on the Internet and in US publications will give you an idea of where you are likely to find the right jobs and the kinds of salaries you can expect. If you are in possession of a solid list of companies, employment agencies and contacts when you arrive in the USA, this will be a great start.

Countless Internet sites, newspapers, professional journals and recruitment agencies exist to help you find the perfect job, but none is a substitute for networking. According to the US Bureau of Labor Statistics, referral is one of the top ways people land new jobs. Knowing someone who knows someone is the most sure-fire way of landing an interview and your dream job. To get in this position you need to be proactive, spreading the word to everyone you know who might have a contact in the States and finding people who work in your field and are prepared to talk to you. Most large companies will have subsidiaries or parents in the USA and the ability to name-drop may just make the difference. Be creative and explore every avenue possible, and don't worry too much about seeming too pushy, since such behaviour is much more accept-able in the USA.

Newspapers and the Internet

Only a few years back, searching the ads in the local Sunday paper was the most popular means by which most people in the USA found their next job. Times have rapidly changed and now the Internet is a much more popular matchmaker for employers and employees, though newspapers are still worth a look to get an impression of the local job climate.

The Internet has literally hundreds of job boards and some of the more popular are listed below. Many are specific to certain industries and a quick search should make it fairly easy for you to find those in your field. Just try searching 'job board' and then 'teachers,' 'medical technicians,' 'programmers' or whatever best describes your field. Many Internet job boards will allow you to post your résumé without applying for a specific position. Employers can then view your credentials without seeing your personal information until you give your approval.

But the newspapers have fought back and many US papers will post their classified ads online either free or free for subscribers. The major newspapers for some of the America's biggest job markets are listed below – the newspapers of smaller towns are easily found via an Internet search engine. The overseas editions of the largest US newspapers, like the *New York Times*, the *Washington Post*, the *LA Times* and *USA Today*, may have some job listings, but it's best to view the local edition where possible. Some UK newspapers, including the *Guardian*, *The Times* and the *Financial Times*, also list US job openings, but mostly they are only useful for finding senior management positions.

Internet Job Boards

- **Careerbuilder (www.careerbuilder.com).** The nation's largest employment network with close to a million job vacancies.
- **Career One Stop (www.careeronestop.org).** Portal for several state and federal job boards.
- **Dice (www.dice.com).** Huge job board for technology professionals.
- **Hotjobs (www.hotjobs.com).** Run by Yahoo!, this large job bank covers many fields and experience levels.
- **Monster (www.monster.com).** The most popular job board in the United States. Hundreds of thousands of jobs advertised by job type and location. Also includes useful résumé and interviewing tips.
- **United States Jobs (www.usajobs.com)** The official job site of the United States federal government, with government job openings across the country. Most positions entail a lengthy recruitment process and some may require citizenship.

Newspaper Websites

- *Atlanta Journal-Constitution*, **www.ajcjobs.com/wl**.
- *Arizona Republic* – for Phoenix, **http://azcentral.gannettonline.com/careerbuilder**.
- *Boston Globe*, **http://bostonworks.boston.com**.
- *Chicago Tribune*, **www.chicagotribune.com/classified/jobs**.
- *Dallas Morning News*, **www.dallasnews.com/classifieds/jobcenter**.
- *Denver Post*, **www.postnewsmarketplace.com**.
- *Houston Chronicle*, **www.chron.com/class/jobs**.
- *Miami Herald*, **www.miami.com/mld/miamiherald/classifieds/employment**.
- *Las Vegas Review-Journal*, **www.reviewjournal.com/employment**.
- *Los Angeles Times*, **www.latimes.com/classified/jobs**.
- *The New York Times*, **www.nytimes.com/pages/jobs**.
- *Philadelphia Inquirer*, **www.philly.com/mld/philly/classifieds/employment**.
- *San Francisco Chronicle*, **www.sfgate.com/jobs**.
- *Seattle Times*,**http://classifieds.nwsource.com/jobs**.

- *Star Tribune* – for Minneapolis, **www.startribune.com/jobs**.
- *Washington Post* – for Washington, DC, **www.washingtonpost.com/wl/jobs/home**.

Recruitment Agencies

Recruitment agencies match tens of thousands of employers and job-seekers each year. Whether they are called 'Recruiters', 'Head-hunters' or 'Placement Firms' they all provide essentially the same service. Most have hundreds of contacts and are often aware of job vacancies before they are advertised. All reputable agencies get paid by the employer once a position is filled, so it is in their best interest to find you a job. Since their fee is often based on a percentage of the salary, they will also often work to get you as much money as possible. There are plenty of agencies that provide their service free of charge to job-seekers, so it is almost never worth paying a recruiter for their services. Be sure to ask up front before a recruiter does any work on your behalf.

Some recruiters specialise in certain fields and if you are particularly strong in a niche area it is certainly worth seeking these out – punching 'recruitment' and your job type and proposed location into an Internet search engine should find them. Some larger firms have offices not only throughout the USA but also in the UK, enabling you to start part of the process at home. The larger networks of recruitment agencies in the United States include the following:

- **I-Recruit (www.i-recruit.com)**. Provides links to hundreds of recruiters sorted by job category.
- **Recruiters Online Network (www.recruitersonline.com)**. Find hundreds of recruiters by field and location and even post your résumé online.
- **Recruiter Network (www.recruiternetwork.com)**. Send your résumé to hundreds of recruiters across the United States.
- **Search Firm (www.searchfirm.com)**. The largest recruitment directory for executives.

Temping and Contracting

With the current instabilities in the job market, temps and contractors have become increasingly common. The distinction between the two is blurry, but contractors usually perform more prestigious jobs and have assignments of six months or longer. Temping, on the other hand, is typically used to refer to shorter-term assignments and usually limited to less skilled administrative or manufacturing jobs. Both types of employment are highly likely to lead to permanent employment if the employer is satisfied with the work being performed, and so are a good way of getting a foot in the door. Sometimes you can effectively fill a job in this way that hasn't even been advertised.

The payroll of both temps and contractors is administered by the agency that finds their position. They are responsible for withholding taxes and sometimes offer additional benefits. Some contractors may even see greater take-home pay than the full-time employees with whom they are working. However, when budget cuts are made, temporary employees are the first to go.

Some of the larger temp agencies with offices across the USA are listed below. It's worth e-mailing them your résumé before you arrive in the States:

- **Account Temps (www.accounttemps.com).** A specialist in placing accounting and finance professionals.

- **Adecco (www.adeccousa.com).** This agency has hundreds of offices throughout the United States placing workers in all sorts of positions. Also try **www.adeccotechnical.com** for technical staffing.

- **Kelly Services (www.kellyservices.us).** Matches all kinds of workers with employers around the world.

- **Manpower (www.us.manpower.com).** One of the world's largest staffing agencies, with offices throughout North America and Europe.

- **Office Team (www.officeteam.com).** Places general administrative staffing around the country.

Direct Contact

If all else fails, or you are looking for a job in a really small part of the market, then sending out your résumé to potential employers is a worthwhile strategy. Cold-calling employers is not recommended; often you will only get to speak to a receptionist, who will insist you submit your résumé. Today just about every US company has its own website, and each is likely to have a section marked 'jobs' or 'careers', or 'working for us'. Here you will find a list of positions they are looking to fill and some general recruitment policy information.

Even if you don't find the perfect match, you can send a potential employer your résumé via e-mail. It costs nothing and takes little time, but bear in mind there are probably hundreds of others doing this too, so this scatter-gun approach is unlikely to yield many results or even responses. But if you can quickly convey that you offer something desirable, it may just pay off and land you the perfect job.

Sending a copy of your résumé on quality paper looks as if you have made a special effort and may help to get you noticed. However, this will quickly become costly and it's worth bearing in mind that most large companies will scan your résumé into their digital database and discard the paper version.

Some online services will offer to 'blast' or 'zap' your résumé to thousands of employers and recruiters for a fee typically between $50 and $100. This is probably only worth it if you don't have time to do the job yourself.

Interviews

The interview is often the most nerve-racking step in the process of finding a job. If you have been contacted for an interview, chances are your credentials are considered suitable, so this is your chance to sell your personality rather than your experience. There are hundreds of books and websites dedicated to interview skills and knowing how to answer every question imaginable. However, the two golden rules are to be yourself and try to ignore your nerves and so be relaxed and alert without being over-confident. Try also to put yourself in the interviewer's position – what would you be looking for? In particular, try to anticipate questions and queries regarding your experiences in the UK and what bearing these might have on working in the USA.

Many US companies now conduct a preliminary interview over the telephone before inviting you for a formal interview. These are normally short and simple and used by the employer to get a feel for whether or not the information on your résumé is accurate, if you are qualified for the job and if you have the basic phone skills necessary for the job. As long you are polite and professional you will be asked to come for a formal interview in person. Certainly avoid being lulled into a sense of informality on the phone, which is tempting. Some people find it helpful to stand when conducting business phone calls.

Arrive at your first interview on time and smartly dressed. Although your interviewer will have a series of questions prepared, the best interviews flow more like a conversation. This doesn't mean that you should chatter nervously about irrelevancies, but does mean you need to try to remain as relaxed and normal as possible. It's important to remember that Americans tend to be much more direct than Brits. Don't be surprised by comments or questions that may seem a bit abrupt at home, and try not to beat around the bush with any of your responses. Also be very wary of using sarcasm or humour, which is much less an understood part of life than it is in the UK and can easily go horribly wrong.

Leaving a good impression with the interviewer involves asking as well as answering questions well. Try to learn as much as possible about the company and the position before you arrive. Have a series of questions to ask the interviewer, as you will almost always be given the chance to ask them. This will demonstrate your enthusiasm. It is quite all right to ask about salary, but try to wait until the interviewer broaches the subject. It is always best to allow them to put a figure on the table but sometimes you will be led into stating a figure first. This can lead to a little game of cat and mouse that you can only win if you come well prepared. Know how much this type of position usually fetches. Know how much you are worth and be comfortable with saying it directly, but without sounding arrogant.

In addition to the typical question-and-answer session, be prepared for anything else that may come your way. Many companies now administer aptitude or psychometric tests. A test may be a simple measure of your typing skills or may involve a series of seemingly irrelevant questions that are used to test whether or not you give the same answer when the question is framed differently. For these types of tests, the important thing to remember is to answer honestly, not give the answer you think they want.

Drug testing for new employees is also becoming an increasingly common part of the recruitment process. Around half the applicants to medium- to large-sized companies will be required to undergo drug screening. Most companies opt for urine testing, which is an inexpensive and fairly inaccurate procedure. Some types of workers, such as those in law enforcement, drivers and heavy equipment operators, will also be subjected to random drug screening.

Conditions of Work

Working conditions in the USA are usually excellent, and great provision is made in law to see that you are fairly treated in the workplace. American workers are rewarded with more pay and, as you move up the ladder in status, more benefits than just about anywhere in the world. But these rewards come at a price and Americans work more hours than any other nation in the industrialised world. The average American works almost 2,000 hours per year – about 250 hours or 32 additional eight-hour days a year more than the average British worker. Beyond stipulating workplace safety, setting bare minimum wage and overtime rates and administering a basic pension and disability scheme, the government does little to regulate the employment sector. Many benefits are provided at the employer's discretion and it is up to individuals to ensure their overall security should they become ill or lose their job.

Contracts

American law does not require a contract to be signed between employer and employee, but most skilled professionals will be required to sign a contract to accept an offer of employment. However, many employees never see a contract or even think of it. Foreigners are often surprised by this and may be afraid to question the practice – which they should generally only do in larger companies and in better-paid positions.

Most employers abide by the terms they present when the job is offered; however, it's always a good idea to have the agreement in writing. And since American employers are not required to provide any benefits or paid time off, if they offer these verbally you may want to request a contract. If you are taking a long-term assignment in the United States with your current employer, you should sign a contract detailing all the terms of the assignment. Employment laws are very different in the United States and you don't want to find yourself in a new country with no medical insurance and less holiday time.

Even if a contract is signed, most employers reserve the right to void the contract within a probationary period of the first 90 days. This is usually only done if the employee proves completely inept or unsuitable or if the information given in the application process proves to be false.

Employment contracts are often long and filled with incomprehensible legal terms. Don't be afraid to take your time reviewing the entire document or to take it to someone more qualified. Many employers will provide an unnecessarily lengthy document, hoping to indemnify themselves in as many circumstances as possible. Usually, there is little you can do to have these clauses removed, but certainly be sure that all the benefits that have been discussed are in writing. The hourly or yearly salary should be clearly stated, along with whether the employee is 'exempt' or 'non-exempt'. Exempt employees are not entitled to the benefits and protection of the Fair Labor Standards Act of 1938 (**www.opm.gov/flsa/law.asp**), including overtime pay. Exempt employees are almost exclusively in management or other well-paid positions and are compensated rather generously for waiving these rights.

Wages

Wages in the United States will seem rather generous once you compare them with those in the UK, particularly when taking into account a lower cost of living. But these costs can vary tremendously depending on where you live: $25,000 per year will not go very far in San Francisco but give you a comfortable life in Alabama. For a comparison of up-to-date costs of living across the USA, check **www.bankrate.com/brm/movecalc.asp**. Bear in mind, when considering your net pay, that in positions of employment where you earn tips this is likely to constitute a considerable portion of your income in this way. Your basic pay will probably be low to reflect this, but should not fall below $2.13 per hour. Then, with tips added, you should be earning at least $5.15 per hour – the current federal minimum wage for all other jobs (though some states have a higher minimum wage; *see* **www.dol.gov/esa/minwage/america.htm**). If not, your employer is legally obliged to make up the difference.

Although every dollar of tips collected is technically subject to taxation, this rarely happens. Most servers report just enough to avoid raising eyebrows at the Internal Revenue Service. Although most recipients would prefer that they didn't, Americans are increasingly adding the tip to their credit card payment. This establishes a paper trail, forcing servers to report their tips.

Pay Rises

Pay increases ('raises') are never compulsory, other than to meet increases in the minimum wage or if they are stipulated in a union or a personal contract. They are certainly never a matter of course and most companies use their annual or six-monthly evaluations to decide whether or not to grant a raise. It may be necessary to remind or even pester a boss for the next raise. This sensitive matter will probably need to be addressed from year to year.

Hours and Overtime

The Fair Labor Standards Act requires all 'non-exempt' employees to be paid a rate of one and a half times the normal hourly rate for any work beyond 40 hours in one week (the 40 hours does not include lunch breaks, which can be either 30 minutes or one hour). Some employees, typically those in unions, receive overtime pay if they exceed eight hours in one day. Night shift workers often receive an extra 10 per cent, though this is not required by law. Skilled 'exempt' workers with higher salaries are normally expected to work 45 to 50 hours a week or more as needed.

The Standard Week

Traditional office hours are 9am to 5pm, but, where the nature of the work allows it, most businesses operate flexitime. Many companies require employees to clock in and out each day, even at the management level.

Holidays

Perhaps the hardest aspect of working in America is the meagre amount of holidays that workers receive. Though employers are not required to pay for any time off, most full-time employees do receive pay for their holidays (vacation) and bank holidays (also called three-day weekends). There are 10 federal holidays observed by all government offices, banks, and schools (*see* **References**, 'Holidays and Celebrations', p.227) and employees entitled to these days who are required to work will typically receive an additional day's pay. Most private offices and businesses will not observe all 10 holidays and employees with private companies can only expect to have New Year's Day, Memorial Day, Labor Day, Thanksgiving, and Christmas Day off.New employees can expect no more than 10 days' annual paid vacation when starting with a company. This will gradually increase to around 20 or 25 days after about 10 years of service.

Insurance and Benefits

Medical Insurance

The United States is the only industrialised nation without a national health insurance programme, and, though excellent healthcare is available, it comes with a hefty price tag. Even those visiting the USA on a holiday should not arrive without some sort of health insurance, and for long-term stays a good insurance plan is equally essential.

Some employers will offer a number of plans to choose from, of which they will pay a portion of the premium, while deducting the rest directly out of your pay cheque. Self-employed and contract workers should make a thorough investigation of available plans. There are many brokers listed in the Yellow Pages under 'health insurance' or 'insurance brokers', or you can try E Health Insurance (**www.ehealthinsurance.com**) to help you pick a plan that is right for you. Volumes have been written about the types of plans available and will be available in local libraries and bookshops.

See **Living in the USA**, pp.151–4.

Life Insurance

Employers are not required to offer life insurance but will generally provide each employee with a policy that, in the event of their death, will provide their next-of-kin with payouts to the value of half their annual salary. Employees will have the option to increase their policy to any level at their own expense.

Maternity Leave

Paid maternity leave is unusual in the USA but under federal law, enshrined in the Family and Medical Leave Act, both men and women are entitled to 12 weeks' unpaid leave without the risk of losing their job. Most employers are fairly sympathetic and flexible, however, and allow parents (dads too) to use a combination of short-term disability, sick leave and vacation time to either ensure income during their maternity leave or in some cases extend it.

Sickness Leave and Disability Benefit

Paid sick leave is not required under federal law, but many companies will allow employees to earn paid sick days. Expect to earn about one day every six weeks.

Disability insurance varies considerably from state to state. Some states require either the employer or employee (or both) to pay into a short-term disability insurance plan administered either by the state or a private insurance company. This is often referred to as workmen's compensation or worker's comp. If unable to work, an employee with the plan will receive a percentage of their pay (around 60 per cent) for a specified period of about six months. Disability benefits are not paid until all accrued sick time is exhausted. Long-term disability is an optional insurance programme similar to short-term disability. Employees are entitled to a percentage of their salary for a period of up to 10 years in the event of a catastrophic illness or injury. Paying into a plan is always a good idea, even if it is not a requirement; monthly payments vary with your salary but are typically only a few dollars a month.

Unemployment Benefits

Each state administers its own unemployment insurance fund, which is backed by a federal unemployment programme. The requirements and benefit schedules vary by state, but some generalisations can be made. With the exception of three states (Alaska, New Jersey and Pennsylvania), which require a nominal contribution from employees, all funding is provided solely by employer-imposed premiums.

In order to receive benefits you must be unemployed through no fault of your own, so resigning, being dismissed for misconduct or leaving due to illness (*see* 'Sickness Leave and Disability Benefit', p.209) will not entitle you to any benefits.

Payments to the unemployed are typically calculated as a percentage of your earnings over the first 12 of the last 15 months. Maximum benefits vary greatly by state but typically reflect that state's cost of living. In 2004, the maximum benefit for an individual in Mississippi was $210 a month while in Massachusetts it was $508.

State law usually limits benefits to 26 weeks, but extensions are made during times of high unemployment. You will be expected to search for work while receiving payments and it may necessary to provide evidence of this, though authorities find this difficult to enforce.

Pensions

Virtually all American workers must contribute to the **federal social security retirement programme**. This means 7.65 per cent of an employee's salary (up to $90,000) is deducted directly from their pay cheque with their employer paying a matching amount (the self-employed pay 15.3 per cent). This programme currently pays retirees over the age of 65 a monthly payment that's calculated on the basis of their lifetime contributions. This is generally fairly meagre, so a private scheme is pretty much essential (*see* **Living in the USA**, 'Retirement and Pensions', pp.155–8).

A reciprocal agreement between the USA and UK (and most EU countries) means that no one is required to pay into state pension schemes in both countries. If you have been working in the USA for a UK employer for less than six years, or if you work in the USA for the UK government, you will continue to pay into the UK scheme. Those working for a US company, the self-employed, or those working more than six years in the USA for a UK company, will pay into the US scheme. Those working in the USA on a J-, M-, F- and Q-type visa are exempt from contributing to the US system.

For further information contact the **US Social Security Adminstration** at **t** 1-800-772-1213, or view their UK agreement pamphlet at **www.ssa.gov/international/Agreement_Pamphlets/uk.html**.

Dismissal and Termination Indemnity

Employers avoid dismissing (firing) individuals without just cause through fear of costly lawsuits and because their own unemployment insurance premiums increase as they lay off more employees. However, almost all employers reserve the right to fire anyone at any time without notice for the usual reasons of misconduct and ineptitude.

Though there is no government regulation determining the level of termination indemnity, most large companies making redundancies will offer a severance package depending on the employee's length of service. Employees of smaller companies may receive nothing. Depending on state unemployment law, severance payments usually delay eligibility for unemployment benefits.

Running Your Own Business

For many, self-employment and the freedoms and rewards that it can bring are fundamental to the American Dream. There are countless tales of penniless immigrants striking it rich in the USA. American laws and culture create an environment that welcomes the entrepreneur – perhaps more than anywhere else in the world. Despite some xenophobia in some parts of the country, a good business that provides customers with what they want should always succeed.

US immigration laws (*see* **Red Tape**, pp.115–126) are particularly friendly to wealthy foreign business-owners. Large business investors ($1 million or more) are typically granted immigrant status if starting or purchasing a business in the United States. Smaller business investors may qualify for an E visa, which can be repeatedly extended as long as the business remains successful.

The lack of government regulation and intervention means that anyone with experience of running a business elsewhere should find it considerably easier in the United States. The regulations that exist vary from state to state, but for small business they are usually easily understood and never much of a hindrance. Once a company goes public, the level of regulations increases and it is best to consult a lawyer.

Types of Business

United States businesses operate under a variety of legal structures, though most will fit into the categories detailed below. The principal difference lies in the tax and legal liability of each owner. None of them is difficult to establish and choosing between them should usually be based on the advice of a business expert or tax attorney.

Sole Proprietorships

Sole proprietorships are the simplest and easiest businesses to start. In almost every state, nothing need be done to open for business. Technically, once any individual conducts any business, even just selling an item on eBay, a sole proprietorship has been established. However, depending on the type of business conducted, certain permits or registration may be necessary. In California, all businesses require a licence even though it is difficult to determine when exactly you go from selling an item to running a business. If your business will operate under a fictitious name, many states will require registration so that there is a record of who owns the business. If your business will be operated out of your home, there may be zoning regulations to consider. Therefore, it is best to check with state and local offices to ensure legal compliance. Registration fees for sole proprietorships are usually less than $100. Permit fees will vary from nothing to hundreds of dollars for businesses selling or distributing liquor or handling hazardous materials.

Any debt, income or lawsuits connected with a sole proprietorship are inseparable from the owner. A separate tax return for the business is not filed. Instead, income from the business is reported as personal income.

Partnerships

Any proprietorship with more than one owner becomes a partnership. Laws pertaining to partnerships are similar to those of sole proprietorships and nothing needs to be done by the owners to legally conduct business. A partnership without a formal agreement between the owners is a **general partnership**. If the business is sued or cannot pay a debt, either owner can be held responsible. If a **limited partnership** is established, one owner has limited personal liability with the company. In either case, both parties can bind the company to a contract. It is therefore essential that you trust the person with whom you form a partnership. It is not necessary to have a written contract with a partner, but it is unwise not to have some sort of formal agreement. If a limited partnership is not done properly, both parties can be fully liable. Also be aware that if a spouse carries on business or shares in profits, he or she may be a partner in the business. Again, it is best to seek professional advice.

Corporations

Incorporating (forming a limited company) provides business owners with several advantages they wouldn't have as a sole proprietorship or partnership. Most notably, a corporation limits their personal liability for debts accrued by the company, or against any lawsuits. It also allows owners to finance their company with any number of shareholders.

The first step to forming a corporation is to file '**articles of corporation**' with the office of the secretary of the state that will be home to your business. These are fairly simple forms that can be completed by anyone, but it is advisable to have a lawyer review the papers before you sign them. For a new small business the whole process will cost between $200 and $1,000 depending on state and lawyer's fees. Contact information for every secretary of state's office can be found on the Internet at **soswy.state.wy.us/sos/sos2.htm**.

Loosely enforced requirements on small corporations such as writing bylaws, issuing stock certificates and holding regularly scheduled meetings are contained in the 'articles of corporation'. These laws apply even if only one person has a vested interest in the company. While it is not necessary to prove to the state that any of this is done, it is advisable to do these things and keep a record of them in the event that your corporation runs into legal trouble (a real risk in the most litigious country in the world). Unless you plan to maintain a very small business, having a business lawyer is highly recommended.

Chairmen of a corporation must ensure that the business maintains formal and organised records for every transaction done in its name. Once a business is incorporated, it will be subject to an entirely different tax code and it is advisable to consult an accountant.

Incorporating a business does not have to be done in the state in which business is conducted. The 'headquarters' of many large companies consists of nothing more than a post office box with no actual business needing to be carried out in the state; nor do any records need to remain there. As a result, a disproportionate number of corporations decide to operate from Delaware with its relaxed incorporation laws, low costs and efficient administrators. Other states may have incentives for you to incorporate with them, and local incorporation experts should be consulted before making the move.

Joint Ventures and Limited Liability Companies

Joint ventures and limited liability companies (LLCs) make up almost all other American businesses. Joint ventures are general partnerships established to carry out one or more business transactions or projects. Beyond this, there is no further relationship. An LLC is sort of a cross between a partnership and corporation. An LLC offers the limited liability of a corporation while taxation is based on each partner's personal gains and losses rather than the corporations a whole.

Starting a Business

True entrepreneurial spirits would settle for nothing less than starting a new business from the ground up. A new business allows for complete freedom in every aspect of a new company. However, though the rewards are potentially infinite, starting a new business is a risky endeavour and most new businesses fail in their first few years. Less risky options are to buy an existing business or set up a franchise, but, whatever you do, securing capital and setting up a business plan are likely to prove crucial.

An ideal place to start investigating the ins and outs of starting and running a small business in the USA is with the federally sponsored **Small Business Administration**, 409 Third Street, SW Washington, DC 20416, **t** 1-800-U-ASK-SBA, **www.sba.gov**. It provides a wealth of information for starting and financing small businesses and has links to similar state-run programmes on its website.

If you already own a successful company in the UK, you'll likely find the United States a very welcoming market for its expansion. The **British American Business Council** (**www.babc.org**), which helps promote US–UK business relationships, and the **UK Trade and Investment** (**www.uktradeinvest.gov.uk**), which supports all UK companies doing business overseas, are two places that may help you get started.

Capital and the Business Plan

The first step to owning your own business is finding the necessary capital to get things off the ground, and creating an excellent business plan is a big part of this process.

Private and governmental financing for new businesses is readily available in the USA, and American and foreign business-owners are often delighted and surprised at the level of help that federal and state programmes offer to small businesses. Banks and government programmes are only interested in one thing – investing in sound business plans that will make money. But if they like your ideas they will readily offer you thousands of dollars in loans and advice each year. In most cases, the level of assistance is the same no matter whether you are foreign or not, but having permanent residency should will increase your chances of assistance. Without your own funds, these programmes will often be your only source of capital, since UK banks will not typically lend money to those starting a business overseas – though they will finance UK businesses expanding into the USA.

To be considered for any business loan you will have to provide a sound business plan. These serve as a road map for your venture. Whether you are asking for $100 or $1 million, your lender will need to know how you plan to spend every dollar. Just like a résumé, this document needs to be impeccable and is best prepared with the help of a professional. Creating a business plan will help in ways you may not have imagined. Putting a plan on paper forces you to think clearly about every detail. You may discover a potential or a pitfall you hadn't considered. It provides you with benchmarks for which you can strive. You will also need to take a hard look at the competition and see where your business might be better. If nothing else, a business plan will help you decide whether or not you want to proceed with your existing idea.

The outline below gives an idea of what needs to go into this 30–40-page document; but for detailed advice on how to write a good business plan *see* www.sba.gov/starting_business/planning/writingplan.html.

The Basic Elements of a Business Plan

Cover page:
- business name
- contact information
- company logo

Executive summary:
- a clear, concise, three-paragraph summary of entire document
- business concept, market background, legal structure, anticipated requested loan amount, anticipated returns, repayment schedule

Overview of proposed business:
- description of the business
- the product or service to be offered
- pricing information

Market background:
- history and status of the existing market

Market potential:
- shortcomings in the existing market
- how this business will differ

Marketing strategy:
- marketing methods used to promote the business

Stage of development:
- current state of the business
- steps needed to get the business running

Operations:
- plan for operations of the business
- production costs, margins, necessary resources

Management:
- organisational structure
- background of key individuals
- personnel needs

Financials:
- estimated production costs
- breakdown of requested funds
- projected revenues

- return on investment
- exit strategies

Appendices:
- any other supplementary documents that support the plan
- personal résumés, references, leases, contracts, site plan

Buying a Business

Buying an existing business is an easier and safer option and ideal for those who prefer a low-risk alternative or think they can see a new way of doing something much more profitably. There is much less time and money involved in start-up and income is likely to begin immediately, through the business's existing customer base. The problem is that the price tag attached to an existing business is likely to directly reflect its profitability. If a business is successful and profits are flowing in, it will come at a significant cost. If you find

Location, Location, Location!

Choosing where to establish your business in the USA is not a matter to be taken lightly in a country where local laws, taxes and regulations can vary drastically from state to state and the business environment – the infrastructure, competition and staff costs – varies between regions.

At the largest scale, the country's division into the 'blue', progressive, left-wing states of the northeast and west coast and the 'red' conservative, right-wing states of the southern and central USA is mirrored in business. The 'blue' states tend to tax and regulate businesses more, while 'red' states have a more *laissez-faire* attitude.

But specialisations also exist within these areas. The northeast has most of America's financial companies; the midwest is a strong manufacturing area with experienced labour and extensive infrastructure; the south is best place to find cheap labour; while the west has the largest number of skilled technology professionals (*see* appropriate sections in **Profiles of the Regions**, pp.35–62).

At an even more localised level there are patterns of growth and development to consider. Some inner-city areas formerly in decline are now being regenerated, forming gentrified areas where small specialist shops, boutiques or restaurants can thrive. Yet in small-town America city centres continue to die, as large corporations develop strip malls of chain retail outlets and restaurants on their fringes.

Clearly you will need to do your homework on every geographic scale, and the development of a business plan will force you to consider these factors. The crucial link to make is interpreting what patterns apply to the success or failure of specifically your type of business.

a business that is quite a bargain, you should be wary and carefully establish the reason. Small local business offered for sale can be found listed in the classified section of most newspapers. Look for 'businesses for sale' or 'business opportunities' near the help wanted section. On the web try **www.businessesforsale.com** and **www.bizbuysell.com**.

The advice of a licensed business broker, which can be found in the Yellow Pages or on the web, is recommended.

Before purchasing a business, investigate it thoroughly. As always, good research is key. A wise business owner will ask you to sign a confidentiality agreement. This restricts you from using the information you acquire for any purpose other than to ascertain the state of the business and forbids you from sharing the information with anyone other than your lawyer or accountant. While there may be many legitimate and potentially profitable businesses on the market, much of what you see advertised will invariably be overpriced, have hidden pitfalls or be an outright scam. In any of these cases you may have legal recourse, but this will no doubt be costly and time-consuming.

Franchises

Investing in a franchise is the cheapest and most straightforward way of obtaining an E-2 visa (see **Red Tape**, p.121). It is also a good stepping-stone for new entrepreneurs. The capital needed to get a new business off the ground can be prohibitive and often the most difficult part of starting a new business. For a fraction of the cost, anyone can buy the rights to a franchise of a proven product or service. Whether you want to sell cheeseburgers, mobile phones or cars, the franchiser will provide most of what is needed, including goods, some advertising and advice on other aspects, such as hiring employees and complying with state and federal law.

The down side of owning a franchise is that it may not provide the level of independence you are seeking. Franchise owners are forced to abide by strict contract details and are allowed little input towards business decisions. Although you can expect to share all profits, the fact that you can buy and sell only franchise products and need to deal with a managerial bureaucracy means that owning a franchise can differ little from being an employee in a large corporation. It is also necessary to consider the risk of the franchiser going out of business or merging with another company. Should this occur, a qualified lawyer would be necessary to pursue maximum recourse.

If you are considering buying a franchise, be sure to research the company extensively. Good sources of information are the **Better Business Bureau** (**www.bbb.org**), and existing franchise holders. There is also an annual **Franchise Expo** (**www.franchiseexpo.com**), which even offers special advice and incentives for international visitors. Be certain to have a lawyer review any contract before you sign.

Employees

As businesses grow, the need to take on staff becomes almost inevitable. Finding the right people will not be easy, and the costs of hiring the wrong person can be high. Fortunately for business owners, US labour laws don't make it difficult to dismiss employees. However, disgruntled employees may make it difficult for you. Among other laws in a prosecutor's arsenal, Title VII of the Civil Rights Act of 1964 'prohibits employment discrimination based on race, color, religion, sex and national origin'. If accused of violating this or any other employment or safety law, the burden of proof will be on the employer. This can costs thousands of dollars in time and legal fees. Therefore, while it is relatively simple to dismiss an employee, it still comes with some risk.

It would therefore be best to hire the right person right away; and the best way to fill a position is often by referral. Advertising through a newspaper or online may result in hundreds of applicants, from whom it may be difficult to choose and necessitate a series of time-consuming interviews.

The paperwork involved with hiring employees can be mind-numbing – hence the size of human resource departments in larger companies. Paying social security and payroll taxes, health and unemployment insurance, certifying a person's right to work and ensuring compliance with the federal **Occupational Health and Safety Administration** (**OSHA**; **www.osha.gov**) are just some of the responsibilities involved with taking on employees. You might like to enlist the help of a human resource service to handle the whole process; some of the larger firms are **ADP** (**www.adp.com**) and **Paychex** (**www.paychex.com**). Smaller companies may want to check with local temp and recruitment agencies, as some offer these services for a fee that may be less than those of the larger firms.

If you need an extra hand but are unsure about hiring a full-time employee, there are a few options. Hiring someone 'under the table' is always a possibility, but the penalties for those who are caught can be severe and it is not recommended unless you know and trust the person well. Temp agencies can provide staff with skills ranging from manual labour to secretarial or computer experts. The hourly cost is high but may be worth it. Hiring a temp may help you decide the extra staff member isn't needed, or it may help you find the perfect person that you choose to hire full time – though the latter will incur a hefty 'finder's fee' from the temp agency.

Taxes

Businesses are taxed according to their classification, and owners of a sole proprietorship or partnership simply file taxes as an individual. Corporations must file wholly separate tax returns unless they choose to establish an 'S' corporation, in which case an individual return is filed. Classification as an 'S' corporation is restricted to businesses with small income and a limited number of shareholders.

Other corporations file a federal tax return very different from that of individuals. It is not recommended that you attempt to do this without the help of a qualified accountant. In most states, a state return must be filed as well. Unlike individual returns, where state taxes are fairly simple to file, corporate state tax can be very complex, since states compete with each other to attract business and all offer different and sometimes archaic incentives.

If your business has a presence on both sides of the Atlantic, it is vital that you see an accountant specialising in international tax law, since most European countries have agreements preventing double taxation on corporate income.

Working Holidays

Young people looking for a 'working holiday' in the USA will find a number of opportunities lasting from a few months to a whole year. Many exchange programmes will sponsor a visa and make all the arrangements before you leave the UK. Applications can take several months to process so it is vital to plan at least six months ahead. Start by contacting one of the sponsor programmes that have an office in the UK.

The biggest sectors involve working with children as an au pair or summer camp counsellor. These positions entail a great deal of responsibility; and in each the notoriously demanding American children will likely test your patience – so a genuine desire to work with children is a vital prerequisit. Every year hundreds of counsellors break off their contracts to return home, despite the penalties that this entails, so the move should not be considered lightly. Generally, too, neither type of job is well-paid, and most au pairs and counsellors will be unable to return home with any savings, particularly if they take time to travel in the USA. All that being said, those who welcome the thought of spending a summer with children of a different culture will find the whole process an excellent way to build up their CV.

Other seasonal areas of work include working at ski resorts and volunteering on environmental projects in exchange for bed and board.

Au Pair Work

Each year thousands of people (predominantly women) come from around the world to serve as an au pair for an American family. Although it is possible to come to the USA and find au pair work in exchange for room and board (technically illegal on a tourist visa), there are enough legal opportunities for those who are qualified. Currently six au pair exchange programmes are recognised by the US Department of State. Requirements and pay are mandated by the US government and so very similar between programmes. To qualify, each candidate must:

- be between 18 and 26 years of age.
- have at least 200 hours of childcare experience.
- have completed secondary school education.
- have no criminal record.
- hold a valid driving licence.
- be able to commit to an entire 12-month period with one family.

Additionally, each candidate will go through a rigorous screening process, including a background check, interviewing and reference checks that may well feel intrusive. Bear in mind that all applicants are potentially entrusted with the care of someone's child. The Louise Woodward case – the 19-year-old British au pair who was convicted of the involuntary manslaughter of an 8-month-old baby – is forever ingrained in the minds of many American parents.

In exchange for their service, au pairs receive a one-year J-1 exchange visa, room and board, plus a fixed pay rate of $139 a month. Other benefits generally include a study allowance, health insurance plan, return flight and an optional 13th month of self-financed travel. Additional pay is given to 'au pairs extraordinaires' who possess qualified childcare or nursing certification. Many au pair hosts are fairly wealthy and provide au pairs with additional cash and benefits, though this is technically illegal.

Any of the following six recognised programmes can be contacted. Four agencies currently have offices in the UK:

- **Au Pair Care**, 600 California St, FL 10, San Francisco, CA 94108, **t** (415)-434-8788, **www.aupaircare.com**.

- **Au Pair in America**, 37 Queens Gate, London SW7 5HR, **t** (020) 7581 7322, **www.aupairinamerica.co.uk**.

- **Au Pair Homestay USA**, EIL 287 Worcester Road, Malvern, Worcs WR14 1AB, **t** (01684) 562577.

- **Euraupair: Intercultural Child Care Programs**, 250 North Coast Highway, Laguna Beach, CA 92651, **t** 1-800-333-3804.

- **Exploring Cultural & Learning/Au Pair Registry (Au Pair Program USA)**, 6955 Union Park Center, Suite 360, Salt Lake City, Utah 84047, **t** 1-800-574-8889.

- **Interchange Au Pair**, 161 Sixth Avenue 13th Floor, New York, NY 10013, **t** 1-800-287-2477.

Camp Counsellors

Summer camps across the USA hire thousands of young people each year through qualified visa exchange programmes. Counsellors supervise children in all their daily activities, from brushing their teeth to team sports. Some camps specialise in certain activities and skilled counsellors are highly sought-after. Soccer (football) camps have become very popular and routinely recruit qualified footballers from overseas. For those with experience with disabled children, specialised camps may offer additional benefits.

Counsellors are required to commit to at least eight weeks of work to obtain a J-1 visa. The air fare to the USA plus room and board are provided, with the registration fee starting at £65. On completion of the job, counsellors will have earned their return air fare to London (if they quit early they need to pay some or all of this back) and $600–$1,000 depending on the counsellor's age and job duties. After the eight-week commitment is filled, the J-1 visa allows for additional travel of up to 10 weeks. Contact:

- **Bunac**, 16 Bowling Green Lane, London EC1R 0QH, **t** (020) 7251 3472, **www.bunac.org**.
- **Camp America**, 37a Queen's Gate, London SW7 5HR, UK, **t** (020) 7581 7373, **www.campamerica.co.uk**.
- **Camp Counselors USA**, 1st Floor North, Devon House, 171–177 Great Portland Street, London W1W5PQ, **t** (020) 7637 0779, **www.ccusa.com**.
- **Camp Leaders**, 57 Seel Street, Liverpool L1 4AZ, **t** 0845 430 1219, **www.campleaders.com**.
- **International Counselor Exchange Program**, 38 West 88th Street, New York, NY 10024, **t** 212-787-7706, **www.international-counselors.org**.

Ski Resorts

Ski enthusiasts the world over flock to the USA each year to fill seasonal jobs in the major ski resorts. Pay is low and expenses are high, but employment with a resort means unlimited skiing when off the clock. Plenty of young Americans are willing to fill these jobs, but some resorts offer a number of positions to foreign applicants.

Students already holding a J-1 visa are eligible to work at most resorts for up to four months. Some larger resorts will sponsor applicants for their H-2B visa. These positions are limited and typically fill before the season begins. You should apply no later than June for positions in the following winter season. Several strong recruitment websites exist for ski industry jobs exist including **www.resortjobs.com**, **www.natives.co.uk**, **www.coolworks.com**, **www.jobsinparadise.com** and **www.skiingthenet.com**. But probably the best strategy to find a job is to contact the resorts themselves – having first carefully examined their websites. Most resorts have sections on their websites about working for them, and about seasonal employment possibilities in particular. The largest sponsor for H-2B visa is **Vail Resorts**, Human Resource Office; Admin Building; 600 West Lionshead Circle; Vail, Colorado 81658, **t** 1-888-SKI-JOB1, **www.vailresorts.com**, which operates four mountains in Colorado and one in

California. Another key place to look is **www.wework2play.com**, which covers several of the largest resorts in the North American ski industry. Links to these and almost all other US ski areas can be found on **www.skicentral.com**.

Short-term Volunteer Projects

See 'Volunteering', 'Working Outdoors', below right.

Volunteering

Volunteering is a wonderful chance to meet new people, become part of a new community and feel positive, by doing some socially or environmentally useful work. Whether it's working with people in need, animals or in the great outdoors, the opportunities to volunteer in the United States are virtually limitless. Additionally, those looking for the perfect job in a small area of expertise may find that volunteering may just enable you to meet someone who can help. Requirements for volunteers vary considerably so be sure to check carefully with each agency before arriving.

To find the right volunteer organisation in your community, check with local churches, libraries, community centres and animal shelters or contact one of these groups that match volunteers with the right organisation:

• **USA Freedom Corps** was founded in 2002 to help match volunteers with organisations in their area based on skills and interests. The Corps works closely with America's government-run domestic volunteer organisations such as Citizen Corps, AmeriCorps and Senior Corps. Contact them at 1600 Pennsylvania Avenue NW, Washington, DC 20500, **t** 1-877-USA-CORPS, **www.usafreedomcorps.gov**.

• **Volunteer Abroad** (**www.volunteerabroad.com/unitedstates.cfm**) lists thousands of opportunities around the world including the United States.

• **Volunteer Match** (**www.volunteermatch.org**) has an online database, which allows for searches of organisations by area, fields of interest and organisational affiliation.

Working with Children

Founded by the United Nations General Assembly in 1946, UNICEF helps children around the globe to grow up healthy, safe and educated. The **United States Fund for UNICEF**, 333 East 38th Street, New York, NY 10016, **t** 800-4-UNICEF, **www.unicefusa.org**, is the oldest of 37 national branches of UNICEF. The headquarters are in New York with offices in Atlanta, Boston, Chicago,

Houston and Los Angles, but volunteer opportunities exist in communities throughout the country.

Big Brothers Big Sisters, 230 North 13th St, Philadelphia, PA 19107, **t** 215-567-7000, **www.bbbsa.org**, provides a fantastic opportunity to mentor a young person in need of role model. Volunteers are paired with youths who typically come from single parent homes. 'Bigs' meet with their 'littles' once a week to serve as a friend and adviser.

YMCA of the USA, **www.ymca.net/kfc/volunteer.htm**, has volunteer opportunities at all of its 2500 US affiliates.

Working with the Elderly

Meals on Wheels (**www.mowaa.org**) provides companionship and delivers hot, nutritious meals to the homes of elderly Americans around the country.

Senior Corps (**www.seniorcorps.org**) is for pensioners who want to give help rather than receive it. Sponsored by the federal government, Senior Corps is a network of programmes that provide seniors with opportunities to share their experience and skills with those in need.

Working Outdoors

America's **National Parks** (**www.nps.gov/volunteer/**) need volunteers for long- and short-term projects every summer, for one day or an entire summer. Positions can be administrative, deal with practical conservation issues or see you attending to the needs of the public; volunteers maintain trails, act as tour guides, or host a campsite.

Similar opportunities exist with the **National Forest Service** (**www.fs.fed.us/fsjobs/volunteers.html**) and within each state's park system.

Volunteer vacation and trail maintenance opportunities also exist throughout the country with the **American Hiking Society** (**www.americanhiking.org**).

Volunteer Abroad (**www.volunteerabroad.com/unitedstates.cfm**) lists thousands of opportunities around the world, including close to 100 in the USA, for a variety of exciting volunteer possibilities. Projects range from working with endangered wildlife, on a dig or with impoverished rural minorities.

Working with Social Services

Citizen Corps (**www.citizencorps.gov**) is the branch of USA Freedom Corps that co-ordinates volunteer activities in the event of a natural or terrorist disaster. Trained and willing volunteers are among the first to respond when disaster strikes.

Habitat for Humanity International (**www.habitat.org**) builds simple, afford-able homes for families in need. Houses are built with volunteer money, material and sweat. Volunteers and home-owners raise homes in as little as one day. This is a great opportunity to learn and share valuable skills.

The **American Red Cross** (**www.redcross.org**) provides humanitarian aid to victims of disasters around the world. In addition to helping people prepare, prevent and respond to natural disasters, the Red Cross is America's largest supplier of blood products to hospitals and international disaster sites.

Reading is Fundamental (**www.rif.org**) helps bring the joy of reading to children. Volunteers distribute books and tutor children living in areas vulnerable to inferior education.

References

The USA at a Glance

Capital city: Washington, DC.

Official name of country: United States of America.

Head of government: President George W. Bush.

Area: 9,158,918 sq km (includes the lower 48 states, and Alaska and Hawaii).

Width of the USA (east–west): 4,421km.

Length of the USA (north–south): 2,572km.

Geographic highlights: The USA encompasses elements of almost all of the world's environments and ecosystems. Three dominant mountain ranges cut through the USA running north–south. They are the Appalachians in the east, the Rocky Mountains just west of the middle and the Sierra Nevada range in the west. The land between these ranges is relatively flat. This is particularly so in the centre of the continent whose northern part is dominated by the presence of the Great Lakes. These five huge bodies of fresh water are surrounded by thousands of smaller lakes.

States within the USA: Alabama, Alaska, Arizona, Arkansas, California, Colorado, Connecticut, Delaware, Florida, Georgia, Hawaii, Idaho, Illinois, Indiana, Iowa, Kansas, Kentucky, Louisiana, Maine, Maryland, Massachusetts, Michigan, Minnesota, Mississippi, Missouri, Montana, Nebraska, Nevada, New Hampshire, New Jersey, New Mexico, New York, North Carolina, North Dakota, Ohio, Oklahoma, Oregon, Pennsylvania, Rhode Island, South Carolina, South Dakota, Tennessee, Texas, Utah, Vermont, Virginia, Washington, West Virginia, Wisconsin and Wyoming.

Languages: The USA has no official language and, as a country built by immigrants, most of the world's major languages are spoken somewhere. Additionally, Native American tribes, especially the larger tribes such as the Navaho in the southwest, maintain their own languages. English is the most common language, although there is also a large Spanish minority, particularly in Florida and California. The 10 most popular languages, based on what is spoken at home, are English (198 million), Spanish (17 million), French (1.7 million), German (1.5 million), Italian (1.3 million), Chinese (1.2 million), Tagalog (850,000), Polish (750,000), Korean (630,000), Vietnamese (500,000) and Portuguese (430,000).

Bordering countries: Canada, Mexico.

Surrounding seas: Atlantic Ocean, Gulf of Mexico and Pacific Ocean; Alaska is surrounded by the Bering Sea, the Chukchi Sea and the Gulf of Alaska.

Population: 290,809,777.

Religion: Predominantly Christian with half the population Protestant and a quarter Roman Catholic; sizeable Mormon, Jewish and Muslim minorities.

GDP growth rate: 3.1 per cent.
GDP per capita: $37,800.
Unemployment: 6 per cent.

Holidays and Celebrations

National Holidays

On national holidays you may find information offices closed, museums open for shorter hours and public transport running Sunday services. Some shops, banks and offices are likely to be closed.

Days that are celebrated nationwide are:

1 January	New Year's Day
Third Mon in January	Martin Luther King Day
Third Mon in February	Presidents' Day
Last Mon in May	Memorial Day
4 July	Independence Day
First Mon in September	Labor Day
Second Mon in Oct	Columbus Day
11 November	Veterans' Day
Fourth Thurs in November	Thanksgiving Day
25 December	Christmas Day

Major Celebrations

January	**Chinese New Year**. In the last two weeks in January or early February, Chinese communities across the USA are awash with colour. The parade in San Francisco is among the most spectacular.
January	**Superbowl Sunday**. The grand finale to the American Football season and the worlds' largest televised sporting event. Watched by millions, many of whom gather in Superbowl parties; as much about the advertising between plays and the half-time show as the sport. The date varies, and is sometimes in early February.
February	**Mardi Gras**. Two weeks in late February or early March are given over to parades and revelry, with the celebrations in New Orleans historically the most flamboyant and hedonistic.
17 March	**St Patrick's Day**. The traditionally Irish strongholds of New York, Boston and Chicago are smothered in a blaze of green. Huge parades are followed by heavy drinking.

March/April	**Easter**. Churches pack out on Easter Sunday and children hunt for painted eggs hidden by the Easter bunny.
5 May	*Cinco de Mayo*. A celebration of all things Mexican, which is heartily embraced by the country's sizeable Hispanic community. The date is significant as the day on which the Mexicans destroyed the French army in 1862.
2nd Sun in May	**Mother's Day**. Mothers all around the nation receive cards and flowers.
3rd Sun in June	**Father's Day**. Fathers are honoured with cards and gifts.
June	**Gay Pride**. Most larger cities have flamboyant parades and events to celebrate gay culture. San Francisco stretches its celebrations out for a whole month.
4 July	**Independence Day**. Every city and town has some form of parade to commemorate American Independence; fireworks follow at night. Oddly, Chicago's celebrations are largely on 3 June.
31 October	**Hallowe'en**. Children and adults alike don fancy dress. Children go trick-or-treating from door to door for candy; adults often head to parties. Costumes are of any nature – the more creative the better – and don't necessarily follow a ghoulish theme.
2 November	**Day of the Dead**. A day of commemoration for dead friends and relatives, largely celebrated by Hispanic communities. Candy skulls and skeletons are popular and not considered in poor taste.
4th Thurs in November	**Thanksgiving**. Modern-day harvest festival, which is as important as Christmas as a family occasion. Families gather to gorge themselves on all-day meals traditionally involving a turkey and a big roast. A huge parade takes place in New York.
25 December	**Christmas**. A mix of religious and secular rituals to commemorate the birth of Christ. Concerts, parties, carols, church services, eggnog and, of course, present-giving.
December	**Chanukah**. An eight-day Jewish holiday whose date is determined by the Hebrew Calendar. Also called Hanukkah.
31 December	**New Year's Eve**. General partying and revelry to celebrate the coming of the New Year.

Regional Climate Charts

Average Seasonal Temperatures (°C)

City	Jan	Feb	Mar	Apr	May	June	July	Aug	Sept	Oct	Nov	Dec
Atlanta, GA	10	13	18	23	26.5	30	31	30.5	28	23	17	12
Baltimore, MD	4.5	6.5	12	18	23	28.5	30.5	29.5	26	19.5	14	7
Birmingham, AL	11	14	19	24	27	30.5	32	31.5	29	24	18.5	13
Boston, MA	2	3.5	8	13	19.5	24.5	28	26.5	23	17	11	4.5
Buffalo, NY	−1	0	5.5	12	19	24	26.5	25.5	21.5	15	8.5	1.5
Charlotte, NC	9.5	11.5	16.5	21.5	25.5	30	31.5	31	28	22	17	11
Chicago, IL	−1.5	1	8	15	21	26.5	29	28	24	17	9	1
Cleveland, OH	0	1.5	8	14.5	20.5	25.5	28	27	23	16.5	10	3
Columbus, OH	1	3.5	10.5	16.5	22	26.5	29	28	24.5	18.5	10.5	4
Dallas-Fort Worth, TX	12	15	20	24.5	28.5	33	36	35.5	31	26	19.5	14.5
Denver, CO	6	8.5	11	16.5	21.5	27	31	30	25	19	11.5	7
Detroit, MI	−1	0.5	6.5	14.5	21	26	28.5	27	23	16.5	9	1.5
Green Bay, WI	−5	−3	4	12	19.5	24.5	27	25.5	20.5	14	5.5	−2
Hartford, CT	0.5	2	8.5	15.5	22	26.5	29.5	28.5	24	18	10.5	3.5
Honolulu, HI	26.5	27	28	28.5	29.5	30.5	31	31.5	31.5	30.5	29	27
Houston, TX	16	18.5	21.5	25.5	29.5	32	34	34	31	28	22	18.5
Indianapolis, IN	1	3.5	10.5	17	23	28.5	30	29	25.5	19	11	4
Jacksonville, FL	18	19.5	23	26	29.5	31.5	33	33	30.5	26.5	23	19.5
Kansas City, MO	1.5	5	11.5	18.5	23	28.5	31.5	30	25.5	20	11.5	4
Las Vegas, NV	14	17	20.5	25.5	31	38	41	39.5	35	28	19.5	14.5
Lincoln, NE	0	3.5	10	18	23	29.5	32	30.5	25	19.5	10	2
Little Rock, AR	9.5	12	18	23	27	31.5	33	33	29.5	24	17	11.5
Los Angeles, CA	20	20.5	21	22	23	25.5	29	29.5	28.5	26	22	20
Louisville, KY	4.5	7	13	19.5	24.5	29	30.5	30	26.5	20.5	14	7
Memphis, TN	9.5	12	17	23	27	31.5	33	33	29	23	16.5	11.5
Miami, FL	24	25	26	28	29.5	31	31.5	31.5	31	29.5	26.5	25
Milwaukee, WI	−3.5	−1	4.5	11.5	18	24	26.5	25.5	21.5	15	7	−0.5
Minneapolis, MN	−6	−3	4	14	20.5	26	29	27	21.5	15	5	−3.5
Nashville, TN	8	10.5	16	21.5	26	30.5	32	31	28.5	23	15.5	10
New Orleans, LA	16	18	22	26	29	31.5	33	32	30.5	26	21.5	18
New York, NY	3.5	4.5	10	16	22	26.5	29.5	29	24.5	18.5	12	6
Oakland, CA	14.5	16	17	19.5	20.5	23	24	24.5	24.5	23	18.5	15
Oklahoma City, OK	8.5	11	16.5	22	26	30.5	34	34	29	23	15.5	10
Orlando, FL	21.5	23	25.5	28.5	31	33	33	33	32	29.5	26	23
Philadelphia, PA	3.5	5	11	17	23	28	30	29.5	25.5	19	13	6
Phoenix, AZ	19	21.5	24.5	29.5	34.5	40	41	40	36.5	31	24	19

City	Jan	Feb	Mar	Apr	May	June	July	Aug	Sept	Oct	Nov	Dec
Pittsburgh, PA	1	3	9.5	15.5	21.5	26	28.5	27	23	17	10	4
Portland, OR	7	10.5	13	16	19.5	23	26.5	26.5	24	18	11.5	8
Raleigh, NC	9.5	11.5	16.5	22	26	29.5	31	30.5	27	22	17	11.5
Richmond, VA	8	9.5	15.5	21	25.5	29.5	31	30.5	27	21.5	16	10
Sacramento, CA	11.5	15.5	18	21.5	26.5	31	34	33	30.5	25.5	17	11.5
Salt Lake City, UT	2	6.5	11	16	22	28.5	33	31.5	26	19	10.5	3.5
San Antonio, TX	16	19	23	26.5	29.5	33	35	35	31.5	28	22	18
San Diego, CA	19	19.5	19	20	20.5	22	24.5	25.5	25	24	21	19
San Francisco, CA	13	15.5	16	16.5	17	18	18.5	19	20.5	20.5	17	13
Seattle, WA	8	10.5	12	14.5	18	21	23	23	20.5	15.5	11	8
St Louis, MO	3.5	6	13	19.5	24.5	29.5	31.5	30.5	26.5	20.5	13	5.5
Syracuse, NY	−0.5	0.5	6	13	20	25	28	26	22	15.5	9	1.5
Tampa, FL	21	21.5	25	28	30.5	32	32	32	31.5	29	25.5	22
Washington, DC	5.5	8	14	19.5	24.5	29.5	31.5	30.5	26.5	20.5	14.5	8.5

Average Precipitation (cm)

City	Jan	Feb	Mar	Apr	May	June	July	Aug	Sept	Oct	Nov	Dec
Atlanta, GA	12	12	14	11	11	9	12.5	9.5	8.5	8	10	11
Baltimore, MD	8	8	8.5	8	9.5	9.5	9.5	10	8.5	7.5	8.5	8.5
Birmingham, AL	13	12	15.5	12.5	12.5	9.5	13.5	9	10	7	11	13
Boston, MA	9	9	9.5	9	8.5	8	7	8	8	8.5	10.5	10
Buffalo, NY	7	6	7	7.5	8	9	8	10.5	9	8	9.5	9.5
Charlotte, NC	9.5	9.5	11	7	9.5	8.5	10	9.5	9	8.5	8	9
Chicago, IL	3.5	3.5	7	9	8.5	9.5	9.5	10.5	9.5	6	7.5	6.5
Cleveland, OH	5	5.5	7.5	8	9	9.5	9	8.5	8.5	6.5	8	8
Columbus, OH	5.5	5.5	8.5	8	10	10	11	9.5	7.5	5.5	8	7.5
Dallas-Fort Worth, TX	4.5	5.5	7	9	12.5	7.5	6	5.5	8.5	9	6	4.5
Denver, CO	1.5	1.5	3.5	4.5	6	4.5	5	3.5	3	2.5	2.5	1.5
Detroit, MI	4.5	4.5	6.5	7.5	7.5	9	8	8.5	7.5	5.5	7	7
Green Bay, WI	3	2.5	5.5	6	7	8.5	8	9	9	5.5	5.5	3.5
Hartford, CT	8.5	8	9	10	10.5	9.5	8	9.5	9.5	9	10	10
Honolulu, HI	9	5.5	5.5	3.5	3	1.5	1.5	1	2	6	7.5	9.5
Houston, TX	8.5	7.5	7.5	8	13	12.5	9	9	12.5	11	9.5	9
Indianapolis, IN	6	6.5	9.5	9.5	10	9	11.5	9	7.5	6.5	8	8.5
Jacksonville, FL	8.5	10	9.5	7	9	14.5	14	20	18	7.5	5.5	7
Kansas City, MO	3	3	6.5	8	12.5	12	11	10	12.5	8.5	5	4
Las Vegas, NV	1.5	1.5	1	0.5	1	0	1	1.5	1	0.5	1	1
Lincoln, NE	1.5	2	5.5	7	10	10	8	8.5	9	5.5	3.5	2.5
Little Rock, AR	8.5	9	12.5	14	13	9	9	8.5	10.5	9.5	13	12
Los Angeles, CA	7.5	8	6.5	2.5	0.5	0	0	0	1.5	1	5	5

Louisville, KY	7.5	8.5	12	10.5	11.5	9	11.5	9	8	7	9.5	9
Memphis, TN	9.5	11	13.5	14	12.5	9	9.5	8.5	9	7.5	13	14.5
Miami, FL	5	5.5	6	7.5	15.5	23.5	14.5	19.5	19.5	14	7	4.5
Milwaukee, WI	4	3.5	7	9	7	8	9	9	8.5	6	6.5	6
Minneapolis, MN	2.5	2.5	5	6	8.5	10.5	9	9	7	5.5	4	3
Nashville, TN	9	9.5	12.5	11	12.5	9	10	9	9	6.5	10.5	11.5
New Orleans, LA	13	15	12.5	11.5	11.5	14	15.5	15.5	14	8	11	14
New York, NY	8.5	8.5	10.5	10.5	11	9.5	11	10	10	9	11.5	10
Oakland, CA	13	11.5	11	4.5	2	0.5	0	0	1	4	9.5	9.5
Oklahoma City, OK	3	4	7	7	13	11	6.5	6.5	9.5	8	5	3.5
Orlando, FL	6	7.5	8	4.5	9	18.5	18.5	17.5	15	6	6	5.5
Philadelphia, PA	8	7	9	9	9.5	9.5	11	9.5	8.5	6.5	8.5	8.5
Phoenix, AZ	2	2	2.5	0.5	0	0	2	2.5	2.5	2	2	2.5
Pittsburgh, PA	6.5	6	8.5	8	9	9.5	9.5	8	7.5	6	7.5	7.5
Portland, OR	13.5	10	9	6	5.5	3.5	1.5	3	4.5	7	13.5	15.5
Raleigh, NC	9	9.5	9.5	6.5	10	9.5	10	10	8	7.5	7.5	8
Richmond, VA	8	8	9	7.5	9.5	9	12.5	11	8.5	9	8	8.5
Sacramento, CA	9.5	7.5	6.5	3	1	0	0	0	1	3	7	6.5
Salt Lake City, UT	3	3	5	5.5	4.5	2.5	2	2.5	3.5	3.5	3.5	3.5
San Antonio, TX	4.5	4.5	3.5	6.5	10.5	9.5	5.5	6.5	8.5	8	6.5	3.5
San Diego, CA	4.5	3.5	4.5	2	0.5	0	0	0	0.5	1	3.5	4
San Francisco, CA	10.5	7.5	8	3.5	1	0.5	0	0	1	3.5	8	8
Seattle, WA	13.5	10	9.5	6.5	4.5	4	2.5	3	5	8.5	14.5	15
St Louis, MO	4.5	5.5	9	9	10	9.5	10	7.5	8	7	8.5	7.5
Syracuse, NY	6	5.5	7	8.5	8.5	9.5	9.5	9	9.5	8	9.5	8
Tampa, FL	5	8	7.5	3	8	14	17	19.5	15	5	4.5	5.5
Washington, DC	7	7	8	7	9.5	8.5	9.5	10	8.5	7.5	8	8

Regional Calling Codes and Post Codes

The international country code for calling the USA from outside is 00 1. When making a call to a number with a different area code from your own, dial 1 first. 800, 866, 877 and 888 numbers are toll-free for interstate callers (hence written as 1-800); local callers should use the local number given. Many 800 series numbers can be accessed from outside the USA, though they will not then be toll-free. Be careful, as 800 numbers could also be Caribbean area codes.

Alabama (AL)
205 – Birmingham, Hoover, Tuscaloosa
251 – Bay Minette, Mobile, Monroeville
256 – Anniston, Florence, Huntsville
334 – Auburn, Dothan, Montgomery

Alaska (AK)
907 – Statewide

Arizona (AZ)
480 – Chandler, Mesa, Scottsdale
520 – Casa Grande, Sierra Vista, Tucson
602 – Phoenix – City
623 – Avondale, Glendale, Peoria
928 – Flagstaff, Lake Havasu City, Yuma

Arkansas (AR)
479 – Fayetteville, Fort Smith, Russellville
501 – Hot Springs, Little Rock, Searcy
870 – Jonesboro, Pine Bluff, Texarkana

California (CA)
209 – Merced, Modesto, Stockton
213 – Los Angeles – Downtown
310 – Inglewood, Santa Monica, Torrance
323 – Hollywood, Huntington Park, Montebello
408 – San Jose, Santa Clara, Sunnyvale
415 – Novato, San Francisco, San Rafael
510 – Fremont, Hayward, Oakland
530 – Davis, Redding, South Lake Tahoe
559 – Fresno, Madera, Visalia
562 – Downey, Long Beach, Whittier
619 – Chula Vista, El Cajon, San Diego
626 – Alhambra, Pasadena, West Covina
650 – Daly City, Palo Alto, San Mateo
661 – Bakersfield, Lancaster, Santa Clarita
707 – Eureka, Santa Rosa, Vallejo
714 – Anaheim, Huntington Beach, Santa Ana
760 – Oceanside, Palm Springs, Victorville
805 – Oxnard, San Luis Obispo, Santa Barbara
818 – Burbank, Glendale, San Fernando
831 – Monterey, Salinas, Santa Cruz
858 – La Jolla, Linda Vista, Poway
909 – Ontario, Riverside, San Bernardino
916 – Folsom, Roseville, Sacramento
925 – Antioch, Concord, Livermore
949 – Costa Mesa, Irvine, Mission Viejo

Colorado (CO)
303 – Boulder, Denver, Littleton
719 – Alamosa, Colorado Springs, Pueblo

720 – Overlay Area Code 303
970 – Durango, Fort Collins, Grand Junction

Connecticut (CT)

203 – Bridgeport, New Haven, Waterbury
860 – Hartford, New London, Torrington

Delaware (DE)

302 – Statewide

District of Columbia (DC)

202 – Statewide

Florida (FL)

239 – Cape Coral, Fort Myers, Naples
305 – Hialeah, Key West, Miami
321 – Cocoa, Melbourne, Titusville
352 – Gainesville, Leesburg, Ocala
386 – Daytona Beach, Deltona, Lake City
407 – Kissimmee, Orlando, Sanford
561 – Boca Raton, Jupiter, West Palm Beach
727 – Clearwater, New Port Richey, Saint Petersburg
754 – Overlay Area Code 954
772 – Fort Pierce, Stuart, Vero Beach
786 – Overlay Area Code 305
813 – Plant City, Tampa, Zephyrhills
850 – Panama City, Pensacola, Tallahassee
863 – Clewiston, Lakeland, Sebring
904 – Fernandina Beach, Jacksonville, Saint Augustine
941 – Bradenton, Punta Gorda, Sarasota
954 – Coral Springs, Fort Lauderdale, Hollywood

Georgia (GA)

229 – Albany, Americus, Valdosta
404 – Atlanta, Decatur, East Point
470 – Overlay Area Codes 404, 678 and 770
478 – Macon, Milledgeville, Swainsboro
678 – Overlay Area Codes 404 and 770
706 – Athens, Augusta, Columbus
770 – Gainesville, Griffin, Marietta
912 – Brunswick, Savannah, Waycross

Hawaii (HI)

808 – Statewide

Idaho (ID)

208 – Statewide

Illinois (IL)
217 – Champaign, Quincy, Springfield
309 – Bloomington, Moline, Peoria
312 – Chicago – Inside Loop
618 – Belleville, Carbondale, Mount Vernon
630 – Aurora, Naperville, Wheaton
708 – Calumet City, Cicero, Tinley Park
773 – Chicago – Outside Loop
815 – Joliet, Kankakee, Rockford
847 – Elgin, Evanston, Waukegan

Indiana (IN)
219 – Gary, La Porte, Rensselaer
260 – Angola, Fort Wayne, Wabash
317 – Franklin, Indianapolis, Noblesville
574 – Elkhart, Logansport, South Bend
765 – Kokomo, Lafayette, Muncie
812 – Evansville, New Albany, Terre Haute

Iowa (IA)
319 – Burlington, Cedar Rapids, Waterloo
515 – Ames, Des Moines, Fort Dodge
563 – Davenport, Decorah, Dubuque
641 – Marshalltown, Mason City, Ottumwa
712 – Council Bluffs, Sioux City, Spencer

Kansas (KS)
316 – El Dorado, Newton, Wichita
620 – Emporia, Garden City, Hutchinson
785 – Lawrence, Salina, Topeka
913 – Kansas City, Leavenworth, Overland Park

Kentucky (KY)
270 – Bowling Green, Owensboro, Paducah
502 – Bardstown, Frankfort, Louisville
606 – Ashland, Pikeville, Somerset
859 – Covington, Lexington, Richmond

Louisiana (LA)
225 – Baton Rouge, Donaldsonville, New Roads
318 – Alexandria, Monroe, Shreveport
337 – Lafayette, Lake Charles, New Iberia
504 – Gretna, Kenner, New Orleans
985 – Hammond, Houma, Morgan City

Maine (ME)
207 – Statewide

Maryland (MD)

240 – Overlay Area Code 301
301 – Bowie, Frederick, Hagerstown
410 – Annapolis, Baltimore, Salisbury
443 – Overlay Area Code 410

Massachusetts (MA)

339 – Overlay Area Code 781
351 – Overlay Area Code 978
413 – Amherst, Pittsfield, Springfield
508 – Brockton, New Bedford, Worcester
617 – Boston, Cambridge, Quincy
774 – Overlay Area Code 508
781 – Lynn, Waltham, Weymouth
857 – Overlay Area Code 617
978 – Fitchburg, Lawrence, Lowell

Michigan (MI)

231 – Cheboygan, Muskegon, Traverse City
248 – Farmington Hills, Pontiac, Troy
269 – Battle Creek, Benton Harbor, Kalamazoo
313 – Dearborn, Detroit, Grosse Pointe
517 – Coldwater, Jackson, Lansing
586 – Mount Clemens, Sterling Heights, Warren
616 – Grand Rapids, Holland, Ionia
734 – Ann Arbor, Livonia, Monroe
810 – Flint, Lapeer, Port Huron
906 – Marquette, Menominee, Sault Sainte Marie
947 – Overlay Area Code 248
989 – Alpena, Mount Pleasant, Saginaw

Minnesota (MN)

218 – Brainerd, Duluth, Moorhead
320 – Hutchinson, Saint Cloud, Willmar
507 – Mankato, Rochester, Worthington
612 – Minneapolis, Richfield, Saint Anthony
651 – Eagan, Red Wing, Saint Paul
763 – Coon Rapids, Elk River, Plymouth
952 – Apple Valley, Bloomington, Minnetonka

Mississippi (MS)

228 – Biloxi, Gulfport, Pascagoula
601 – Hattiesburg, Jackson, Meridian
662 – Columbus, Greenville, Tupelo

Missouri (MO)

314 – Florissant, Kirkwood, Saint Louis
417 – Branson, Joplin, Springfield
573 – Cape Girardeau, Columbia, Jefferson City
636 – Chesterfield, Festus, Saint Charles
660 – Kirksville, Maryville, Sedalia
816 – Independence, Kansas City, Saint Joseph

Montana (MT)

406 – Statewide

Nebraska (NE)

308 – Grand Island, North Platte, Scottsbluff
402 – Lincoln, Norfolk, Omaha

Nevada (NV)

702 – Henderson, Las Vegas, Laughlin
775 – Carson City, Elko, Reno

New Hampshire (NH)

603 – Statewide

New Jersey (NJ)

201 – Bayonne, Hackensack, Jersey City
551 – Overlay Area Code 201
609 – Atlantic City, Trenton, Willingboro
732 – Long Branch, New Brunswick, Toms River
848 – Overlay Area Code 732
856 – Camden, Cherry Hill, Vineland
862 – Overlay Area Code 973
908 – Elizabeth, Flemington, Phillipsburg
973 – Morristown, Newark, Paterson

New Mexico (NM)

505 – Statewide

New York (NY)

212 – New York City – Manhattan
315 – Syracuse, Utica, Watertown
347 – Overlay Area Code 718
516 – Long Island (Nassau – Hempstead, Levittown, Valley Stream)
518 – Albany, Glens Falls, Plattsburgh
585 – Batavia, Geneva, Rochester
607 – Binghamton, Elmira, Oneonta
631 – Long Island (Suffolk – Commack, Islip, Southampton)
646 – Overlay Area Code 212
716 – Buffalo, Jamestown, Niagara Falls
718 – New York City – Bronx, Brooklyn, Queens, Staten Island

845 – Middletown, Newburgh, Poughkeepsie
914 – New Rochelle, White Plains, Yonkers
917 – New York City (Cellulars and Pagers)

North Carolina (NC)
252 – Greenville, New Bern, Rocky Mount
336 – Greensboro, Lexington, Winston-Salem
704 – Charlotte, Concord, Gastonia
828 – Asheville, Boone, Hickory
910 – Fayetteville, Jacksonville, Wilmington
919 – Chapel Hill, Goldsboro, Raleigh
980 – Overlay Area Code 704

North Dakota (ND)
701 – Statewide

Ohio (OH)
216 – Cleveland, Euclid, Lakewood
234 – Overlay Area Code 330
330 – Akron, Canton, Youngstown
419 – Lima, Mansfield, Toledo
440 – Lorain, Mentor, Parma
513 – Cincinnati, Hamilton, Middletown
567 – Overlay Area Code 419
614 – Columbus, Reynoldsburg, Westerville
740 – Marion, Portsmouth, Steubenville
937 – Bellefontaine, Dayton, Springfield

Oklahoma (OK)
405 – Norman, Oklahoma City, Stillwater
580 – Ada, Enid, Lawton
918 – Bartlesville, Muskogee, Tulsa

Oregon (OR)
503 – Astoria, Portland, Salem
541 – Eugene, Medford, Pendleton
971 – Overlay Area Code 503

Pennsylvania (PA)
215 – Lansdale, Levittown, Philadelphia
267 – Overlay Area Code 215
412 – Bethel Park, Mc Keesport, Pittsburgh
484 – Overlay Area Code 610
570 – Pottsville, Scranton, Williamsport
610 – Allentown, Reading, West Chester
717 – Harrisburg, Lancaster, York
724 – Indiana, New Castle, Washington

814 – Altoona, Erie, Johnstown
878 – Overlay Area Codes 412 and 724

Rhode Island (RI)

401 – Statewide

South Carolina (SC)

803 – Aiken, Columbia, Rock Hill
843 – Charleston, Florence, Hilton Head Island
864 – Anderson, Greenville, Spartanburg

South Dakota (SD)

605 – Statewide

Tennessee (TN)

423 – Chattanooga, Johnson City, Morristown
615 – Franklin, Murfreesboro, Nashville
731 – Dyersburg, Humboldt, Jackson
865 – Knoxville, Oak Ridge, Sevierville
901 – Covington, Memphis, Somerville
931 – Clarksville, Columbia, Cookeville

Texas (TX)

210 – Alamo Heights, San Antonio, Universal City
214 – Dallas, Irving, Plano
254 – Killeen, Temple, Waco
281 – Same as Area Code 713
325 – Abilene, Brownwood, San Angelo
361 – Corpus Christi, Kingsville, Victoria
409 – Beaumont, Galveston, Jasper
430 – Overlay Area Code 903
432 – Alpine, Midland, Odessa
469 – Overlay Area Codes 214 and 972
512 – Austin, Georgetown, San Marcos
682 – Overlay Area Code 817
713 – Houston, Pasadena, Sugar Land
806 – Amarillo, Lubbock, Plainview
817 – Arlington, Cleburne, Fort Worth
830 – Eagle Pass, Kerrville, New Braunfels
832 – Overlay Area Codes 281 and 713
903 – Longview, Sherman, Tyler
915 – Dell City, El Paso, Sierra Blanca
936 – Huntsville, Liberty, Nacogdoches
940 – Denton, Mineral Wells, Wichita Falls
956 – Brownsville, Laredo, Mc Allen
972 – Same as Area Code 214
979 – Angleton, Bay City, Bryan

Utah (UT)
385 – Overlay Area Codes 801
435 – Logan, Saint George, Vernal
801 – Ogden, Provo, Salt Lake City

Vermont (VT)
802 – Statewide

Virginia (VA)
276 – Bluefield, Bristol, Martinsville
434 – Charlottesville, Danville, Lynchburg
540 – Fredericksburg, Harrisonburg, Roanoke
571 – Overlay Area Code 703
703 – Alexandria, Arlington, Manassas
757 – Norfolk, Virginia Beach, Williamsburg
804 – Petersburg, Richmond, Tappahannock

Washington (WA)
206 – Mercer Island, Richmond Beach, Seattle
253 – Auburn, Kent, Tacoma
360 – Bellingham, Olympia, Vancouver
425 – Bellevue, Everett, Renton
509 – Kennewick, Spokane, Yakima

West Virginia (WV)
304 – Statewide

Wisconsin (WI)
262 – Kenosha, Racine, West Bend
414 – Milwaukee, Wauwatosa, West Allis
608 – Janesville, La Crosse, Madison
715 – Eau Claire, Superior, Wausau
920 – Green Bay, Oshkosh, Sheboygan

Wyoming (WY)
307 – Statewide

Dictionary of American–English Terms

A

Appetizer	Starter
Area code	Dialling code
Arugula	Rocket as in the plant used in salads
Asphalt	Tarmac
Attached home	Semi-detached house
Attorney	Lawyer

B

Baby carriage	Pram
Baking soda	Bicarbonate of soda
Band-aid	Sticking plaster
Bangs	Fringe
Bankroll (to)	To foot the bill
Barrette	Hair slide
Baseboard	Skirting board
Bathrobe	Dressing gown
Bathroom	Toilet
Bell pepper	Red, green or yellow pepper
Beltway, loop	Ring road, circular road
Bill	Banknote, piece of paper currency
Biscuit	Scone
Blacktop	Tarmac
Blinkers	Indicators on car
Blush	Rosé, light pinkish wine
Bobby pin	Hair grip
Bouillon cube	Stock cube
Boxcar	A covered railway wagon with a door for loading
Breakdown lane	Hard shoulder
Brown bag lunch	Packed lunch
Bum	Tramp, layabout
Burglarize	Burgle, steal

C

Candy	Sweets
Carnival	Travelling fair or circus
Carousel	Merry-go-round
Carpenter's level	Spirit level
Casket	Coffin
Cattle guard	Cattle grid
Checking account	Current account
Chesterfield	Settee, sofa
Chips	Crisps
Cilantro	Coriander
Closet	Walk-in cupboard or wardrobe
Clothes pin	Clothes peg
Collect call	Reverse charge call
Comforter	Quilt, eiderdown, bedspread
Condominium, condo	Block of flats
Consignment	Second-hand goods sold on commission
Cooler	Cool box

Corn	Sweet corn, maize, corn-on-the-cob
Corn starch	Corn flour
Cotton candy	Candy floss
Cotton swab	Cotton bud
Cream of wheat	Semolina
Crosswalk	Pedestrian crossing
Cuban	Floridan term for a sandwich with roast pork, ham and Swiss cheese
Cupcake	Fairy cake

D

Deductible	Excess, in terms of insurance payouts
Delivery truck	Van
Denatured alcohol	Methylated spirits
Diaper	Nappy
Dime	10 cent coin
Dish pan	Washing-up bowl
District attorney	Public prosecutor or procurator fiscal in Scotland
Divided highway	Dual carriageway
Docent	Curator, guide in a museum, historic house or art gallery
Doctor's office	Surgery
Drapes	Curtains
Drugstore	Pharmacy, chemist
Dumpster	Skip
Duplex (house)	Semi-detached house

E

Eggplant	Aubergine
Elementary school	Primary school
Entrée	Main course
Excise laws	Licensing laws
Expressway	Main road

F

Fall	Autumn
Fanny	Behind, *derrière*
Fanny pack	Bumbag
Faucet	Tap
Fava bean	Broad bean
Fedora	Trilby
Feminine	Napkin
Fender	Wing of a car, mudguard on bicycle
First floor	Ground floor

Flashlight	Torch
Flatware	Cutlery
Four-way stop	Crossroads where, in the absence of traffic lights, priority is given to vehicles in order of arrival
Furnace	Central heating boiler

G

Galoshes	Wellington boots, wellies
Garter belt	Suspenders
Grade crossing	Level crossing
Graham crackers	Digestive biscuits

H

Heavy cream	Double cream
Hidabed, hideaway	Sofa-bed
High school	Secondary school
Hobo	Tramp
Hood	Bonnet

I

Incorporated	Limited, as in limited company
Instalment plan	Hire purchase

J

Janitor	Caretaker
Jack	Socket
Jelly	Type of jam
Jell-o	Jelly
Jumper	Short dress

K

Kerosene	Paraffin

L

Lawyer, advocate, attorney	Lawyer, solicitor, barrister
License plate or license tag	Number plate
Lima bean	Butter bean
Line	Queue
Love seat	Settee, sofa
Luggage rack	Roof rack

M

Mean	Bad-tempered
Military time	24-hour clock

Muffler	Silencer in vehicle exhaust system
Mutual fund	Unit trust

N

Nickel	5 cent coin
Notions	Haberdashery items
Number sign	Hash mark

O

Oil pan	Sump
On-ramp, off-ramp	Slip road
Overalls	Dungarees
Outlet	Socket

P

Pacifier	Dummy used to stop small children crying
Paddle	Bat for table tennis and similar games
Panhandler	Beggar
Pantihose/pantyhose	Tights
Pants	Trousers
Pavement	Paved area
Penny	Cent
Period	Full stop in punctuation
Petroleum	Crude oil
Pitcher	Jug for liquid
Plastic wrap	Cling film
Plexiglas	Perspex
Potato chips	Crisps
Pot holders	Oven gloves
Pound sign, number sign	Hash sign, i.e. #
Preserves	Jam, marmalade
Professor	Lecturer
Public school	State school
Purse	Handbag

Q

Quarter	25¢ coin

R

Realtor	Estate agent
Realty	Estate agency
Restroom	Toilet
Résumé	Curriculum vitae (CV)
Retirement fund	Superannuation

(American) revolutionary war	American war of independence
Robe	Dressing gown
Rotary	Roundabout
Round trip	Return
Row house	Terrace house
Rutabaga	Swede

S

Sack lunch	Packed lunch
Sales tax	VAT
Sanitary napkin	Sanitary towel
Saran wrap	Cling film
Savings and loan trust	Building society
Scallion	Spring onion
Scotch tape	Sellotape
Second floor	First floor
Sedan	Saloon type of car
Seeing eye dog	Guide dog
Semi-trailer	Articulated lorry
Server	Waiter or waitress
Senior	Pensioner
Shade	Blind
Sherbet	Sorbet
Shrimp	Prawn
Silverware	Cutlery
Ski mask	Balaclava
Slacks	Trousers
Slowpoke	Slowcoach
Snaps	Press studs
Snowbird	Tourist from a cold region who spends the winter somewhere warm
Snow peas	Mangetout
Social security number	National insurance number
Soda	Fizzy soft drink
Sports utility vehicle (SUV)	Large four-wheel drive vehicle with comfortable interior
Station wagon	Estate car
Stemware	Wineglasses
Stick shift	Gear lever
Streetcar	Tram
Strip mall	Parade of shops
Stroller	Pushchair, baby buggy

Stub	Counterfoil
Submarine, sub	Sandwich in long roll
Suspenders	Braces
Switchback	Hairpin bend

T
Teller	Cashier
Townhouse	Terrace house
Traffic circle	Roundabout

U
Unemployment compensation	Dole, unemployment pay or benefit

V
Variety meats	Offal
Vest	Waistcoat
Veterans' day	Remembrance day

W
Walker	Zimmer (frame)
Water heater	Immersion heater
Wax paper	Greaseproof paper
Welfare	Benefit
White-out	Tippex
Wrench	Spanner

XYZ
Yard	Garden
Zee	Zed
Zip code	Postcode
Zucchini	Courgette

Films

Annie Hall, 1977. One of a clutch of extremely watchable Woody Allen films. Here his unique comic genius is coupled with a spot of romance.

Birth of a Nation, 1915. Hugely influential silent film, ground-breaking in both its use of close-ups and extreme racism.

Blade Runner, 1982. Smooth and moody sci-fi *film noir* set in a futuristic LA, by Ridley Scott. The 1991 director's cut is even better.

Blue Velvet, 1986. Disturbing film in which director David Lynch critiques suburban middle-class values.

Chinatown, 1974. A silky film in which Roman Polanski observes LA via down-at-heel private eye Jack Nicholson.

Citizen Kane, 1941. Orson Welles' masterpiece, which portrays the rags-to-riches story that lies at the heart of the American Dream – though he finds only misery in financial fortune.

Do The Right Thing, 1986. Racial tension in a hot Brooklyn summer stylishly explored by Spike Lee, one of the most accomplished African-American directors of all time.

Double Indemnity, 1944. Fatalistic *film noir* in which an insurance executive is corrupted by a femme fatale. A Billy Wilder classic.

Easy Rider, 1969. Dennis Hopper stars in the film he directs, teaming up with Peter Fonda to produce the ultimate 1960s road-movie.

Farenheit 9/11, 2003. A polemic yet powerful Michael Moore documentary takes a critical look at the state of the nation.

Fargo, 1996. Quirky, hugely entertaining and dark Coen-brothers movie set in a wintry and highly evocative Minnesota landscape.

The Godfather, 1972. The father of all modern gangster films, as powerful now as when it was made.

It's a Wonderful Life, 1946. Much more than just a Christmas classic, that asks some fundamental questions about American priorities amid a rich tapestry of small-town 1940s American life.

The Night of the Hunter, 1955. Magical Depression-era tale and one of Hollywood's most offbeat successes.

The Searchers, 1956. Classic John Ford Western, with John Wayne hunting down an Indian chief who butchered his friends.

Singin' in the Rain, 1952. Exuberant and energetic musical, set in Hollywood and including a whole host of catchy numbers.

Some Like it Hot, 1959. Upbeat farce, inspired by the St Valentine's Day Massacre, with Marilyn Monroe.

Sunrise, 1927. Extravagantly beautiful lighting effects make this tale of a country boy led astray by a streetwise city girl a compelling silent film.

Taxi Driver, 1976. Twisted tale of infatuation featuring Robert De Niro and Jodie Foster; directed by Martin Scorsese.

The Wild Bunch, 1969. The best bloodthirsty Western from the Peckinpah stable.

Further Reading

Archdeacon, Thomas J., *Becoming American: An Ethnic History* (Free Press, 1983)

Barlett, Donald and Steele, James, *America, What Went Wrong?* (Doubleday, 2004)

Barth, Gunther, *Fleeting Moments: Nature and Culture in American History* (Oxford University Press, 1990)

Brogan, Hugh, *The Penguin History of the United States of America* (Penguin, 1985)

Brook, Stephen, *New York Days, New York Nights* (Picador, 1985)

Bryson, Bill, *Made in America* (Transworld, 1998); *The Lost Continent* (Transworld, 1999); *Notes from a Big Country* (Black Swan, 1999)

Carroll, Peter and Noble, David, *The Free and the Unfree: a New History of the USA* (Penguin, 1977)

Carver, Raymond, *Will You Please Be Quiet Please?* (Vintage, 1992)

Faul, Stephanie, *Xenophobe's Guide to the Americans* (Oval Books, 1999)

Frazier, Ian, *Great Plains* (Faber and Faber, 1991)

Hoggart, Simon, *America: a User's Guide* (HarperCollins, 1990)

Jones, Roger, *Getting a Job in America* (How to Books, 2003)

Keillor, Garrison, *Lake Wobegon Days* (Faber and Faber, 1998)

Kerouac, Jack *On the Road* (Penguin, 1957)

Liebman, Henry G., *Getting into America* (How to Books, 2004)

Melville, Herman, *Moby-Dick* (Penguin Popular Classics, 1994)

Milner, Clyde A. and O'Connor, Carol A. & Sandweiss, Martha A., *The Oxford History of the American West* (OUP, 1994)

Moon, William, *Least Heat, Blue Highways* (Little, Brown & Company, 1999)

Moore, Michael, *Stupid White Men* (Penguin, 2004)

Proulx, E. Annie, *Accordion Crimes* (Simon & Schuster, 1996)

Thomas, G. Scott, *Life in America's Small Cities* (Prometheus Books, 1994)

Twain, Mark, *Roughing It* (Penguin Popular Classics, 1982)

Walmsley, Jane, *Brit-Think Ameri-Think: A Transatlantic Survival Guide* (Penguin, 1987)

White, Edmund, *States of Desire: Travels in Gay America* (Dutton, 1983)

Chronology

15,000 years ago	First human settlers arrive on the American continent from Siberia
10th century AD	The Vikings arrive in the Americas and establish a colony in Greenland
1492	Christopher Columbus stumbles on the Caribbean islands in search of a route to India
1496	John Cabot explores the coast of Newfoundland
16th century	Other Spanish explorers explore the south of North America and start the first permanent settlement in St Augustine, Florida, in 1565; French explorers make expeditions in search of the Northwest Passage
17th century	Spanish missionary activity along the Rio Grande in New Mexico; the Spanish consolidate power at Santa Fe
1607	The first enduring British colony founded at Jamestown, Virginia
1615	Tobacco found in Virginia
1620	Puritans fleeing persecution disembark from *Mayflower* in New England; those who survive establish a colony
17th century	The Dutch set up several colonies, including one at the mouth of the Hudson River, later New York City; the French explore inland, and develop a foothold in the Great Lakes Region
18th century	By the 1760s the population of colonists in today's USA is 1.6 million, a huge increase on the 250,000 who lived there in 1700
1756–63	The Seven Years' War encourages European countries to look at the profitability of their colonies; Britain raises local taxes in its American colonies and there are boycotts of British goods and some unrest
1774	The Boston Tea Party – locals dressed as Native Americans hurl an incoming cargo of tea from British vessels into the sea
1776	Declaration of Independence
1781	British surrender to George Washington at Yorktown; finally leave in 1783
1787	First Bill of Rights drawn up
19th century	Expansion westwards; attempts to control Mexico; industrial boom and transport revolution; unrest over slavery

1812	Declares war against the British
1835	Erie Canal completed, which links New York City with Great Lakes, cementing New York as the country's commercial centre
1860	Republican Party comes to power with Abraham Lincoln as president
1861–65	American Civil War
Late 19th century	Immigrants pour into the USA from Europe and Asia
1903	Wright brothers achieve the first successful powered flight
1911	Hollywood acquires its first movie studio; jazz and blues become nationally popular at this time
1914–18	The USA join the First World War and more than 100,000 American are killed
1920s	The country enjoys new-found wealth and freedoms, and considerable economic success, but organized crime proliferates
24 Oct 1929	The New York Stock Exchange crashes on 'Black Thursday'; redundancies follow and there is mass unemployment
1930s	Franklin D. Roosevelt introduces New Deal policies
7 Dec 1941	Bombing of Pearl Harbor brings the USA into the Second World War
1957–75	Vietnam War
1960s	Civil rights and women's movements; massive internal migration
1962	Cuban Missile Crisis
1972	Watergate Affair
1980s	Republican domination, with Ronald Reagan president
1990s	Democrat Bill Clinton in office
2000	George Bush (jr) elected president
11 Sept 2001	Terrorist attacks on the World Trade Center

American Presidents

Washington, George	1789–97
Adams, John	1797–1801
Jefferson, Thomas	1801–1809
Madison, James	1809–17
Monroe, James	1817–25

Adams, John	1825–9
Jackson, Andrew	1829–37
Van Buren, Martin	1837–41
Harrison, William Henry	1841
Tyler, John	1841–5
Polk, James	1845–9
Taylor, Zachary	1849–50
Fillmore, Millard	1850–53
Pierce, Franklin	1853–7
Buchanan, James	1857–61
Lincoln, Abraham	1861–5
Johnson, Andrew	1865–9
Grant, Ulysses S.	1869–77
Hayes, Rutherford B.	1877–81
Garfield, James	1881
Arthur, Chester	1881–5
Cleveland, Grover	1885–9
Harrison, Benjamin	1889–3
Cleveland, Grover	1893–7
McKinley, William	1897–1901
Roosevelt, Theodore	1901–1909
Taft, William H.	1909–13
Wilson, Woodrow	1913–21
Harding, Warren	1921–3
Coolidge, Calvin	1923–9
Hoover, Herbert	1929–33
Roosevelt, Franklin D.	1933–45
Truman, Harry	1945–53
Eisenhower, Dwight	1953–61
Kennedy, John F.	1961–3
Johnson, Lyndon	1963–9
Nixon, Richard	1969–74
Ford, Gerald	1974–7
Carter, Jimmy	1977–81
Reagan, Ronald	1981–9
Bush, George H.W.	1989–93
Clinton, William J.	1993–2001
Bush, George W.	2001–present

The USA on the Internet

Alabama
- **Alabama Bureau of Tourism and Travel – www.touralabama.org**

Alaska
- **Alaska Division of Tourism – www.travelalaska.com**
- **Anchorage – www.anchorage.net**

Arizona
- **Arizona Office of Tourism – www.arizonaguide.com**
- **Phoenix – www.phoenixcvb.com**

Arkansas
- **Arkansas Tourism Office – www.arkansas.com**

California
- **California Division of Tourism – www.gocalif.com**
- **Los Angeles – www.lacvb.com**
- **San Diego – www.sandiego.org**
- **San Francisco – www.sfvisitor.org**

Colorado
- **Colorado Tourism – www.colorado.com**
- **Denver – www.denver.org**

Connecticut
- **Connecticut Tourism Division – www.ctbound.org**

Delaware
- **Delaware Tourism Office – www.state.de.us**

District of Columbia
- **Washington DC, Convention and Visitors Bureau – www.washington.org**

Florida
- **Visit Florida – www.flausa.com**
- **Miami – www.tropicoolmiami.com**

Georgia
- **Georgia Department of Industry, Trade and Tourism – www.georgia.org**
- **Atlanta – www.atlanta.com**

Hawaii
- **Hawaii Visitors Bureau – www.gohawaii.com**

Idaho
- **Idaho Travel Council – www.visitid.org**

Illinois
- **Illinois Bureau of Tourism – www.enjoyillinois.com**
- **Chicago – www.chicago.il.org**

Indiana
- **Indiana Tourism Development Division – www.enjoyindiana.com**

Iowa
- **Iowa Division of Tourism – www.state.ia.us/tourism**

Kansas
- **Kansas Division of Travel and Tourism – www.kansas–travel.com**

Kentucky
- **Kentucky Department of Travel Development – www.kentuckytourism.com**

Louisiana
- **Louisiana Office of Tourism – www.louisianatravel.com**
- **New Orleans – www.neworleanscvb.com**

Maine
- **Maine Division of Tourism – www.visitmaine.com**
- **Portland – www.visitportland.com**

Maryland
- **Maryland Office of Tourist Development – www.mdisfun.org**
- **Baltimore – www.baltconvstr.com**

Massachusetts
- **Massachusetts Office of Travel and Tourism – www.mass-vacation.com**
- **Boston – www.bostonusa.com**

Michigan
- **Michigan Travel Bureau – www.michigan.org**

Minnesota
- **Minnesota Office of Tourism – www.exploreminnesota.com**
- **Minneapolis – www.minneapolis.org**
- **St Paul – www.stpaulcvb.org**

Mississippi
- **Mississippi Division of Tourism Development – www.mississippi.org**

Missouri
- **Missouri Division of Tourism – www.missouritourism.org**
- **St Louis – www.explorestlouis.com**

Montana
- **Travel Montana – www.visitmt.com**

Nebraska
- **Nebraska Tourism Information Center – www.visitnebraska.org**

Nevada
- **Nevada Commission on Tourism – www.travelnevada.com**
- **Las Vegas – www.lasvegas24hours.com**

New Hampshire
- **New Hampshire Office of Vacation Travel – www.visitnh.gov**

New Jersey
- **New Jersey Division of Travel and Tourism – www.state.nj.us/travel**

New Mexico
- **New Mexico Department of Tourism – www.newmexico.org**
- **Santa Fe – www.santafe.org**

New York
- **New York State Division of Tourism – iloveny.state.ny.us**
- **New York City – www.nycvisit.com**

North Carolina
- **North Carolina Division of Travel and Tourism – www.visitnc.com**

North Dakota
- **North Dakota Tourism Office – www.ndtourism.com**

Ohio
- **Ohio Division of Travel and Tourism – www.ohiotourism.com**

Oklahoma
- **Oklahoma Department of Tourism – www.travelok.com**

Oregon
- **Oregon Tourism Commission – www.traveloregon.com**

Pennsylvania
- **Pennsylvania Office of Travel – www.dced.state.pa.us/visit**
- **Philadelphia – www.pcvb.org**

Rhode Island
- **Rhode Island Tourism Division – visitrhodeisland.com**

South Carolina

- **South Carolina Parks, Recreation and Tourism – www.travelsc.com**

South Dakota

- **South Dakota Department of Tourism – www.travelsd.com**

Tennessee

- **Tennessee Department of Tourist Development – www.state.tn.us/ tourdev**

Texas

- **Tourism Division – traveltex.com**

US Virgin Islands

- **US Virgin Islands Tourism – www.usvitourism.vi**

Utah

- **Utah Travel Council – www.utah.com**

Vermont

- **Vermont Travel Division – www.travel–vermont.com**

Virginia

- **Virginia Tourism Corp. – www.virginia.org**

Washington

- **Washington State Tourism – www.experiencewashington.com**
- **Seattle – www.seeseattle.org**

Washington, DC

- **Washington DC, Convention and Visitors Bureau – www.washington.org**

West Virginia

- **West Virginia Division of Tourism – www.state.wv.us/tourism**

Wisconsin

- **Wisconsin Tourism and Travel Information – www.travelwisconsin.com**

Wyoming

- **Wyoming Division of Tourism – www.wyomingtourism.org**

Appendix 1

99 Questions from the US Naturalisation Test 256

99 Questions from the US Naturalisation Test

1. What are the colours of our flag?
2. How many stars are there in our flag?
3. What colour are the stars on our flag?
4. What do the stars on the flag mean?
5. How many stripes are there in the flag?
6. What colour are the stripes?
7. What do the stripes on the flag mean?
8. How many states are there in the Union?
9. What is the 4th of July?
10. What is the date of Independence Day?
11. Independence from whom?
12. What country did we fight during the Revolutionary War?
13. Who was the first president of the United States?
14. Who is the president of the United States today?
15. Who is the vice-president of the United States today?
16. Who elects the president of the United States?
17. Who becomes president of the United States if the president should die?
18. For how long do we elect the president?
19. What is the Constitution?
20. Can the Constitution be changed?
21. What do we call a change to the Constitution?
22. How many changes or amendments are there to the Constitution?
23. How many branches are there in our government?
24. What are the three branches of our government?
25. What is the legislative branch of our government?
26. Who makes the laws in the United States?
27. What is Congress?
28. What are the duties of Congress?
29. Who elects Congress?
30. How many senators are there in Congress?
31. Can you name the two senators from your state?
32. For how long do we elect each senator?
33. How many representatives are there in Congress?

34. For how long do we elect the Representatives?
35. What is the executive branch of our government?
36. What is the judiciary branch of our government?
37. What are the duties of the Supreme Court?
38. What is the Supreme Law of the United States?
39. What is the Bill of Rights?
40. What is the Capital of your state?
41. Who is the current governor of your state?
42. Who becomes president of the U.S.A. if the president and the vice-president should die?
43. Who is the chief justice of the Supreme Court?
44. Can you name the thirteen original states?
45. Who said, "Give me liberty or give me death"?
46. Which countries were our enemies during World War II?
47. What are the 49th and 50th states of the union?
48. How many terms can a president serve?
49. Who was Martin Luther King, jnr.?
50. Who is the head of your local government?
51. According to the Constitution, a person must meet certain requirements in order to be eligible to become president. Name one of these requirements.
52. Why are there 100 senators in the Senate?
53. Who selects the Supreme Court justices?
54. How many Supreme Court justices are there?
55. Why did the pilgrims come to America?
56. What is the head executive of a state government called?
57. What is the head executive of a city government called?
58. What holiday was celebrated for the first time by the American colonists?
59. Who was the main writer of the Declaration of Independence?
60. When was the Declaration of Independence adopted?
61. What is the basic belief of the Declaration of Independence?
62. What is the National Anthem of the United States?
63. Who wrote the Star-spangled Banner?
64. Where does freedom of speech come from?
65. What is the minimum voting age in the United States?

66. Who signs bills into law?
67. What is the highest court in the United States?
68. Who was the president during the Civil War?
69. What did the emancipation proclamation do?
70. What special group advises the president?
71. Which president is called the "Father of our Country"?
72. What immigration and naturalization service form is used to apply to become a naturalized citizen?
73. Who helped the pilgrims in America?
74. What is the name of the ship that brought the pilgrims to America?
75. What were the 13 original states of the United States called?
76. Name 3 rights or freedoms guaranteed by the bill of rights?
77. Who has the power to declare war?
78. What kind of government does the United States have?
79. Which president freed the slaves?
80. In what year was the Constitution written?
81. What are the first 10 amendments to the Constitution called?
82. Name one purpose of the United Nations.
83. Where does congress meet?
84. Whose rights are guaranteed by the Constitution and the Bill of Rights?
85. What is the introduction to the Constitution called?
86. Name one benefit of being a citizen of the United States.
87. What is the most important right granted to U.S. citizens?
88. What is the United States capitol?
89. What is the White House?
90. Where is the White House located?
91. What is the name of the president's official home?
92. Name one right guaranteed by the first amendment.
93. Who is the commander in chief of the U.S. military?
94. Which president was the first commander in chief of the U.S. military?
95. In what month do we vote for the president?
96. In what month is the new president inaugurated?
97. How many times may a senator be re-elected?
98. How many times may a congressman be re-elected?
99. What are the 2 major political parties in the U.S. today?

Answer Sheet

1. Red, white, and blue
2. 50
3. White
4. One for each state in the union
5. 13
6. Red and white
7. They represent the original 13 states
8. 50
9. Independence Day
10. July 4th
11. England
12. England
13. George Washington
14. George W. Bush
15. Dick Cheney
16. The electoral college
17. Vice president
18. Four years
19. The supreme law of the land
20. Yes
21. Amendments
22. 27
23. 3
24. Legislative, executive, and judiciary
25. Congress
26. Congress
27. The Senate and the House of Representatives
28. To make laws
29. The people
30. 100
31. (insert local information)
32. 6 years
33. 435

34. 2 years
35. The president, cabinet, and departments under the cabinet members
36. The Supreme Court
37. To interpret laws
38. The Constitution
39. The first 10 amendments of the Constitution
40. (insert local information)
41. (insert local information)
42. Speaker of the house of representatives
43. William Rehnquist
44. Connecticut, New Hampshire, New York, New Jersey, Massachusetts, Pennsylvania, Delaware, Virginia, North Carolina, South Carolina, Georgia, Rhode Island, and Maryland
45. Patrick Henry
46. Germany, Italy, and Japan
47. Hawaii and Alaska
48. 2
49. A civil rights leader
50. (insert local information)
51. Must be a natural born citizen of the United States; must be at least 35 years old by the time he/she will serve; must have lived in the United States for at least 14 years
52. Two (2) from each state
53. Appointed by the president
54. Nine (9)
55. For religious freedom
56. Governor
57. Mayor
58. Thanksgiving
59. Thomas Jefferson
60. July 4, 1776
61. That all men are created equal
62. The Star-spangled Banner
63. Francis Scott Key
64. The Bill of Rights
65. Eighteen (18)

66. The president

67. The Supreme Court

68. Abraham Lincoln

69. Freed many slaves

70. The cabinet

71. George Washington

72. Form n-400, "Application to file petition for naturalization"

73. The American Indians (Native Americans)

74. The Mayflower

75. Colonies

76. (a) the right of freedom of speech, press, religion, peaceable assembly and requesting change of government.

    (b) the right to bear arms (the right to have weapons or own a gun, though subject to certain regulations).

    (c) the government may not quarter, or house, soldiers in the people's homes during peacetime without the people's consent.

    (d) the government may not search or take a person's property without a warrant.

    (e) a person may not be tried twice for the same crime and does not have to testify against himself.

    (f) a person charged with a crime still has some rights, such as the right to a trial and to have a lawyer.

    (g) the right to trial by jury in most cases.

    (h) protects people against excessive or unreasonable fines or cruel and unusual punishment.

    (i) the people have rights other than those mentioned in the Constitution. Any power not given to the federal government by the Constitution is a power of either the state or the people.

77. The Congress

78. Republican

79. Abraham Lincoln

80. 1787

81. The Bill of Rights

82. For countries to discuss and try to resolve world problems; to provide economic aid to many countries.

83. In the capitol in Washington, D.C.

84. Everyone (citizens and non-citizens living in the U.S.)

85. The preamble
86. Obtain federal government jobs; travel with a U.S. passport; petition for close relatives to come to the U.S. to live
87. The right to vote
88. The place where Congress meets
89. The presidents official home
90. Washington, D.C. (1600 Pennsylvania Avenue, NW)
91. The White House
92. Freedom of: speech, press, religion, peaceable assembly, and requesting change of the government
93. The president
94. George Washington
95. November
96. January
97. There is no limit
98. There is no limit
99. Democratic and Republican

Index